# DEAF
# ADOLESCENTS

# DEAF ADOLESCENTS

## Inner Lives and Lifeworld Development

MARTHA A. SHERIDAN

*Foreword by* Irene W. Leigh and Patricia E. Spencer

Gallaudet University Press     *Washington, D.C.*

Gallaudet University Press
Washington, D.C. 20002
http://gupress.gallaudet.edu

*Library of Congress Cataloging-in-Publication Data*

Sheridan, Martha.
   Deaf adolescents : inner lives and lifeworld development / Martha A. Sheridan.
      p. cm.
   Includes index.
   ISBN 978-1-56368-369-5 (alk. paper)
   1. Deaf children—Case studies. 2. Deaf children—Interviews. 3. Deafness—Psychological aspects—Case studies. 4. Deafness in children—Case studies. I. Title.
HV2391.S55 2008
305.9'082—dc22                                                      2007038582

To touch a life, to lift a soul, to love, to teach, to learn,
In that we find we are whole . . .

To my loving family, Michael and Chris;
To my late parents, Joseph and Marilyn Sheridan;
And to Alex, Angie, Danny, Joe, Lisa, Mary, and Pat.
You have touched my life in ways you can never know.

# Contents

# FOREWORD

In her earlier book, *Inner Lives of Deaf Children*, Martha Sheridan introduced us to Danny, Angie, Joe, Alex, Lisa, Mary, and Pat. Using her considerable professional skills to encourage them to communicate freely, Dr. Sheridan asked the children to tell us their own stories. As a result, we learned about their families, their challenges and joys, and their hopes and dreams for their future as "grown ups." Dr. Sheridan gave us a careful analysis of these stories, pointing out the various ways that the children and their families confronted and negotiated issues of communication, relationships, and identity within and beyond the family and educational settings.

*Inner Lives of Deaf Children* was unique and groundbreaking in a number of ways. First, rigorous qualitative research methods were employed to condense and draw themes from the stories that the children told. Dr. Sheridan's combination of scholarly rigor and human focus is rare in research in general and especially in research focused on deaf children. Second, the researcher grew up deaf herself. In conjunction with her professional training, this undoubtedly increased the depth of her communication with the children and enriched her understanding of the meanings, emotional and otherwise, that they expressed. The resulting descriptions revealed Dr. Sheridan's unique ability to interpret the children's stories in ways that demonstrated the fascinating and positive complexities of their lives.

*Deaf Adolescents: Inner Lives and Lifeworld Development* takes us all a step further. We are now privileged to visit these children again, although at this stage of their lives they might not appreciate being called "children." They are adolescents now—teenagers. They have grown physically, mentally, and emotionally. They have accrued more experiences and have been through many changes at school, with peers, in their communities, and within their own families. Again, Dr. Sheridan allows them to tell us, in their own words, what all of these experiences have meant to them and how they have adjusted and accommodated to the challenges they face daily. Now, the future, adulthood, is becoming a reality, and the adolescents' concerns, hopes, and plans are beginning to take shape as they continue to make their way through the complicated world of adolescence.

Both the adolescents' stories and Dr. Sheridan's conceptual and theoretical analysis of what the adolescents present have deepened and broadened. Dr. Sheridan provides a framework for analysis of similarities and differences among the teenagers by referring to their unique "lifeworlds"—that is, the synthesis of their experiences, their relationships, and their truths; the intersecting physical and psychological systems of self, family, community, and beyond; the ways they view their current reality, and the possibilities they see for their futures. Yes, all of these teenagers are deaf, and, as will be clear in the book, communication accessibility is a critical and increasingly important influence as they mature and encounter more complex environments. It becomes inescapably clear that Angie, Joe, Alex, Pat, Mary, Danny, and Lisa are unique persons with unique gifts, challenges, needs, plans, and hopes. The diversity in their comments and the portrayals of their lifeworlds prove the fallacy of referring to "deaf children," "deaf adolescents," or "deaf people" as labels reflecting monolithic, homogeneous groups.

Although the adolescents' lifeworlds are fascinating, this book gives us much more than a collection of individual stories. Using the approach of following a small and diverse set of individuals from childhood to adolescence allows us, the readers, to see how attitudes, experiences, and personal characteristics interact and evolve over time. A gifted scholar, Dr. Sheridan shares with us how these individuals' development illuminates and refines theories of maturational processes. Her focus on adolescents who are deaf both clarifies and expands our current thinking about maturation during this stage of life in general—for deaf as well as for hearing persons. Dr. Sheridan helps us see how various deaf and hard of hearing identities wax and wane over time depending on individual experiences, therefore illustrating the various ways in which unique individual characteristics and experiences interact in the process of internalizing identities.

We are pleased to have this opportunity to "catch up" with the lives of the children to whom Dr. Sheridan introduced us earlier—and to have at the same time the opportunity to "catch up" with her thinking and conceptualizing about interrelating factors that are influencing these individuals and, perhaps, have influenced our own lives as well. Since Dr. Sheridan plans to continue exploring developmental issues with this cohort through adulthood as part of a planned longitudinal study, we look forward to meeting Angie, Joe, Alex, Pat, Mary, Danny, and Lisa again when they have reached the next stage in their lives, namely adulthood, hoping that they will again allow us entry into their lives and anticipating Dr. Sheridan's continuing contributions as she integrates these children's expressions of their life-worlds with ever more elegant theories of development and identity.

We love the stories themselves—the words of these open and articulate teenagers—and we know that we still have much to learn from them and from the author. We are thrilled to have even a peripheral role as observers as this uniquely powerful, longitudinal study unfolds. We are confident that you, the reader, will be engaged and enlightened by this fascinating journey into the lifeworlds of these very special teenagers.

IRENE W. LEIGH
PATRICIA E. SPENCER

# Acknowledgments

Let me begin these acknowledgements by saying, "It takes a child to teach a village." First and foremost on my thank-you list are the teenagers who participated in this study—Alex, Angie, Danny, Joe, Lisa, Mary, and Pat—who gave unselfishly of their time and opened up their hearts and minds to teach others about the multiple meanings of being a deaf adolescent. For this, I am eternally grateful. I thank their parents and families for their willingness to open their homes and lives to this research process. For this, the world is more enlightened.

I wish to gratefully acknowledge the Gallaudet Research Institute for their financial and technical support of the research, which made this book possible. Qualitative research should always involve a method of establishing trustworthiness in the research process, and to that end, I thank my peer debriefers, Dr. Irene Leigh and Dr. Teresa Mason. I owe very special thanks also to Dr. Patricia Spencer, whose encouragement, intelligence, and insight have been great sources of objectivity and support. Thank you also to my good friend Dr. Barbara White and my anonymous external reviewer for their careful review of my manuscript prior to its publication.

I thank Ivey Pittle Wallace and the staff of Gallaudet University Press, the faculty and staff in the Gallaudet University Department of Social Work, and my dear friends for your ongoing support of this project. I owe special thanks to Jean Parmir and Linda Williams for their professional and technical assistance and for their endurance in the face of computer crashes and technological panics.

And finally, my loving family, husband Michael and son Christopher, made many trips through the house to find me buried under books and papers in our home office, where they offered lots of welcome hugs, kisses, and warm cups of coffee. Thank you, guys, for your patience, support, and enduring love!

# 1

# The Dance of Adolescence

Dance is not an imitation of life, but life itself.
—Peter Wisher (1911–1995)

WE CAN use many metaphors to describe the place and experience of our adolescent lives. Adolescence is a time of change on the continuum of life. Late in my adolescence, when I entered Gallaudet University, I was fortunate to have been a dance student of Dr. Peter Wisher, who used to say, "Dance not an imitation of life, but life itself."[1] Adolescence is a part of that dance in life.

Life as a dancer under the direction of this wise teacher was quite memorable. Once, backstage at the Kennedy Center for the Performing Arts, we found ourselves taking part in a performance with some of the most famous entertainers in the world. We were quite impressed to be in the presence of these prominent performers, one of whom was Louise Fletcher, who had won an Academy Award for her portrayal of Nurse Ratchet in *One Flew Over the Cuckoo's Nest*. We were awestruck when we realized that this great and accomplished woman actually seemed quite nervous as she paced back and forth backstage rehearsing her speech. Expressing what each of us was thinking at the time, a fellow dancer, Kathy Jones, looked to Dr. Wisher in wonder and asked, "*She's* nervous?"

He responded, "Of course she's nervous. That's what makes her great. She cares about her performance."

---

1. Peter Wisher's quotation was perhaps based on this statement by Havelock Ellis: "Dancing is the loftiest, the most moving, the most beautiful of the arts, because it is no mere translation or abstraction from life, it is life itself."

1

Some would say this is true of the dance of adolescence as well. In adolescence, all the world is a stage, and our performance incorporates all of our rehearsals up until that point. Though adolescence may not be the conscious rehearsal that Fletcher's was, it is nonetheless a movement in time that becomes a rehearsal tied to a future performance in life where there are no guarantees.

Adolescence is a time of tremendous growth, a gradual moving away from childhood to a life of increasing independence and responsibility as an adult. Adolescence is a time of letting go but also of holding on, a time of preparation and development, and a time of reaching out to grasp what lies ahead. Properly nourished by their own and environmental resources, adolescents will carry on through life with the right amount of inner strength to succeed.

## SETTING THE STUDY IN MOTION

Growing up deaf in hearing schools, in an educational environment that provided no communication access, and in an era where many children like me were educationally deprived by a system unprepared for us, I missed out on the opportunity to maximize what an education could offer.[2] At some point in time, perhaps beginning in my upper elementary or middle school years and climaxing in high school, I developed a conscious awareness that access to education was empowering, but I did not reap equal benefits from my education.

Coming to Gallaudet University in Washington, D.C., for my undergraduate education proved my hypothesis that an accessible education would be empowering for me. Gallaudet is the world's only liberal arts university for deaf and hard of hearing students. Faculty, students, and staff at Gallaudet use American Sign Language (ASL) to communicate in an environment that is designed to meet the visual language needs of deaf and hard of hearing college students. I prepared to come to Gallaudet by learning ASL. When I returned home for Thanksgiving recess of my freshman year, I proclaimed to my family, "I've learned more in three months at Gallaudet than I learned in four years in a hearing high school."

---

2. See Oliva (2004) for a description of the experiences of deaf children in mainstream classes.

But my learning was not just academic. I finally learned about myself as a deaf person in an environment with other students who were also deaf. My self-awareness and my identity changed dramatically when I was at Gallaudet. I was no longer a "different" kind of person with a hearing "problem" in a world where no one, me included, understood what that difference meant. At Gallaudet I was validated as a person, as a deaf person, and as a person of worth with much to contribute to the world. My immersion in this deaf academic and community environment verified for me that being deaf was a gift, a part of my diversity in a diverse world where diversity should be celebrated.

Establishing an identity is said to be a primary and necessary task of adolescence (Erikson, 1959). There are, however, individual and social, cultural, and linguistic variables that influence this process. The unique psychosocial factors inherent in my life as a deaf adolescent included the fact that I had no reference group of deaf people in my environment. I felt different, yet I didn't understand what that difference was. I had no role models, no peers, and no adults in my environment who understood or could explain that disparity. Yet beneath this sense of separation was an emerging, intuitive longing to touch and explore a new horizon. I asked myself, am I deaf?

Hard as it is to believe, no one had ever told me I was; only that I couldn't hear. Perhaps this was because people close to me were hearing, and like me, they had no role models from whom to learn what it meant to be deaf. But I needed to explore that part of myself; I was bursting at the seams in search of my concept of self. And yes, Gallaudet was where I found my "fit," where I started on a journey and resolved this feeling of difference, where I ended my adolescence and established the beginnings of my identity as a deaf person. Gallaudet was where I acquired the tools that would prepare me for later stages of life.

In addition to my own personal and academic experiences as a deaf person, I became socially immersed in the deaf community, surrounded by close friends, acquaintances, and colleagues who were also deaf. My graduate studies in social work at the University of Maryland and Ohio State University and my professional presentations and publications focused on the developmental, psychosocial, and existential aspects of being deaf. In my professional practice as a social worker, I had a glimpse into the lives and experiences of deaf children, adolescents, and adults, as well as their families, at various points in their life cycles and in a range of experiences and situations in life. I learned that in the midst of all the developmental theories created and explored by world-famous scholars on a quest to understand human life and human behavior, many of them had not considered applications to multiple cultures. Nor did these theorists consider the implications of environmental factors on the growth and development of deaf people, their families, and communities.[3]

This is not to imply that deaf people have more difficulties in development. Perhaps the more appropriate question to consider is whether we use similar or different means to arrive at the same, or different, ends. The *means* being the pathways we take through the process of human development in the temporal context of our environments and the *ends* (although development never ends) being developmental actualization and identity or identities across time. Another appropriate question to ask is, what developmental pathways and spaces are conducive to productive, healthy, satisfying, actualized deaf lives?

Much of the research on deaf children focuses on their educational and cognitive development. Much less has been done on their social development (Meadow-Orlans, 1990). Further, much of the literature and research on deaf children describes the perceptions that others have of them, yet there is so much to learn from the children themselves by listening to their stories and descriptions of their lives. In my previous book, *Inner Lives of Deaf Children* (Sheridan, 2001), I presented interviews of seven children between the ages of seven and ten. I conducted phenomenological interviews with this diverse group of deaf and hard of hearing children to identify similarities (themes) and differences in their *lifeworlds*. *Lifeworlds* refers to the individual and collective elements and realities that are present within the participants' existential experiences, their relationships, and their truths. The term includes not only what exists, but what they see as possible. It includes all elements of the self, their environments, and their relationships. It includes the dynamics of their activities and interactions with both animate and inanimate objects and the context of time and space in their lives. Lifeworlds also involve the dynamics of the children's interactions and the reciprocal influences of various systems levels (i.e., individual, family, and small groups, as well as cultural, organizational, and political systems).

---

3. A more in-depth discussion of these theoretical issues will be presented in chapter 2.

I set out to respect the voices of the children, to let them be our teachers, and to learn, through their narratives, their perspective on "what it is like to be a deaf child in a hearing world that imposes communication, language, and cultural biases" (Sheridan, 2001, p. 10). I wanted to learn what belief systems they had related to belonging and culture, as well as how they viewed their relationships with their parents and significant others and the grief that the literature has stated their parents experience upon discovery that their child is deaf. I wanted to know what views the children had of themselves, what meanings they attributed to their environmental experiences and relationships, what they reported their experiences to be, and what their worldviews were.

## WHY A FOLLOW-UP STUDY?
## LEARNING MORE ABOUT THE DANCE

At the end of *Inner Lives of Deaf Children*, I recommended further research to explore the experiences and perspectives of deaf adolescents using research methods similar to those used in this study. The purpose was to lead us to a deeper understanding of the developmental issues and tasks faced by deaf children and adolescents in their formative years. At that time I had not considered doing such a follow-up study myself. This changed, however, when I received a letter from the mother of one of the children in my study. She thanked me for including her child in the book and told me she had shared it with the staff at her child's school, where it was well received. Then she wrote, "If you ever consider another research paper or book, I thought a follow-up of the children you used in your book would be of great interest. How they have grown and matured would be good to see" (Name withheld, personal communication, 2001). Colleagues agreed and encouraged me in that direction. That's when I knew that I was about to begin a new longitudinal quest for knowledge.

Thus the purpose of this follow-up study is to revisit the children presented in *Inner Lives of Deaf Children* during their adolescent years (between the ages of thirteen and seventeen), to explore the experiential themes they report to exist in their lifeworlds and how they and their families cope with these themes. I was interested in finding out how and if their perspectives on their lifeworlds had changed as they developed to this point in their adolescent lives. Framing this research around the same questions that guided my previous study, I wanted to learn from them what they had to say about being deaf adolescents, about their belief systems of belonging and culture, how they perceived themselves and others in their lives, what they reported their experiences to be, what meanings they ascribed to these experiences, and what thoughts they have about their futures. This has turned into a longitudinal study of the same cohort of deaf students seven years apart. Phase I was the initial research reported in *Inner Lives of Deaf Children*; this book reports phase II, the current follow-up study on their adolescent experiences. Future studies exploring similar research questions at various developmental points in the lives of these participants are planned.

Each of the teenagers in this book has stories to tell about his or her own individual dance. Angie refers to her adolescence as a time of "mulling things over." She talks about all the tasks she needs to accomplish to prepare for adulthood—learning to budget her money, to deal with interpersonal relationships, and, literally and figuratively, to drive: "So I need to start getting ready for my temporary license." Lisa tells us how hard she is training to prepare for the athletic challenges that await her in high school.

All of the participants in this study are faced with tasks and situations that lead them to rely more on themselves and others outside of their family (i.e., friends and mentors who begin to play more significant roles in their lives). Mary tells us about the challenges she faces and the connections she has among her friends and in her community outside of her family. Joe talks about the effort he puts forth on and off the football field and how he has had to learn to pull himself up by his own bootstraps and be responsible for his growth and survival when he finds himself forced onto shaky ground. Pat shares how he bides his time as he looks to the future and values the time he spends with his deaf friends. Danny, true to his inner basketball player, reviews the plays he has made and strategizes his game plan in view of transitions old and new at this pivotal point in his life.

Sometimes in the midst of all this uncontrollable growth, it just seems like too much. Like Alex, they may ask, "Can I take a break?" or "Can we skip that one?" But while they survive the challenges of adolescence, they are also relishing its joys and privileges. They cherish and delight in the laughter and joy of their many friendships, they share loving stories about pleasurable experiences with their families, they take pride in their multiple talents, and they amuse themselves and others with their sense of humor and their fun-loving nature. They are gregarious, responsible, and creative, and I am honored to have had the chance to spend this time with them.

My goals in undertaking this study were to learn about the experiences and perceptions of deaf adolescents and to find out in what ways their experiences and perceptions were similar to or different from those of their childhood seven years ago. In the pages of this book you will find their stories. We will learn from each of these teenagers at this pivotal point in their lives what it means to be a deaf adolescent in the context of today's world. We will learn about their strengths, their beliefs, their hopes and dreams, their likes and dislikes, their day-to-day experiences, how they are similar, and how they are different from each other. We will also examine the similarities and differences they reveal in their views at two developmental points in their lives—as children (between the ages of seven and ten) and as adolescents (between the ages of thirteen and seventeen).

# 2

# Theoretical and Developmental Contexts

## Continuity, Change, and Transcendence

"Who are *you*?" said the Caterpillar.

This was not an encouraging opening for a conversation. Alice replied, rather shyly, "I—I hardly know, sir, just at present—at least I know who I *was* when I got up this morning, but I think I must have been changed several times since then."

—Lewis Carroll, *Alice in Wonderland*

ADOLESCENTS ARE deeply involved in active self-exploration and self-discovery, a process of defining and establishing their individual social and personal identities based on their many life experiences, influences, and roles. As adolescents grow physically, their awareness and understanding of the world, themselves, and others increases. Differences in others' responses and social expectations occur as these changes emerge. Social roles and responsibilities change. Psychological processes change as adolescents are faced with these new physical and social challenges. At the same time, there are temporal and historical influences on adolescents and their environments (Cobb, 1995; Germain, 1987; Hill, 1973; Sheridan, 2001).

Many theories have contributed to our understanding of the stages of human growth and development. Human behavior theory occurs within the context of sociocultural, political, and temporal variables in history. As these variables (i.e., values and norms) change over time, we critique and adapt our theoretical perspectives. Qualitative research is time and context bound (Lincoln & Guba, 1985), and good qualitative researchers describe and consider biopsychosocial and temporal contextual issues. The following section explores professional and popular literature on adolescents in general and deaf adolescents in particular to explain what we know about deaf adolescents in an adolescent world.

## THEORIES OF HUMAN DEVELOPMENT: UTILITY FOR THE LIFE CYCLE OF THE DEAF PERSON AND DEAF ADOLESCENTS

### Life-Stage Theory

Life-stage theories propose specific tasks and challenges that human beings confront at various points in development throughout life. Psychological, social, cognitive, and moral development have all been delineated in life-stage theories. This section will review some of the implications of life-stage theories for the deaf adolescent as discussed in the literature.

*Identity and Individuality.*  Life-stage theorists refer to adolescence as the stage in the life cycle in which humans search for and establish an identity (Erikson, 1959). Not all adolescents arrive at their identities in the same way—some do so gradually after a period of exploration, and others do so more abruptly; some adolescents are relatively unconcerned about identity resolution while others struggle with it (Marcia, 1966, 1976). Adolescence is a time of preparing for new social roles and relations and adopting socially responsible behaviors, values, and ethics (Havinghurst, 1972).

In regard to deaf adolescents, individual, family, and social issues influence the deaf adolescent's attempt to resolve the crisis of identity versus identity diffusion. Most deaf children (approximately 90 percent) are born to two hearing parents. Certainly, the parents' knowledge, experience, and comfort levels are factors in their adjustment to the unexpected responsibility of being a parent of a deaf child. While hearing adolescents and their parents typically face conflicts in values as the teenager attempts to establish individuality, Schlesinger (1972) suggests that deaf versus hearing cultural values may be a source of tension when both parents are hearing and have hearing-centered goals and hopes emotionally invested in their child's future. However, this degree of tension depends on many variables, such as adaptation, coping skills, the strengths of the individuals involved (including communication skills), and the strength and security of parent-child attachment.

Identity development for deaf adolescents may necessitate a process of assessing and resolving diverse perspectives on what and who they should be, where they fit in, and what this means in terms of choices for their futures. Based on cultural and racial identity development models, Glickman (1996) proposes four possible cultural identities that the deaf person may adopt and transition through.

1. *Culturally hearing*: A hearing identity that mirrors the ways hearing people behave and views deafness as a disability to be surmounted.
2. *Culturally marginal*: An identity that lacks social embeddedness in either a hearing or deaf environment.
3. *Culturally deaf*: An awareness of and positive acceptance of one's deafness, so that the deaf person pursues positive relationships with a social group of deaf peers.
4. *Bicultural*: An identity that reflects comfort in both deaf and hearing environments.

*Cognitive, Social Development, and Social Construction Theories.*   Human behavior, cognition, and development cannot be understood without understanding the developmental social and cultural contexts within the person's environment (Vygotsky, 1978). Debates in cognitive theory have centered around the roles of nature (i.e., individual characteristics) versus nurture (environmental influences) in human development. Piaget (1952), in his stage theory of cognitive development, described adolescence as a period of formal operational thought, where reasoning becomes more abstract and more formal in terms of thinking through problems. Bruner, Goodnow, and Austin (1956) emphasized the importance of interpersonal and environmental interaction in cognitive growth.

Throughout history, deaf people have had to transcend the pathologizing labels of professionals in psychology and education in relation to cognition. The early views of sign language as inferior to spoken language and presumptions that spoken language is necessary for formal thought have been blamed for social and cultural views of deaf people as socially and intellectually inferior (Moores, 2001; Padden & Humphries, 2005). Later investigations (i.e., Furth, 1964) centered around the cognitive development of deaf people have led to the conclusion that deaf people have the same capacities for cognitive development as hearing people.[1] Where cognitive delay exists in deaf people with properly functioning internal mental structures (Vygotsky, 1978), it is restrictive, nonstimulating environments not conducive to cognitive growth that lead to these delays (Scheetz, 2001). The work of Akamatsu, Musselman, and Zwiebel (2000) suggested that interaction of intrapersonal factors of the deaf child are also important in cognitive development because deaf children are active participants in environmental exchanges.

According to Vygotsky's social construction theory, a person's interaction with the environment determines development, including how one mediates social interactions. Vygotsky was a pioneer in that he viewed deaf children from a sociocultural strengths perspective rather than from the earlier deficit model (Pintner & Patterson, 1917).

Another stage theory and aspect of cognitive development is Kohlberg's (1963) theory of moral development. Kohlberg (1963) outlined six stages of moral reasoning and suggested that complete moral development, which stretches though adolescence into adulthood, is not achieved by most people. There is a dearth of research on moral development, values, and values clarification among people who are deaf and hard of hearing. While deaf people have been shown to be socially competent, as in other areas of development, they generally have fewer opportunities to experience the environmental stimulation that enhances moral development (Scheetz, 2001). Providing opportunities for negotiating and bargaining in social interactions with peers may help improve a deaf child's moral development (Brice, 1985). The final chapter of this book will provide the reader with some recommendations for such opportunities.

## Conflict Model

Most life-span theorists (e.g., Erikson, Kohlberg, Havinghurst) assume that society provides equal support to all groups and communities. Their theories do not fully consider the social, economic, and political conditions that may have an impact on human development for populations at risk of oppression. Gould's (1987) conflict model of development argues that life-stage models overestimate personal motivation and interpersonal or intrapsychic forces and give insufficient attention to intergroup tension and

---

1. See Andrews, Leigh, & Weiner (2004); Schirmer (2001); Scheetz (2001); Marschark (2003); and Rönnberg (2003) for in-depth discussions of cognitive correlates and the deaf person.

imbalances in power, resources, and opportunities for oppressed groups experiencing subordinate status in society.

An abundance of research, professional and popular literature, and anecdotal evidence testifies to the imbalance of power and discrimination that deaf and hard of hearing people face in society (see Lane, 1992; Ladd, 2003). Many historical and political forces in Western society have worked to suppress attempts by deaf people to validate and promote the existence of their cultures and languages. Social and institutional neglect, social inequities, and discrimination against deaf and hard of hearing people, along with other disability groups, has been so widespread that legislation has been enacted to prohibit it (e.g., the Rehabilitation Act of 1973, the Americans with Disabilities Act of 1990).

Oppressed groups face different and additional challenges as they develop throughout life than do members of dominant groups. The divergent cultural values, standards, and differences between deaf and hearing people create cultural tensions that

> may cause oppressed individuals to be faced with unhealthy choices and conflicts where there is an exacerbated dissonance between what they would like to be and who they think they are on the one hand and who society thinks they "ought" to be and who they are perceived to be on the other. (Corker, 1996, p. 38)

Deaf people are not afforded the stimulating opportunities for development within their environments that hearing people can access. With this in mind, it would be insufficient and unethical to simply compare a deaf person's developmental achievements to those of hearing people and draw conclusions about successful development based on those comparative observations. Traditionally, when baselines for hearing people have been used as the norm, reports on research into the development and the lives of deaf people have been viewed as deviant or negative (Sheridan, 2001). In addition, the problem-focused nature of the professions working with deaf people, the collection of the perceptions of others about deaf people rather than from deaf people themselves, and the lack of appropriate language and communication qualifications and inadequate psychosocial and cultural knowledge of researchers and other professionals have led to conclusions of negative personality, social, and cognitive characteristics in deaf people (Lane, 1992). In spite of this, the fact that deaf people have been able to adapt, cope, and not only survive but transcend a frequently inaccessible and oppressive environment evinces a collective and individual strength (Sheridan, 2001). It is critical for researchers to explore, identify, and embrace the individual and collective strengths of deaf and hard of hearing people.

It is important to view adolescent development as evolving on a developmental continuum connected to childhood and adulthood rather than as a separate and unconnected period of growth (Cobb, 1995; Germain, 1987; Hill, 1973), and for deaf persons, adolescence still is a time of interacting and interdependent biopsychosocial transitions.

## DEAF ADOLESCENTS IN CONTEXT

In *Inner Lives of Deaf Children*, I explored various contexts for studying the development of deaf children, including demographics, technology, validation and advancement of ASL, new visions of self and others, legislation, education, images of deaf people in arts and media, socioeconomic advances, community services, consumer organizations, and new approaches to research and professional practice. Many of these variables can be applied to deaf adolescents today. Exploring the biopsychosocial, temporal, and other contextual factors, such as contemporary cultural, global, and political issues, will lead to better understanding of modern deaf adolescents.

### Biopsychosocial and Temporal Forces

When people think of adolescence, they often think of puberty and the biological changes that teenagers experience—the surge in physical growth, hormonal changes, and sexual dimorphism. Puberty occurs at different rates for different teens, but the completion of the biological and physical processes of adolescence now occurs earlier than it did in the early twentieth century. These biological forces interact with social and psychological influences.

Today's adolescents have experienced a unique set of sociocultural and temporal forces different from those that faced previous generations. They have grown up with highly scheduled and structured lives and face increasing parental and societal pressure to attain higher academic achievement, adapt to changing curricular requirements, and pass state assessment tests.

Perhaps two of the most profound contextual variables influencing the lives of American teenagers in recent years have been the sudden changes in their psychological and physical world caused by the terrorist attacks of

September 11, 2001, and the deep reaches and rapid changes of technology in society.

On September 11, 2001, American children and teenagers watched on national television the brutal attack on their seemingly secure and peaceful nation. Within a relatively short period of time, they saw their fathers, mothers, brothers, sisters, other relatives, and others in their communities called to serve in wars in Afghanistan and Iraq. The interviews for this book took place in the spring and summer of 2002, and the teenagers in this study were very attuned to world events and the terror attacks of September 11, 2001. They mentioned the World Trade Center, the Pentagon, international perceptions of America, a desire to capture those responsible for the attacks, our country's involvement in Iraq and Afghanistan, the response of their schools, and relatives who were affected one way or another by the attacks on New York City.

Today's adolescents entered school at the dawn of the information age. Many teenagers are more computer literate than their teachers and parents. They represent a generation of "tech-savvy" *digital children* (Paige, 2005). They are increasingly reliant on immediate access to communication and information through instant messaging, text pagers, cell phones, fax machines, video technology (including the expanding use of videophone communication), and the Internet. Increased educational and social pressures for technological sophistication have created a digital divide between socioeconomic classes and often between today's youth and their parents.

With the historic Television Decoder Circuitry Act of 1990, deaf adolescents and young adults today are the first generation to grow up with closed-captioned television, which has brought immediate access to the world around them. It is important to note here that the level of access to information via captioned media coincides with the deaf child's reading abilities. Hearing children continue to have greater access to information through auditory means such as radio, incidental communication, and non-captioned media. The current generation of deaf adolescents has witnessed and experienced the beginnings of captioning in movie theaters, real-time captioning in meetings and educational settings, computer-assisted note taking, automatic speech recognition technologies, advances in hearing aid technology, and the increasing number of deaf children and adolescents with cochlear implants. They are also the first to grow up with access to telecommunications and access to 911 emergency dispatch systems.

*Education and Legislation*

In the past thirty years school placement options for deaf and hard of hearing students have changed enormously. Federal laws such as the Education for All Handicapped Children Act of 1975 and the Individuals with Disabilities Education Act of 1990 (IDEA) have mandated a decentralizing shift from deaf-only schools towards integration into nonspecialized educational settings. Educational policy makers seek to place students with disabilities in the *least restrictive environment*, but this placement varies depending on the disability. Whether referred to as *mainstreaming* or *inclusion*, arguments as to the restrictiveness of these environments for deaf students abound (Nash, 2000; Oliva, 2004; Ramsey, 1997; Schick, Williams, & Kupermintz, 2006). While other disability groups inclusion as appropriate, liberating, and empowering, advocates within the Deaf community describe the oppressive social isolation and lack of communication in educational programs designed for children who can hear as inappropriate and a violation of deaf students' civil rights (Schirmer, 2001).[2]

In a 2000–2001 survey of deaf and hard of hearing students, 75.3 percent reported attending mainstream educational programs (Karchmer & Mitchell, 2003). The remaining 24.7 percent attended special schools or centers such as residential or day schools for deaf students. This is an enormous change from the 1975–1976 annual survey, where nearly 50 percent of the participants were enrolled in day or residential programs for deaf students.[3] Some residential schools have closed, and others are adapting to these greatly decreased enrollments. Residential schools have traditionally been a vehicle for the transmission of Deaf culture across generations. Their decreasing enrollment is a source of concern to many Deaf people, who fear the consequence will be the loss of their culture. At a time when more and more deaf and hard of hearing students are fully or partially mainstreamed in programs designed for hearing students and the demand for interpreters is growing, the United States is experiencing a severe shortage of qualified, professional, educational interpreters.

---

2. When capitalized, "Deaf" refers to a cultural identity that stems from the use of American Sign Language; "deaf" refers to an audiologic condition.

3. See Sheridan (2001) for a historical review of the philosophies, placements, policies, and trends in the education of deaf children.

As the interviews with the participants in this study were occurring, the *No Child Left Behind Act* (NCLB) was signed into law by President George W. Bush in January of 2002. NCLB was created to end the achievement gap between rich and poor and white and minority students. It mandates improvements in the academic performance of all students—hearing, deaf, disabled, and nonnative English speakers—by 2014. NCLB holds schools accountable for what their students are learning. To do this, states and school districts across the nation are required to reexamine their standards, use research methods to determine what works best for student learning, set targets for improvement, introduce rigorous achievement testing, and allow parents the option of choosing different schools if theirs is low performing. NCLB was applied to high schools in 2005. NCLB also mandates a National Education Technology Plan.

*Community*

As can be seen from the preceding sections, societal changes have influenced and necessitated change in the communities of deaf and hard of hearing people as well. Historical, social, and cultural changes in the Deaf community parallel the changes that have occurred in larger social systems (Padden & Humphries, 2005). The establishment of schools for the deaf brought large numbers of deaf adults and deaf children together for the first time. American Sign Lanuage flourished and grew in these institutions and led graduates to seek out other Deaf people when they left school. They founded Deaf clubs to meet their social and cultural needs. In the years before telecommunication device for the deaf (TTYs) and captioned films and television, Deaf community members regularly attended Deaf club functions to exchange news, perform skits and plays, and play sports. Memberships in Deaf clubs have dwindled due not only to advances in technology that have provided new means of communication and information access (Andrews, Leigh, & Weiner, 2004; Padden & Humphries, 2005) but also because of changes in mobility (Katz, 1996) and employment patterns, which have given rise to a deaf middle class in the suburbs with access to their own professional organizations (Padden & Humphries, 2005). Technologies such as instant messaging, digital pagers, and videophones have also provided new avenues for socialization and networking that previously could only be achieved through face-to-face contact. Where once the Deaf clubs were the only place Deaf people could enjoy accessible entertainment, now movie theaters show captioned films, television programs and DVDs are captioned, and theatrical performances are interpreted. Home entertainment, professional conferences, athletic events, festivals, meetings, and electronic communication are now more prevalent means of maintaining a sense of community (Erting, Johnson, Smith, & Snider, 1994).

The Deaf community has always lived with social contradictions, including the competing interests of the medical and cultural perspectives of deaf people. American Sign Language is used by more people, both deaf and hearing, now than it ever has in history. At the same time, the very powerful medical sciences profession continues to reach for a cure for deafness through advances in cochlear implants and molecular genetics (Andrews, Leigh, & Weiner, 2004; Padden & Humphries, 2005). Changes in educational programming for deaf children, an increasingly multicultural society, the rise in the number of deaf people attending college, increasing numbers of deaf people in a wider variety of professional fields, and technological and scientific advances will continue to diversify the Deaf community. Today this changing Deaf community is faced with new challenges of self-definition and cultural and linguistic survival. *Inner Lives of Deaf Children* introduced the concept of a *panethnic* Deaf community that encourages collaboration and unity around issues common to the diverse groups of deaf and hard of hearing people and our communities. The concept of *Deafhood* has been introduced by Ladd (2003) as a process whereby deaf people positively reconstruct their existences and environments, develop and actualize their own individual and collective self-concepts, and transcend historical and existing forces of oppression. This term is offered in contrast to the term *deafness*, which is said to reflect a medical view of deaf people. Deafhood is, at this point in time, a source of much discussion in both grassroots and academic circles and will, no doubt, have historical impact on the Deaf community and in professional and academic circles.

## Community Resources

Decreases in public funding for social service programs and the economic stresses caused by changes in health insurance coverage have forced changes in the delivery and availability of social and mental health services for deaf and hard of hearing people, making access to such services more difficult for many. In spite of these economic trends, and in the spirit of community empowerment, many community-based social service programs for deaf and hard of hearing people have sought to become autonomous, deaf-centered, and self-sustaining by transitioning out of the traditional agencies serving the general hearing population, where most have historically been housed. Community service centers for the deaf, which in the past received funding from state departments of rehabilitation to provide sign language interpreting and other social services, have had to find creative means of surviving in the face of economic challenges.

Residential schools for deaf children have contributed to the creation and maintenance of the American Deaf community for almost two hundred years. These schools have passed along the cultural values, norms, traditions, language, and behaviors of American Deaf culture. With greater numbers of deaf children and adolescents mainstreamed in hearing schools, and the closure of several residential schools, it is increasingly important for community agencies to take a greater role in meeting important social and cultural needs of deaf and hard of hearing people of all ages. In addition to continuing to provide the traditional communication, vocational, and life-long education and service needs of deaf and hard of hearing people of all ages, these organizations can support the social and cultural centers of their local Deaf communities. Deaf and hard of hearing people can and do take great pride in owning and operating their own community organizations.

## Diversity, Race, and Ethnicity

Today's youth are growing up in an increasingly diverse society, and cultural pluralism is becoming more accepted (Cobb, 1995). However, many forms of discrimination continue, and the economic inequality between the wealthy and the poor continues to widen, with disproportionate numbers of people of color, immigrants, and refugees likely to be poor (Heyman, 2000). On the fiftieth anniversary of the *Brown v. Board of Education* decision in 2004, then U.S. Secretary of Education Rod Paige noted that "fifty years later, we are still struggling. Access has not always meant achievement. Equality requires quality" (Paige, 2004). Deaf and hard of hearing children and adolescents as a whole, particularly those who are members of diverse racial and ethnic groups, have not escaped this inequality. Just as schools for hearing children were once separated by race, so were schools for deaf children, and just as the educational system has failed to make up for this painful historical fact, so have educational programs for deaf children. Moores (2001) discusses the need for greater emphasis on the needs of ethnic minorities within the Deaf population because our estimates have been historically low, thus leading to underestimates of need. As a result, the educational services provided to deaf members of ethnic minority groups have been inferior to the services provided to deaf students in general (Moores, Jatho, & Dunn, 2001).

## New Visions of Self and Others: Self-Concept Development and Deaf Adolescents

Identity theorists suggest that identity development is a central task of adolescence. As cognitive abilities mature, the self-concept becomes increasingly more abstract, which allows adolescents to better differentiate their sense of self and identity from that of others. Adolescents grow in their ability to reflect on their psychological characteristics, their understanding of themselves, and their fit in various situations. Developing identity and self-understanding, however, is a continuous process, not a one-time event limited to a specific life stage, for both deaf and hearing people.

Numerous studies have examined the self-esteem of deaf and hard of hearing people of all ages. The basis for much of this research is the assumption that we compare ourselves to others and that one component of poor self-concept is the perception that we are lacking in comparison (Cates, 1991). Researchers have long been concerned with the assumption that deaf children and adults may be adversely affected by the negative labeling and stigma they are afforded in their families and in society (Brooks & Ellis, 1982; Beck, 1988; Mindel & Vernon, 1971, 1987; Goffman, 1974; Powers, 1990). Deaf adolescents who identify with both deaf and hearing peers have been found to be more self-critical than those who are more integrated into a deaf peer group (Cole & Edelman, 1991). An opposing view suggests that minority group members are provided with a protective buffer when they participate in a community that shares their minority group membership (Rosenberg, 1989). In another study, profoundly deaf adolescents demonstrated no difference in the level of self-esteem from their hearing counterparts (Martinez & Silvestre, 1995).

The results of my interviews with the cohort of deaf children presented in *Inner Lives of Deaf Children* challenge the traditional negative beliefs and expectations that deaf children will internalize society's stigma.

> The children who were interviewed had many positive experiences, relationships, self-perceptions, and expectations for themselves, as well as healthy coping styles. Their themes of attachment, domesticated others, infinity, and pathways contradict many of society's expectations that

without speech and hearing, deaf and hard of hearing children will not be happy, intelligent, fully functioning, and contributing members of society . . . The children in the study seemed secure in their relationships with their parents and sure of their love and acceptance even though some of them acknowledged their parents had needed to learn new methods of communication and sometimes worried about them. (pp. 208–209)

These participants also presented themes that reflect their views of themselves and others and their relationships with these others (i.e., acceptance and domesticated others, alienation and disparate others), as well as how they determined the identities of deaf, hearing, and hard of hearing individuals (i.e., covert and overt identity) (Sheridan, 2001; see chapter 11, this volume).

While these children recognized their multiple strengths, they also acknowledged their difficulties. Obsessing over what is perceived by society as negative, what society perceives as deviating from the dominant cultural norm, or unrealistic expectations at the expense of individual and collective strengths can have devastating effects on individuals and communities. A healthy and balanced sense of self-esteem is different from a grandiose, unrealistic sense of oneself—which critics of the self-esteem movement are observing in many of today's youth (Smith & Elliott, 2001). I believe we need to be realistic about individual and collective strengths and limitations. While it is important to understand what limitations exist and how we can develop programs and policies to overcome them (or as Ladd [2003] says, to reconstruct them) we can do the most good by emphasizing and putting our individual and collective community strengths to responsible use to defeat the unrealistic and negative expectations and labels that society has imposed on deaf people in research and practice.

Language has also been explored as a factor in the development of self-esteem (Beck, 1988; Kusche, Garfield, & Greenberg, 1983; Bat-Chava, 1993; Desselle, 1994; Wallis, Musselman, & MacKay, 2004). Furthermore, while researchers have looked at the self-esteem of deaf children with hearing versus deaf parents and concluded that deaf children and adults with deaf parents appear to have higher self-esteem than those with hearing parents (Bat-Chava, 1993; Desselle, 1994; Searls, 1993; Yachnik, 1986), they have not investigated this phenomenon with regard to hard of hearing parents (Mitchell & Karchmer, 2004). One factor in this phenomenon may be related to the compatible parent-child language and communication matching. There are a variety of parent-child dyads (two hearing parents and one deaf child; one or two hard of hearing parents and one deaf child; two deaf parents and one deaf child; one hearing parent, one deaf parent, and one deaf child; etc.) that can be investigated while examining the relationship between self-esteem and communication and language (Erting, Prezioso, & Hynes, 1990).

## Friendships and Peer Groups

In adolescence, friendships and peer relations change and become increasingly important. Relationships progress from being superficial in childhood to more intimate and self-disclosing, allowing adolescents to explore and discover themselves in relation to others. At the same time, they are progressing towards individuation and separation from their parents. The coping skills of adolescents evolve to include more complex assessments of stressful situations. Cliques and crowds take on new meanings. Cliques often involve small groups of friends with similar values while crowds provide opportunities for socialization with others outside of their immediate group.

Given a nurturing and accessible social environment that meets the deaf adolescent's visual communication needs, the deaf adolescent may experience these same processes. However, these nurturing and accessible visual social environments are not always available to the deaf teenager. The narratives of the participants in this study attest to the comfortable and uncomfortable situations they face as they seek to establish this level of intimacy with their friends and peer groups, deal with the lack of communication in their social environments, perform increasingly complex assessments of themselves and others in their lifeworlds, and go through the process of adolescent individuation and separation from their parents and families as they look to the future.

## Family Life

The large majority of deaf children and adolescents have hearing parents. Discussions of family dynamics and issues in the literature traditionally focus on deaf children and adolescents with two hearing parents and their hearing siblings all living in the same household. Variations in this pattern of family construction are rarely discussed (e.g., one hearing and one deaf parent, single-parent families, families with deaf grandparents or other relatives). These discussions are based on the assumption, which is statistically correct, that most hearing parents have no previous experience with deaf people and do not expect to have a deaf child. Some attention has been given to families with deaf parents and deaf children and more recently to deaf-parented families of hearing children. This may be due, in part, to our understanding that deaf parents are more attuned to their child's language and developmental needs and that children and adolescents with deaf parents tend to have higher self-concepts and academic achievement because of their early exposure to language (Mitchell & Karchmer, 2004). In addition, these discussions rarely consider minority-parented families. With the growth of minority populations, more consideration and responsiveness is needed for minority families with deaf members (Meadow-Orlans, Mertens, & Sass-Lehrer, 2003) and in this instance with deaf adolescents.

Hearing parents who have no previous experience with deaf people go through their own developmental issues as they grow in their understanding of their deaf child and Deafhood. A dual developmental process takes place—that of the family in response to its deaf member(s) and the child's development in the context of the family and society. Language, communication, ongoing educational issues, the adolescent's developing identity as a deaf person, contextual situations in life requiring advocacy and anticipated vocational opportunities/needs, and culture-specific issues all play into the family's developmental lifeworld. Ideally, parents and family members will achieve linguistic and communication competence, and this in turn will facilitate positive development in the deaf adolescent. Angie told us in *Inner Lives of Deaf Children* that hearing parents would worry about their deaf children, but Danny said they would "learn and learn and learn." The adolescents' narratives in this book will shed further light on their family experiences.

## FRAMING THE STUDY

As in *Inner Lives of Deaf Children*, this study of deaf adolescents is framed in a symbolic-interactionist and ecological perspective of development that continues to observe the deaf person in the biopsychosocial and temporal context of the environment in an effort to understand the deaf adolescent's perspectives of self and others in their lifeworlds. This approach takes into consideration the strengths and limitations of the person, as well as the daily reciprocal influences between people and their environments. It supports the notion of varied developmental paths and the inherent unpredictability of one's life events (Germain, 1973).

Deaf children typically have two hearing parents. Only a small minority of deaf children have two deaf parents. Thus, multigenerational continuity in families, which is assumed in ordinary identity development theories, is absent in the large majority of families of deaf and hard of hearing children. Excepting the similar developmental experiences of cross-racial adoptees and gay or lesbian individuals, the absence of this multigenerational continuity is one of the factors differentiating life span development of deaf people from most other populations (Calderon & Greenberg, 2003; Corker, 1996; Sheridan, 2001). At the core of this discussion is the importance of intimate belonging in families and with peers, and attachment to a social network in adolescent identity development (Calderon & Greenberg, 2003; Foster, 1994; Sheridan, 2001).

## Symbolic Interaction Theory

Symbolic interaction theory sees human behavior and self-concept as shaped by the symbolic meanings we derive from interactive situations with others (Cooley 1902; Mead, 1934). In essence, we come to view ourselves according to how we interpret others' perceptions of us. This theory defines the self as a process that is created and re-created in each social situation we encounter (Berger, 1963). Symbolic interaction is continually at play in our individual social development and self-concept across the life span.

As a minority group, deaf and hard of hearing children grow up in a society that in large part has labeled them as inferior. These messages are communicated to the deaf child in a variety of interactive exchanges. Symbolic interaction theory allows for the possibility that a child may interpret a sender's message in a variety of ways. One possibility is that the child may interpret negative messages as the sender intended, and then proceed to internalize and act on them. And indeed narratives shared by deaf children and adults reflect many such interpretations. Alternatively, the child may interpret a message in a way that was not intended, and the sender and receiver may walk away from the interaction with radically different meanings. While disparate interpretations of interactions happen with everyone, there is increased opportunity for misinterpretation of intended meaning in interactions between deaf and hearing people who do not share a common language. Many of these situations occur on the playground between deaf and hearing children, in the classroom between deaf children and untrained teachers, at the dinner table with hearing family members who do not include the deaf child in their conversations, and in the work environment of deaf adults. Thus, as we attempt to understand the lifeworlds, perceptions of self, relationships, and experiences of deaf and hard of hearing people across the life span, it is important to listen to the meanings that deaf people ascribe to the interactive situations that become their lived realities.

As we act upon the interpretations and meanings we derive from situations, we thereby contribute to the development of our cultures and societies. Social change occurs through the process of symbolic interaction. A good example is found in the 1988 Deaf President Now movement at Gallaudet University in Washington, D.C., the only liberal arts university in the world for deaf students. When the university's board of trustees selected yet another hearing president, students, alumni, faculty, staff, and community advocates saw this as reinforcing their collective sense of discrimination and oppression. The Deaf community acted upon this interpretation with an effective social change—a protest that resulted in the university's first deaf president and a shift to a board of trustees with a majority of deaf members. Since that time, smaller organizations, schools, and agencies serving deaf and hard of hearing people have followed this new social norm of deaf leadership for their programs.

*Ecological Development Perspective*

The ecological development perspective includes the notion that "human beings evolve and adapt through their transactions with every aspect of their environments." Through these interactions, an individual "and the environment continuously and reciprocally influence, shape and change each other" (Germain, 1987, p. 407). Life transitions hold the potential for challenge and growth, yet resources and exchanges between a person and the environment may hinder or stress this potential (Germain, 1980). In the last few decades, researchers have placed increasing emphasis on the impact of the deaf child's environment on the developing person (Harvey, 1989, 2003; Meadow & Dyssegaard, 1983; Vernon & Andrews 1990; Schlesinger & Meadow, 1972; Ladd, 2003). In addition to the family and parental factors, school and community resources and community collaboration are important in ensuring and strengthening the deaf child's developing identity and adaptation (Calderon & Greenberg, 2003).

Harvey's model (1989, 2003) for mental health practice with people who are deaf and hard of hearing emphasizes the importance of biopsychosocial systems that the person interacts with throughout life. He also presents ecological issues to consider in transitional periods across the life span of what he calls the Deaf and hard of hearing ecosystems. Observing that there are differences in the developmental patterns and environments of deaf and hard of hearing persons, he asserts the need for mental health professionals to recognize and work with these differences in psychotherapeutic assessment and treatment settings. While Harvey's work focuses on the problems a deaf person confronts in life within the context of the environment, my research aims to accomplish the following:

1. Reveal the everyday experiences, perspectives, issues, strengths, beliefs, and themes common to a diverse cohort of deaf and hard of hearing children in the context of their biopsychosocial and temporal environments as they develop through life.
2. Be broad in scope and not focused on identifying problems in life.
3. Inform a broader spectrum of professionals outside of the mental health realm.
4. Allow the participants to narrate their own developmental experiences, to be their own voice.

*Existential Theory*

Existential theory examines one's attitude toward, and the meanings one derives from, situations in life (i.e., Frankl, 1969) and "celebrates the absolute uniqueness of each individual" (Walsh, 2006, p. 250). Existential theory frames this study as we learn about the existential meanings that the participants assign to their interpretations of the situations they face in their lifeworlds. We can observe the processes by which they assume personal and collective responsibility to creatively defy and transcend whatever challenges they face. This research allows us to examine the process of their being in the world, of relating to others, and of their hopes for the future. Rather than adopting an oppressive pathologizing approach to knowledge building, it allows us to examine their individual and collective strengths, capabilities, and resiliencies.

PREVIOUS RESEARCH studies on the developmental aspects of being deaf or hard of hearing in the world have neglected to apply research methodologies that pull from the strengths of the participants and allow deaf people to share what is important to them. This study will enhance our knowledge and perhaps even correct what we *think* we know about deaf adolescents by listening to the voices of these participants themselves. Here we will see what they tell us about how they see themselves and others in their lifeworlds and about what it means to be a deaf adolescent in the modern world. We will learn what they can teach us about their development. Rather than fitting deaf adolescents into existing theoretical molds, we will see what this study has to offer as we work towards theories of development specific to the lifeworlds of deaf and hard of hearing people.

# 3

# *We Meet Again*

DOROTHY: What kind of a horse is that? I've never seen a horse like that before!

GUARDIAN OF THE EMERALD CITY GATES: And never will again, I fancy. There's only one of him and he's it. He's the Horse of a Different Color you've heard tell about.

—*The Wizard of Oz*[1]

IN MY presentations to groups I have always said that no two deaf or hard of hearing people are alike. We have as much to learn from their shared perspectives and similarities as we do from their differences. The similarities and differences among the children I interviewed in *Inner Lives of Deaf Children* (2001) are still apparent. As adolescents, they remain unique in their own right and yet continue to share similar experiences, perceptions, likes, dislikes, hopes, and dreams for their futures. This chapter will explain my approach to discovering what these differences and commonalities are.

## RESEARCH METHODS AND ANALYSIS

Qualitative research allows for the discovery of themes and theory through an inductive process of analysis. Qualitative research reports consist of quotations and narratives from the participants in the study. This method helps us to understand the meaning and worldviews that people bring to their interactions with their environments.

My ultimate goal in studying this group of teenagers was to understand how they see themselves, others, and the society with which they interact—all the components of their lifeworlds. I took a phenomenological

---

1. Text taken from Langley, N., Ryerson, F., & Woolf, E. A. (1989). *The Wizard of Oz: The screenplay*. Based on the book by L. Frank Baum (1939). New York: Delta.

approach, which allowed me to see how they interpret their experiences in interactions with others, as well as how the meanings they ascribe to these experiences form the basis of their socially constructed realities (Greene, 1978; Berger & Luckmann, 1967). The data I collected are descriptive rather than numerical (i.e., qualitative rather than quantitative). Thus, within this book, you will find the descriptive narratives shared by the participants in this study.

Naturalistic data are needed to help us understand the nature of the interactions between deaf children and their environments (Moores, 2001). The research method used in this study allowed me to consider the perspectives, experiences, and uniqueness of each adolescent in the study and the contexts of his or her individual and subjective lifeworld. This method also allowed me to identify common themes emerging from the study. From an ethical and social justice standpoint, this empowering approach to research gives voice to the perspectives of a population of children at risk for oppression and discrimination; it is not dependent on the perspectives of others in the children's lifeworlds. There is what ecological theorists (e.g., Germain, 1973) call a *goodness of fit* for naturalistic research into the lifeworlds and perspectives of deaf people throughout the life course.

Traditionally, researchers have doubted the capacity of children and adolescents, whether hearing or deaf, to provide accurate information in self-reports (Stone & Lemanek, 1990). Taking what appeared to be an easier and more accessible route, researchers have typically over-relied on adults (i.e., parents and professionals) for information on various issues of interest pertaining to deaf youth (Sheridan, 1996, 2001). Only recently have researchers begun to obtain self-reports from children (Stone & Lemanek, 1990).

Children's self-understanding develops cognitively. They move from the "concrete, physicalistic, and situation-specific views of the self to abstract, psychological, and trait-like self definitions" (Stone & Lemanek, 1990, p. 25). By the age of eight, children are more aware of themselves and have a more global sense of themselves (Harter & Pike, 1984). After the age of eight, children improve in their ability to report thoughts and feelings, and self-reports become more meaningful and accurate. In adolescence, interviews and self-reports may become richer because of teenagers' ability to critically analyze their thoughts and feelings and the reactions of others (Stone & Lemanek, 1990). The narratives of the deaf adolescents in this study were considerably richer than the narratives from their earlier interviews.

This study looks not only at deaf adolescents' perceptions of self, but also at their perceptions of others in their lifeworlds. Toward adolescence, a child's understanding of the behavior of others develops similarly to their understandings of themselves, moving from the concrete to the abstract, with an increasing "ability to describe and explain the behavior of others, to attribute causes of behavior to situational or dispositional factors, and to generate inferences about the intentions, abilities, and feelings of others" (Shantz, 1983, as cited in Stone & Lemanek, 1990, p. 29)

In the initial interviews (phase I), the participants were between the ages of seven and ten. These children were selected through a process of maximum variation sampling, a nonrandom sampling technique that allows for the selection of participants from diverse backgrounds. This diversity was useful in portraying and preserving the uniqueness of each child and simultaneously allowing for identification of common themes. In phase II, the same cohort of children, now teenagers between the ages of thirteen and seventeen, was revisited, and no new sampling procedures were used. The primary methods for identifying themes in both the previous study and this one were observation and analysis of the transcripts of fourteen videotaped interviews (two interviews for each participant).

The interview techniques in this study included direct and projective questioning. In phase I, art (drawing) and storytelling techniques were used in the first meeting with each child. The children were also asked direct questions. In both phases of the study, the participants were also asked to share stories that reflected their interpretation of photographs from magazines. These photographs depicted children and teens in various settings, situations, and activities, alone, in groups, or with family members. The children and adolescents commented on such things as the activities, feelings, identities, and experiences of the characters in the photographs.

In phase II, similar techniques were used with the adolescents, but instead of being asked to draw pictures, they were given the opportunity to talk about what they would depict in a movie or a book they could create about deaf teenagers. I used a scripted interview guide in both studies to facilitate open-ended questions. This gave me the flexibility to ask for deeper information as the participants shared their unique experiences, as themes emerged, or when I needed clarification and further elaboration. Each interview began as follows:

*Phase I (Ages 7–10)*

—Can you draw a picture of a deaf boy (girl) for me?
—Tell me a story about that deaf child.
—Tell me a story about the deaf child's family. (Similar questions about school, friends, communication, vacations, etc.)

*Phase II (Ages 13–17)*

—If you could make a movie or write a book about deaf teenagers and tell people about what it is like to be a deaf teenager, which would you prefer, a book or a movie?
—In that movie (book), what would you want to tell people about deaf teenagers? (Similar questions were asked about self, school, family, friends, communication, etc.)

Before beginning phase II, I obtained written consent from the parents, just as I had done in the earlier study. I also sought and obtained consent from the teenagers themselves. All seven of the participants returned for this second phase. Some of the interviews took place during the spring of 2002, but most occurred during the summer months of that year, when the participants were on their summer break.

While most of the interviews took place in the adolescents' homes, for the convenience of the participants and their families, a few occurred in the taping studio of a residential school or another site familiar to the teens and their families. Following each interview, I recorded my observations in a field journal to document the research process and context.

I adapted my communication to the needs and preferences of each participant by using ASL, simultaneous communication (signing and talking), or oral communication (speaking and lipreading). A certified sign-to-voice interpreter was present during the interviews to provide audio voice-over on the videotapes of the interviews. This same sign language interpreter transcribed the tapes to text. This process was beneficial for two reasons. First, it sped up the process by allowing me, as the researcher doing the data analysis, to begin interpreting the data as each transcript arrived. Second, having the same person do the voice-over and the transcriptions increased the likelihood of accuracy over an outside transcriptionist. As I received each transcript, I checked it for accuracy against the videotapes. If I disagreed with the interpretation, the interpreter and I discussed the dialogue and reached an agreement on what was said. If we were both unclear about what was said, I contacted the participant to clarify what he or she intended to communicate. I then entered the interview data into a qualitative research software program (ATLAS.ti) for coding and categorizing.

To establish the credibility of this study, I used multiple informants to identify themes and different methods of data collection, such as interviewing with direct questioning and probing, interviewing using projective measures (interpretation of pictures), and observing the teenagers in their environments. Peer debriefing was used in multiple ways throughout the study to lend to credibility.[2]

Because of our earlier work together, the adolescents and I entered phase II of the research with an established level of trust. When I became concerned that I would bring my knowledge of the phase I results into the analysis process of this study, I met with my peer debriefers. It became clear that the emergence of similar codes and categories was unavoidable. These similarities definitely appeared in the data provided by the informants and were not mental constructions I created to match themes that had emerged in the previous study.

Though no assumptions of transferability can be made about this research, I have provided detailed descriptions of the time and context of the interviews to allow future investigators to check for any similarities in other contexts.

## WE MEET AGAIN

Alex, Angie, Danny, Joe, Lisa, Mary, and Pat are teenagers now. I am honored to be welcomed back into these children's lives after they so graciously opened themselves up to my inquiry when they were younger. As I prepared for the interviews, I wondered how much they had grown over the past seven years and if their perspectives had changed. I had much respect

---

2. Two professors in behavioral sciences fields at Gallaudet University also served as peer debriefers in this study. Meetings and e-mail correspondence with these two peer debriefers clarified process, trustworthiness, and data analysis issues. They also verified the utility of the interview script and pictures selected for projective interview methods. In addition, the peer debriefers met with me at the end of the coding process, prior to the development of categories, to help ensure neutrality in the categorization of codes, to discuss the organization of the data, to determine future steps in methodology and interpretation, and to develop a sense of direction in the analysis, all of which are useful functions of peer debriefers (Lincoln & Guba, 1985).

for, and had enjoyed my meetings with, each and every one of them, and I looked forward to seeing them all again. But none of that forethought prepared me for finally coming face-to-face with them and finding many of them at or above eye level with me, and I wondered if that was a predictor of the psychosocial growth they would reveal in their interviews. I was impressed with their openness, their willingness to share, and their skillfulness in teaching others what it means to be a deaf teenager.

Many changes have taken place in their lives since the phase I interviews. Some of them have moved, some of them have parents who have remarried, and all of them have experienced changes in educational programs or schools. In the original study (phase I) the parents of four of the children were divorced or in the process of divorce. Since that time, most of them have remarried, and two of the children now have step- or half-siblings.

Three of the children in the original study attended residential schools and four were mainstreamed. In phase II, three were mainstreamed and four attended residential schools. Lisa moved from a school with an English-based sign philosophy (Signed English) to an oral residential school where only speech and speechreading are used. At the time of her phase II interviews she was preparing to enter high school in a mainstream setting where Signed English would once again be used. Alex moved from a residential school for the deaf to give mainstreaming a try but then returned to his residential school. Pat and Danny moved from one residential school to another. Mary had remained in a mainstreamed total communication program through middle school and was preparing to enter a public high school.[3] She looked forward to attending the residential school part-time for some of her classes. Like Mary, Angie and Joe were mainstreamed and were attending a public high school. In addition, Angie transitioned from one hearing high school to another, where she remained mainstreamed and reported that this change has been a positive experience for her.

One of the advantages of qualitative research is that it allows researchers to describe their cases and apply their findings to the unique realities of the informants. Readers will come to know these seven delightful teenagers more in chapters 4 through 10, which include excerpts from each of their interviews. However, a brief profile of each participant is provided here.

---

3. *Total communication* is a communication philosophy that incorporates a variety of methods tailored to meet the communication needs of the deaf child (e.g., sign language, voice, fingerspelling, lipreading, writing, amplification, gesture, etc.).

*Angie*

Now seventeen, Angie was ten years old at the time of the original study. She is profoundly deaf and has always been mainstreamed with other deaf children in a public school that follows a total communication philosophy. She communicates in ASL, and both of her parents, who are hearing, use Signed English. Angie is Asian and an only child. Prior to the original study, Angie was diagnosed with Attention Deficit Hyperactivity Disorder (ADHD). Although uncertain, it appears most likely that Angie became deaf as a result of an unknown illness in her infancy.

*Alex*

Alex, who was seven at the time of the first study, was fourteen years old when we met again. He was born profoundly deaf, for reasons unknown. His parents are hearing. He has one sibling who is hard of hearing and another who is hearing. His parents were divorced at the time of the original study. His mother has since remarried, and he has additional half-siblings. Alex's mother is a proficient user of ASL. Other family members reportedly also use ASL. Alex transferred from an ASL-English bilingual residential school to a public school mainstream program using a classroom interpreter. He has since returned to a residential program after it was determined to be the best fit for his educational needs. He is Caucasian has no additional disabilities.

*Danny*

Danny was nine years old at the time of the original study and is now sixteen. He has been profoundly deaf from birth, from genetic causes. At the time of the phase I interviews, Danny's parents were divorced. His mother has since remarried, and he now has several step-siblings. His parents, sister, and all of his step-siblings are hearing. Danny has continued to attend residential schools that espouse an ASL-English bilingual philosophy. He communicates in ASL. His mother and reportedly his father and sister are adept at ASL. Danny says that his step-siblings can sign "some" and fingerspell. He is Caucasian.

*Joe*

Now sixteen, Joe was ten when we met for our first interview. Joe considers himself hard of hearing and has the most hearing of any of the participants in the study. He became deaf at the age of five months from an unknown cause. His parents are divorced and his mother has remarried. He lives with his mother and stepfather and attends a hearing public high school, where he is mainstreamed with other deaf adolescents. He has always attended public school total communication programs. All of Joe's family members are hearing. He communicates with his family primarily through speech, but he and his mother both sign. Joe is African American.

## Lisa

Lisa was born profoundly deaf, but the cause is unknown. At the time of the original study Lisa was ten years old and mainstreamed in a public school total communication program. She is now seventeen years old. Lisa's family has always communicated orally with her; soon after her childhood interviews, she transferred to an oral-only residential program. At the time of the adolescent study, she was in the process of transferring to a hearing public high school where she would be mainstreamed. Lisa's mother, father, and siblings are hearing. Lisa communicates orally, but in our interviews she used a few supplemental signs and gestures to facilitate communication with me. Lisa is Caucasian.

## Mary

Mary is profoundly deaf from birth. Both of her parents and all of her siblings are deaf and native ASL users. Mary was eight years old when we met for our first interviews, and she was fourteen at the time of this adolescent study. She spent her elementary school years attending a total communication day school for deaf children and was mainstreamed in a hearing school with an interpreter for some of her classes. When we met again for the adolescent interviews, she was looking forward to a change from being completely mainstreamed in a hearing high school to splitting her days between the hearing high school and a residential school for deaf students for some of her classes. Mary's parents are divorced, and one parent was preparing for remarriage at the time of the adolescent study. Mary is Caucasian.

## Pat

At the time of the original study, Pat was a ten-year-old residential student. He was born profoundly deaf, from unknown causes. His siblings and parents are hearing. He has mild Tourette syndrome and ADHD. In both of our interviews, Pat used ASL. Both of Pat's parents have sign language skills. In the first study, his mother reported that his hearing family members were learning to sign and made an effort to sign with him at home. At the time of the adolescent study, both of his parents demonstrated the ability to communicate with Pat in sign. Pat is Caucasian, and he has always attended residential schools for deaf children with ASL-English bilingual communication philosophies. Pat was seventeen years old at the time of this adolescent study.

AND SO we begin: "If you could make a movie or write a book about deaf teenagers, what would you want to tell them?"

# 4

# *Mary*

The older I get, the more I want to socialize with peers who are deaf like me and can talk, and talk, and talk with me. I like that.

—Mary

ON MY way to pick up Mary at her house, I recalled meeting her for the first time seven years ago—a polite, bright, talkative eight-year-old child. When I pulled in her driveway, Mary's mother came out on the porch of the small yellow rambler and waved hello. She explained that Mary was eating and would be out in a few minutes, and she offered me a seat on the front porch, where we chatted. The youngest child, a lively, small, nine-year-old, also deaf, came to the door and signed to his mother, who introduced us. Facing them while she was talking with me, I turned to see who had appeared next to me and was pleasantly surprised to see Mary standing there with a smile on her tanned face, busily eating her dinner, which she held on a plate in front of her. Like the other children, she had grown considerably during the seven years since we had last met. As I chatted with her and watched her chat with her family, it became apparent that she was code switching more between ASL and English than she did when we met previously. In our earlier interviews, when she was eight years old, she signed mostly in English.

I looked at Mary's nine-year-old brother and said, "Yes, I remember you were two when we met before, and that you were babbling in sign language and imagining you were using a fax machine."

Mary and her mom laughed. They chatted about how they were rearranging the house, and Mary and her youngest brother teasingly bickered over who was going to get the bigger bed. I was impressed with the fun sense of humor that they shared.

Mary and I left for our drive to the school, where we had a reserved interview room waiting for us. It was still rush hour, and I was a bit concerned about driving in the traffic. Mary knew exactly how to get to the freeway and to the school from her home and offered suggestions for routes. I wanted to chat with her like we did seven years ago in the car on our way to the interviews, but with the traffic and the fact that this time we were taking the freeway, that wasn't possible. Things were much quieter in the car this time around.

Mary said she didn't remember much about our previous interviews: "All I remember is going into the place, and getting ice cream."

I smiled at the memory and asked her if she would like to go for ice cream again, and she said, "Sure!"

When we arrived at the school, Mary surveyed the grounds, the buildings, and the people in the cars we passed. This was the alma mater of several of her family members. This was a different setting than the living rooms of the other children. We met here at Mary's mother's suggestion due to all the family activity at home. However, Mary was connected here and seemed right at home.

In our session, Mary was quick and to the point in her responses. Because she was quite open and articulate, she didn't require much probing. Appropriate to her developmental age, Mary has grown in the depth of her responses, but as can be expected, I suspect they were also more "learned" and less imaginative than in her previous interviews. A fluent bilingual communicator in ASL and English, Mary was cooperative, confident, polite, aware, and mature for her age.

Mary illustrates for us the importance of socialization experiences common to all adolescents, yet she instructs us on some very important and unique experiences of deaf adolescents. She talks about the awkwardness of using an interpreter to talk with a boy she is interested in and the inability of her hearing teachers in her mainstreamed classrooms to accurately construe the meaning of her behaviors in interactions with hearing students even with a sign language interpreter present. She demonstrates, as a child of deaf parents, that she feels the same sense of aloneness, detachment, and dissatisfaction that deaf children of hearing parents feel in situations that are communicatively inaccessible or unfulfilling. She emphasizes the importance of her deep sense of attachment, identity, and fulfillment in relationships and interactions with others who are like her in their communicative, cultural, and social preferences. Mary's interviews indicate her developing identity as an individual and an individual who is deaf.

## SCHOOL

It became apparent in her interviews that Mary's views of her mainstream educational experiences have changed. Mary previously attended a day school for deaf students utilizing a total communication approach. She is now primarily, except for homeroom and a few classes, mainstreamed with all hearing students using a sign language interpreter. In our meetings of seven years ago, she reported that her experiences in hearing settings were simple and positive. Today, she admits to challenges in her mainstreamed education where she is not always comfortable. She readily admits that she feels much more at ease in the company of deaf peers but says she tolerates the mainstream experience for the sake of her education. She says her experience at her hearing high school has been an adjustment because it's a different culture and people who go there are "rich." She is excitedly preparing for a transition that would allow her to attend the bilingual residential school for deaf students for part of her school days this coming fall. "I have always wanted to do that, ever since I was in middle school!" A taxi will pick her up and take her to the deaf school and then take her home after school. She looks forward to participating in athletics at the residential school.

Mary smiles as she begins to share her account of what it means to be a deaf teenager. She seems to be saying that some hearing people think being deaf means minimal noise distraction, yet she understands that being deaf is more multifaceted than this.

> I would tell them what it's like to be me, deaf, and a teenager, going to a public, mainstream school. For example, sometimes I feel insulted if hearing people say, "Oh, I wish I were deaf like you." I understand, because we can't hear the noises in class or in the hall. But really it wouldn't be that way. If people are deaf they can't listen to music, and we miss out on some talking and conversation in the hall around us.

Mary also implies that she sometimes feels misjudged in classroom interactions with hearing students. She finds it difficult to communicate with her hearing peers and desires the company of deaf people where communication is easier. She signs her last sentence forcefully as if in frustration.

> Sometimes during class, someone will be talking to me, and the teacher gets mad and the interpreter will nudge me to let me know that the teacher says we have to be quiet because she's going to take away points for class participation. But I'm not doing anything. Sometimes I feel bad,

but sometimes I wish I were with deaf, communicating with friends. It's easier than someone coming up to me and talking, or I talk, and they don't understand, so I give up and write and show that to them so they'll understand me.

Part of what Mary was trying to convey in the paragraph above relates to the complexity of communication for her with hearing students and teachers at school. She seems to be saying, although the example above may not have been the best example, that because her teacher doesn't understand sign language or other nuances of communication with deaf people (e.g., eye contact, the lag in timing with interpreted communication) she feels misunderstood and maybe sometimes defenseless in these situations. Then she shares how a very personal and common teenage experience is so dissimilar for her.

MARY: But sometimes I want . . . if there's a guy, if there's a cute guy that I like, that I want to flirt with . . . but I have to ask the interpreter to tell him. Not really flirt for me . . . But he doesn't really create what he wants to say for me, but he creates it for the interpreter because she's interpreting for me. They're not used to it.

I'm really quiet in class, but when I socialize with other deaf kids at my school, we talk and go on and on. I feel like that. So, they'd get an idea of what it's like to be a deaf teenager. Sometimes people will have parties, and I can't go because if I go, who will talk for me? How can I communicate? I don't really go out often with hearing friends. Only with deaf family and friends. I socialize like that.

MS: So, it sounds like you are saying that sometimes it's specifically a challenge to be a deaf teenager in a public school with hearing kids?

MARY: It is. Maybe if there were some sign language at my school, if they offered ASL and people would take it, then I could communicate through their awareness of sign language; it wouldn't be so much of a challenge. I could help them learn, and they could help me, so it would be more equal. This hasn't happened yet. This fall they're going to set up ASL. I know that some of my friends are going to take it so they can communicate with me more easily.

Mary tells me there were six deaf students in her school this past year but that this fall there will be ten who are her age, and she is happy to have a bigger peer group. She talks about her typical day, waking up at five o'clock in the morning to catch a six o'clock bus to go across town to her school, where all of the students in her homeroom are deaf. Even with the increasing number of deaf peers her age, Mary is often the only deaf student in her classes.

> MARY: We're there [homeroom] for about fifteen or twenty minutes. We talk about things we're supposed to do and so forth. Then about seven thirty, I go into my first period class. Right now it's instructional reading. Next is a physics class . . . First period I'm alone. Second period, physics, I'm with the other guy, Kyle, who is hard of hearing. The two of us are together. He's more of an oral student, but he uses some sign language. The two of us are together that period. Then the next period is study hall, and I'm alone. I start with . . . one of my interpreters sits across from me. I write and do work and so forth. Fourth period is gym, and I'm alone again.

> MS: You mean the class is hearing and you're the only one who's deaf?

> MARY [nods]: I'm the only one who's deaf. In gym now, we're playing tennis, so we're outside. That's boring for me because I'm not really into tennis. Then fifth period is algebra. That's about half deaf and half hearing. Then at lunch with me, from my homeroom, there are a couple. After lunch is math again, with one interpreter, one-on-one. Then sixth and seventh periods are like two classes in one. Really it's two periods of two classes but in one room. It's called World Studies for English and Social Studies. It's world history and all that. Then after that, I get on the bus at two thirty. We go to middle school to pick up one guy. We wait for him until three o'clock to pick him up, from two thirty, thirty minutes waiting on him. Then I get home around four o'clock . . . [She signs this with a sigh.] So I arrive home, I do my homework, I talk with my friends, I go out and play sports. I tend to go to bed around ten o'clock.

Mary has conveyed to us that she finds herself alone in many situations related to school. She is often alone in the company of hearing classmates without deaf peers, she would be alone if she went to parties that hearing students have, she doesn't indicate a strong connection with the hard of hearing classmate who is "really more oral," she seems to feel alone when her behaviors are misunderstood; and she feels alone in the distinct situation of wanting to talk to a boy she likes but having to do so through an interpreter. All of this seems to reflect a theme in Mary's current educational experience.

> MS: And you said that next year you'd be going to the deaf school for three classes?

MARY [*nods*]: I *always* wanted to do that. Since I was in middle school I've always wanted to. Because my sister, when I was in eighth grade and my sister was in ninth grade, she joined the deaf school for two classes. She loved it, but she didn't do it again for some reason. I don't know why. Since then, I've always wanted to be here, and this year, before I graduated I wanted to and my mother said no. But this year I begged and begged, and she permitted me to come this fall.

Because at my school communication is not so great. I'm like a Deaf community person. I have to socialize. Really socialize and talk with my peers. I like that. So in the fall I'm going join classes at the deaf school. So, it should be interesting. I'll see what it's like to socialize with deaf peers, instead of hearing people in their group. I want to see what it's like in deaf classes with a deaf teacher. No interpreter, one-on-one, with the whole class, with no communication. It will be easier for me to make presentations, because I tend not to like to give presentations in front of hearing classmates because they're all hearing and I'm deaf. They don't understand what I'm saying. They're only listening through an interpreter, and I don't really like that. Sometimes it's hard and I feel uncomfortable. For a long time I've wanted that.

## SOCIALIZATION

For teenagers, stories about school, peer relations, and socialization are interrelated. Between childhood and adolescence, socialization activities and priorities change. For deaf teenagers, communication is a conscious issue in their relationships. It's interesting to see how the following exchange reflects Mary's growth and her conscious recognition of greater comfort, ease, and depth in her relations with signing deaf peers. She has an established identity group.

MS: When we met some time ago, in your stories it seemed that it was very easy for you to join hearing friends, to chat with them, to play with them, whether they were deaf or hearing. But now it seems you feel a little bit different.

MARY [*nodding in agreement*]: I think that, too. Before, when I was little, it was fun. I didn't mind because we played. It didn't matter if we couldn't communicate, because we didn't need to. As I got older, communication became more important because teenagers like to talk. We like to gossip; we like to talk about boys. I don't like to be left out of that because most of them don't like to learn sign language. I do have some friends who are older who already know sign language from middle school and elementary school. But I guess the older I get, the more I want to socialize with peers who are deaf like me and can talk, and talk, and talk with me. I like that.

Mary's socialization sometimes includes her deaf teenage siblings.

MARY: Last year at homecoming, that was when I was with my old boyfriend. And when the two of us went out for my school homecoming. So the two of us, and my sister and her now ex-boyfriend, and two of my other friends, we all got together. The two of them were guys named TJ and Kevin. The two of them were going solo. We got together and had a lot of fun. We went out to dinner and went dancing until eleven o'clock or twelve o'clock. Then I went to a friend's house and stayed overnight there. We partied most of the night and enjoyed ourselves. It was really fun.

MS: Sounds like a good time. Everyone in the group that evening was deaf?

MARY: All of us are deaf. Actually two are hard of hearing—no, three are hard of hearing and the rest of us are deaf.

MS: Do you sometimes have parties with a mix of deaf and hearing friends together?

MARY [*jerks her head back a bit, tightens her neck muscles*]: Not . . . Well, yes, I have, yes, I have. My birthday party, for example, some of my hearing friends and some of my deaf friends got together. I liked it because it was kind of interesting to see them socialize with each other and communicate through their knowing sign language by the hearing people and their knowing lipreading by the deaf people. Looking at the two groups, it was interesting. It was really very interesting because the hearing people got to understand the perspective that deaf people have, how we party. The deaf people saw hearing people and got to understand what they're like. It was interesting.

MS: Interesting. Your hearing friends might have gotten to know you a little better from interacting?

MARY: Yeah, see the real me. Yes.

MS: Okay. Is there anything more you'd like to add about your friends?

MARY: I think . . . Let me think about it . . . Last year I went on an eighth-grade school trip to Williamsburg, Virginia. We drove eleven hours. On the drive I got a lot closer to my boyfriend. We stayed for four or five days. With close friends, taking the trip, being roommates with some of my friends. I got to know their real sides, what they were like. It was interesting. I really enjoyed going to Jamestown. I picked on them; we teased each other. They got to know the real me more, you know. I taught them more sign language. It was easier to learn to communicate because there was nothing around. We communicated for a long time. It was nice.

MS: Were there deaf and hearing people in the group?

MARY: Really, last year I was the only one who was deaf . . . They were all hearing. I was the only one. But I still had fun. One of the parent chaperones interpreted, luckily. We went to visit the museums. That was one area that was very interesting to go into. For me personally, I'm fascinated with the history. They have four or five books related to that. To be there, touch it, I loved that. To see and get a vision of how awful that period was. Then we went to visit several other historical sites; it was beautiful. There was a lot to see. We were on a boat trip late into the night. It was fun. My friends teased and played around that night. It was fun. We played games. Another time, I went to visit Gallaudet University. That was interesting! That was cool . . . Normally we have eleven deaf and hard of hearing middle school students who go for the weekend and visit Gallaudet University. Sort of a special open house.

I like it if I'm with deaf friends. Mostly I'm with deaf friends two times a month because we have our club meetings for teens only to get together. At the meetings we talk about general things, about what things we have to face every day. Some of the things we talk about are drugs; we talk about sex, how we deal with hearing people and the hearing world. That sort of thing.

Most of the time when I get together with a group of hearing friends, we tend to do something. But sometimes they're frightened to go to a movie because I won't be able to understand it. I tell them I don't care. If there's action, I don't care. Or sometimes if it's boring, I can lipread a little and understand. With lipreading and action I can get the idea. I don't need to be insulted by going to a movie. It's fine with me.

But with deaf people we get together and go bowling. We go anywhere, to parties, to people's houses. We have sleepovers. We watch movies, rented movies. We do anything, really. I like to get together with my deaf friends more because it's wide open. Whatever, it's flexible. We fool around, we don't care what hearing people think. We play around, tease, fool around.

But with hearing people, if they know sign language well enough we can tease each other and play and fool around. But most of the time I would normally do that with deaf friends.

## FAMILY

Born profoundly deaf to a hard of hearing father and deaf mother in a family where members from multiple generations are deaf, Mary's first language was sign. She tells me, "The only thing interesting about me is my family, that's all. My brothers and sisters, sometimes they drive me crazy, maybe they bother me most of the time, but I still love them." Mary updates me on her current family situation. She shared with me that her family is undergoing another transition. At the time of our previous interviews, her parents were going through a divorce; this time her father is about to remarry. Mary admits that this is sometimes a difficult situation, and while she is a pleasant, optimistic child, I sense an underlying sensitivity to the situation, and she readily volunteers that she wishes the divorce never happened. Despite this tragedy, Mary's family stories clearly present a strong sense of attachment, open communication, good conflict resolution skills, good humor, and an abundance of love for each other. Her family is unmistakably resilient, fun loving, and good natured.

She goes on to share more with me about events in her family since we last met, decisions that both of her parents have made about living arrangements, and how she and her siblings are responding. Mary acknowledges her family's resilience.

My mom's doing pretty well. My sister travels for swimming—my older sister. She swims like me and my brother; all four of us are on swim teams really . . . Problems. We have overcome problems before, nothing new.

Let me think. Stories about my family. Let me see. I have several. One example, last year during my spring break, we went on a camping trip with my dad. We went to an area in southern Tennessee, really far south. Lots of curvy, hilly roads. My sister had her temporary license at that time. My dad made her drive, a good way to break her fear of driving. She was paranoid about the hills and curves. We took two cars, and I was in the other car. They were following, and I liked looking back and seeing my sister going so slowly up and down! When we got there, we really enjoyed it. It was small, just a cute little cabin, divided into rooms, very laid back. We stayed there for a few days. It was a really nice place.

Also, three years ago, when I was in seventh grade, my mom took us kids to South Carolina. We drove the whole way. Hours! We got kind of grouchy with each other, but when we got there, we really enjoyed it! We really enjoyed that week! We got together and went to the beautiful beaches. My brother thought since he tans easily he didn't need any lotion. He didn't realize the sun is closer there. We played and spent the whole day there. My sister went swimming and screamed "Eek." She saw a fish, an ugly black fish. We found seashells. I fell asleep, and I got burned all down my legs really badly. Two stripes down my legs. It looked like a car had driven over my back . . . It was so funny. My—all my girlfriends were making fun of me because I was so stupid to fall asleep on the beach.

But the most funny part is my brother thought he was smart, he knew everything, he didn't need lotion. So we went to the beach and he was swimming all day. When we went home, guess what. My brother had a huge blister on his back. He was so sore. He couldn't bend, he moved like a robot. It was funny. He complained the whole night. That next day, we went bowling, and he wanted to bowl. He looked so funny moving like a robot. My sister looked like an apple, red from head to toe except for white strips from her suit. It was fun! Good memories to look back on. Funny things! "You remember the time you got that huge blister on your back?" Funny! It was nice.

Looking at a picture of a man and a woman that I brought along as a storytelling prompt, Mary says,

This looks like a mother and son. They're close, hugging each other. Mothers and sons are always close. They're laughing because they're relaxed, taking a break or something. It looks like my father and my grandmother.

Further demonstrating her affectionate family ties, she says the following about a picture of a man and a woman with a baby.

Mary: It looks like a mom and dad who have a little kid, and the baby is grouchy. But it looks like they have a lot of love, the parents do, because they want to see what's wrong and take care of him. They could be either deaf or hearing,

MS: So it doesn't matter if they're deaf or hearing, there's still a lot of love in the family?

Mary: Yep. You always can love in a family; it doesn't matter.

MS: Your family is deaf. Is your relationship with your brothers and sisters the same as a deaf person from a hearing family or is it different?

MARY: It's probably different because we're all deaf. We argue and communicate the same way, equally. We yell at each other, we get on each other. But I think with hearing . . . a deaf sister with a hearing sister is probably different. One would look at the other and talk, and the other would say, "I don't understand, I don't understand." You know. When they argue, "What did you say? What did you say?" You know. I think it's probably different.

Mary reported that when they have family reunions now, the hearing cousins group together and just talk while the deaf cousins form another group and sign. They ignore each other. She reported being annoyed by the hearing cousins' lack of signing in the presence of her deaf family members. In the following section on communication, we will see that she recognizes more separation and difference in the deaf and hearing diversity of her extended family now than she did in our interviews seven years ago.

## COMMUNICATION

MARY: I think in the movie I would want to tell them that they should not be afraid to talk to me, to a deaf person. They shouldn't think, "That person's deaf, I'm hearing, it's impossible for the two of us to communicate because I know nothing about how to sign. They don't know how to talk." But you have to remember that there's paper and pencil. You can use that. And if not, try body language or gestures. For sure, you really can be understood. Speak slowly. Talk slowly enough for the deaf person to easily lipread. It's easy, really. Sometimes I find out . . . I heard from friends that there was a guy who liked me, but he was afraid to approach me because I'm deaf. I said, "So, I don't care, I'll approach him, I'll talk to him." Just take steps. It's nice. It's nice. They shouldn't be afraid to try to talk to a deaf person. We don't bite, really.

Well, at first, when I approached a hearing person I didn't know, I would probably be shy at first, knowing how it would feel, how it would feel to talk to a deaf person, me. Sometimes I'd be shy, say hello. Sometimes I'd write. But after a while, we'd be used to each other and write easily and be more open. That's me; I'm very open. Just write easily. For one example, if I'm online and I meet people, they think I'm hearing and can talk. Then after a while I'll tell them I'm deaf and they say, "Oh really? I don't mind." Some of them are rude, you know? "You're deaf?

Oh my God, what am I doing talking to you? Get out of here." They're not used to it.

MS: That really happens?

Mary: Yes, sometimes. But most don't care; it's no big deal. You're a person; I'm a person; we're the same. That's the nice thing about the Internet. You can overlook whether someone is deaf or hearing. But sometimes, for some deaf people, it's very obvious that they're deaf because you can see that. You can see that they don't use proper English. I went to a good school growing up, a mainstream program. My English is pretty good, so most of the time they think I'm hearing. But sometimes when I go into a chat room they'll think I'm hearing because of the way I talk. I'll say, "No, I'm deaf." They say "No," and I say, "I'm really deaf." Sometimes, one thing that's bad about me is I always tend to tell people if something is wrong or inappropriate, I'll tell them they need to change that. They will say I'm insulting them. I don't mean to be, I'm trying to help, but sometimes they don't get the idea that way. That's not my problem; it's on them.

When I'm with deaf people, we talk for hours and hours on end. Really, when I'm with deaf people, we never stop talking. We go on and on. Yes, you can ask my parents about that, for sure. Last year in April, I went into the deaf school for the Academic Bowl meeting. I went in. I was a roommate with three girls, my sister and other classmates. We were sitting in the room. For example, say it was around ten o'clock at night. We'd talk until three o'clock or four o'clock in the morning. When I'm with other deaf people, we never stop talking. We go on and on. It's a lot easier for me to communicate. With hearing people, it's limited, so I tend to just say forget it. With deaf people we can go on and on taking turns. I like that.

It's like in this picture. The girl, I think she's hearing, but if she were deaf, she probably wouldn't be very enthusiastic about participating in sports after school because it's hard to communicate with other hearing peers. If she transferred to a deaf residential school, she would probably be more enthusiastic about talking. Probably like me, because when I'm at school, I'm more quiet and down to earth. But when I socialize with deaf people, I talk and chat and socialize more.

My family's mostly deaf, but there are some hearing relatives. But they know sign language, so we chat and socialize. The family interacts a lot. I like it. Most of the time it is comfortable, but some, I have some cousins who are hearing. They're not enthusiastic about sign language. They get together in a group, a hearing group, and ignore the deaf people. It makes me mad because it's hard for me. There are only us kids who are deaf, me and my brothers and sisters. All of the . . . of the other kids are hearing, so we get left out. I don't really enjoy going out when the family gets together. They know how to sign, but they don't do it. They're too busy talking to each other instead of signing and telling us what they're talking about. [*She makes a dismissive gesture.*]

MS: How does that make you feel?

MARY: Left out. Not involved in the family well. Shunned.

MS: A while ago, when we met before, there was one picture that kids looked at, and they tended to say that when a deaf person is in a situation where she doesn't understand the communication, she's waiting or whatever, that's not an accessible situation. They tended to feel bored. [*Mary nods.*] Do you still feel that way in situations like that?

MARY: Yep. Almost . . . most of the time when we get together with my [hearing] family [members].

MS: How do you handle that?

MARY: Ignore it. They ignore me; I ignore them. My brothers and sisters, we get together and play with each other.

MS: But if you were the only one, would you still ignore it or would you do something different?

MARY: I'd probably try to talk and gesture. If they weren't enthusiastic, I'd get a book and read,

MS: How would you feel?

MARY: I'm used to it. It's no big deal, really. Because when kids are little, they play with each other a lot, but as they grew older and become teenagers, that disappears. I don't know . . . Because we want to talk and gossip, but the hearing kids don't want to sign. Forget it.

Although Mary expresses a great deal of enthusiasm about her opportunities for in-depth communication with her deaf peers, she also tells us that in the right context, where everyone is adept in their communication skills, intense and interesting conversations are possible.

MARY: This is Gallaudet University. They're sitting in a circle and chatting, it seems like. Maybe in the cafeteria area. They would be talking about something interesting because it's an intense discussion about something, because of their facial expressions and their physical gestures and actions.

MS: So you think they're Gallaudet students. Does that mean they're all deaf?

MARY: No. Probably not all, because Gallaudet lets in some hearing kids, but they all know some sign language. They're enthusiastic about learning sign language. They would enjoy themselves, chat, socialize, go out bowling, see movies, eat.

## THE FUTURE

As they were when we met seven years ago, Mary's perceptions of her future and vocational potential continue to be positive.

> Right now, I'm thinking about being an English teacher for deaf students. Maybe an English professor at Gallaudet University. I don't know . . . I think I would like that. Because I myself am interested in writing. I've written a lot of stories and some poems. I'm interested in writing and drawing. I'm a good artist. I like that. But mostly I'm aiming toward an English teacher. I'm interested in that.
>
> I wrote a romantic story about a boy who met a girl and how they got together. It's not done yet. I stopped about eleven pages later and put it aside and have left it since then. I'll pick it up and start writing, and I'll write again when I can . . . I'm doing others, too.

Mary's interpretations of three young people dressed in costumes that represent various vocations reveals the following about her perceptions of the vocational potential of deaf people:

MARY: Interesting picture. It looks like three kids showing what they want to be in the future. This guy looks like a building inspector. This one's a scientist related to animals or something. The other one is an adventurer. He likes adventure, travel, finding things.

MS: Is that something that you and your friends are thinking about in the future?

MARY: I have some friends who want to be scientists, but building inspector, I don't know anyone who wants to do that. Travel, I don't know. Myself, I would like to travel as a tourist, things like that. But exploring and investigating, no.

MS: You said some of your friends want to be scientists. Are those friends deaf or hearing?

MARY: Hearing.

MS: Hearing friends. How about your deaf friends? What do they want to do?

MARY: I don't know. I haven't really had deaf friends so far that have talked in depth about what they want for the future. Most deaf people I know don't want to go to college. They want to lay back and get subsidized every month. I don't know. Me? I want to go to college of course. Get my degree in English, maybe do social work. I don't know, I'll decide later.

Similar to a man in one of the photographs she studies, she tells me that her deaf sister wants to be an architect but that this is an unusual career choice for a deaf person.

In my opinion, he's probably hearing because I don't know a lot of deaf architects. Or anyone that's really fascinated with architecture. My sister is the only one. She's the only one who wants to do that in the future.

Looking at another photograph of a man, Mary decides he must be deaf because of his stance. Mary shrugs as she considers what his life might involve.

Maybe he's in a TV show and they're sitting talking, taking turns one by one, waiting for his turn to speak out. Probably he works at some place related to kids, because he looks like he likes kids. I don't know. He's not married. No ring. [She laughs.]

She examines another photograph, and although she can't distinguish any features in this picture as indicators of the girl's hearing status, she focuses in on other features.

MARY: She might major in sports, because she looks like a sports type of person. Physical Education or something related to physical education things.

MS: Okay. Thank you. If she were deaf, would she go to a hearing college . . .

MARY [*mouths*]: She could [do] either.

MS: . . . or a deaf college?

MARY [*mouths*]: Could. If she's hearing or deaf, she could go to a hearing college if she wants to.

MS: What do you think she would prefer?

MARY: It's hard to tell. It depends how she grew up. Maybe she grew up in an oral program; if she's used to it, she'd probably go to a hearing college, but unless she knows something about Deaf culture and is herself deaf, she might go to find out.

To sum up her discussion on the employment prospects of deaf and hard of hearing people she says,

I would say that . . . really deaf people can basically do everything hearing people can do, because there are no barriers. Nothing. I just met a woman who is a deaf pilot. She can fly planes. And there are other things we have to do. If people, deaf people, say, "I can't do that because hearing people can do that but I can't," maybe they're afraid to do it. You just have to try. If you can't, at least you tried. That's all I want to say.

## PERCEPTIONS OF SELF AND OTHERS

Throughout our interviews, Mary's stories reveal many things about her perceptions of herself, of other deaf people and their families, and of hearing people. This section highlights some examples of Mary's views of herself and these other "characters" in her life.

### Perceptions of Self

Earlier Mary was telling us about the book she was working on. I asked her to tell me about the characters in her story.

MARY: The girl's character is somewhat like me. More, very blunt, her approach is very open. The guy is like I would imagine a guy I went with, you know? It's how I would meet my future boyfriend, something like that.

MS: You consider yourself very direct and —— ?

MARY: Sometimes I'm very direct, really . . . I'm open, very open like my mother. Sometimes I'm a little quiet, but I'm direct sometimes. One of my parents comes from a family with a strong history of deafness. The other one is mixed, but somehow I was born deaf. My brothers and sisters were born deaf. One is hard of hearing, but we're all deaf, really . . . Inherited, from my parents' families. I'm the third generation in one family, and the second generation in the other.

## Perceptions of Others

*Parents' Perceptions of Their Deaf Baby.* Consistent with the earlier study, Mary continues to see a strong sense of attachment between parents and their deaf children regardless of whether parents are deaf or hearing. But she recognizes that hearing parents would face challenges and go through a process of questioning and learning.

MS: In general, parents, whether they're deaf or hearing, when a baby is born deaf, how do the parents feel?

MARY: Oh, they love the baby. I remember seeing my parents when my two little sisters were born. They loved them the moment they saw them. They look at the baby as, "Deaf or hearing, this is my baby who was born, whatever. I suffered for this baby and I love her."

MS: Okay, and if parents are hearing, is there any difference or is it the same?

MARY: They would probably be very happy to have a baby of their own. But if they're hearing and the baby is deaf, they might feel, "What happened? Why is he deaf?" I don't know.

MS: And if your parents were hearing, would that be their response, or what?

MARY: No, I don't think so. They'd just love the baby; whether it was hearing or deaf wouldn't matter.

*Siblings' Perceptions of the Deaf Person.*
Most of the time, at the residential school for example, I know several deaf kids from hearing families, and some of them [the families] look down on them [the teenagers]; they're deaf, so they send them away to

school. They think they know nothing, they're obtuse, you know, dumb. They send them away. And when they come home they don't really socialize; they're not enthusiastic about signing, most of them. But some, they are hearing families, but they love them regardless. They go to the residential school for culture, to learn about the culture, to understand them as deaf. They're eager to sign themselves. There are different kinds of people, really. Most of the time I see different kinds.

*General Perceptions of Hearing People toward the Deaf Person.*
Most of the time in my hearing school, mainstream, it's no big deal, but sometimes, some [hearing] people don't want to know sign language. They just talk and say that's fine or write and are satisfied with that. But some [hearing people] need to know how to chat more, to be closer and chat. They're very enthusiastic. But some just don't care.

*Deaf Teenagers' Perceptions of Mainstreamed Peers.*
Some of them are very critical of hearing people. Sometimes they'll insult me. "What do you go to a hearing school for? You should go to the residential school. You shouldn't go to the hearing school. You don't like yourself and Deaf culture." I'll just tell them, fine. I want to go to that school for a good education. A good education, that's what I want. But deaf . . . I'm deaf, and I go to the residential school to visit because I love Deaf culture. But I want the education I get at a hearing school.

## Deaf or Hearing: Overt Indicators

Mary's observation of one of the photographs tells us that, like Danny, she observes the stance, the sense of fashion, and the presence of material goods as overt indicators of whether one is deaf or hearing.

> She looks like she's a teenager, maybe in ninth grade or eighth grade. I think she has a good family because she has nice clothes; she looks good. She looks young. It looks like a summer dress, good, stylish clothes. I think she's probably hearing . . . Because most deaf people, girls I know, don't dress like that. We dress kind of down to earth, not wear fancy, nice clothes, more down to earth.

She also has overt indicators of hearing status for families:

> MARY [*looking at a picture*]: It looks like Christmas dinner, or [*looks more closely*] maybe not. A fancy dinner with the family all together. They have two happy families. The food looks good. It looks like the mother and some friends who have joined them are talking about something. The

kids are relaxed, getting food. One kid is trying to open the window, I think. The husband is looking down at his kid or something.

MS: Okay. Do you think that family is deaf or hearing?

MARY: Hearing. You tend to see hearing families act like that. You don't see deaf families do that. When deaf families get together, they tend to talk a lot and use large gestures to get people to pay attention and look at them. They seem very laid back, more laid back. Deaf people tend to use large gestures and have more to talk about. They discuss and tease and enjoy. This looks laid back.

When I show Mary the next picture she begins to laugh.

MARY: It looks like a guy from the seventies. The clothes he's wearing, the tight shirt and the flared pants, his shoes are out of fashion. It looks like he's wondering about something. I don't know, wondering about something. I think he's deaf . . . Maybe because of the way he's sitting, sprawled back, [*demonstrates*] looking to the side. I think he might be deaf.

MS: Do deaf people tend to sit differently from hearing people?

MARY: My thinking is probably. I don't know. Looks like the way his arms are spread out, he could sign. I don't know. That's my opinion.

As planned, we stopped for ice cream on the way home. Mary had a double scoop of chocolate marshmallow, and I mint chocolate chip. She had mentioned in her interview that she may want to go to Gallaudet and major in English and be an English professor there and write a book. She also mentioned the possibility of being a social worker. We talked about these careers.

As we approached her house again in the evening, returning from our interviews, we could see her sister and her little brother playing soccer in the front yard. We parked on the street and got out of the car, and as we entered the yard, her sister said hello. I greeted her, and she asked if I had a few minutes to talk about Gallaudet. Of course I did, and she told me she was interested in applying. I answered her questions about such things as our honors program, admissions, and open houses. One sibling was interested in law school, and we discussed the number of deaf lawyers and the internship possibilities in D.C.

I turned around, and the oldest girl showed me a van pulling up to the house and said, "My father."

Mary came up to me holding a little boy with brown hair and blue eyes who bore a striking resemblance to her, and she said, "My son."

I grinned at the likeness and her teasing and said, "I'm confused, another little one?"

Her father laughed at his daughter's humor and the resemblance as well. The little boy grinned and waved as Mary responded with a chuckle, "He's our neighbor."

There was a lot of good-natured humor and teasing with this family as we stood out in the yard and chatted. I told Mary I would look forward to staying in touch and hoped to see her again in seven years. She replied that she would be willing to participate again and maybe would be at Gallaudet then.

ℰಖ

MARY WAS very reality based in her stories. She was realistic about what she saw in the photographs. She shared many stories about her relationships with friends, family, and school, as well as her communication experiences.

Mary is very absorbed in her day-to-day teenage routine at home, at school, and among friends. She had many insights to share, and, as can be expected, many of her perspectives have changed since her childhood interviews. In our previous interviews when Mary was eight years old, she described play relationships with hearing children and cousins as simple and easygoing. Now she appreciates that communication in relationships at this time in her life is of great importance and recognizes that as a child she was focused on play and that communication was less significant to her. Mary's relationships with her deaf peers and family members are comfortable and important to her. She expresses discomfort with hearing cousins and classmates who do not sign. As a child, she taught hearing peers and cousins to sign; now she recognizes that she has a social group to turn to where communication is accessible. She also sees the need for sign language classes in her hearing school.

As will be seen with Danny, Mary perceives differences in fashion and stances as indicators that a person is hearing. She stated that deaf people are more down to earth in their fashion choices and examined posture and stance of people in the photographs for clues to their identities.

Since her childhood interviews, Mary's perception of and insight into her future have grown in detail. Seven years ago she saw herself as a helper, a school bus driver, a schoolteacher, or a hospital worker. Now she sees herself in the teaching role as a college professor of English. Her desire to be a helper or work in a hospital fits her current interest in a career in social work. She anticipates attending college and recognizes a range of positive vocational options for deaf adults.

Mary continues to have a strong sense of herself as person. She knows where she is comfortable, where she fits in and has a variety of strategies for coping with uncomfortable and inaccessible situations. She makes friends easily. She recognizes her talents, loves and respects her family, and feels loved and respected in return. She communicates well in both ASL and English. She is autonomous and insightful and has a fun-loving sense of humor passed on from her family.

# 5

# Danny

I'd like to be the first deaf person in professional basketball.

—Danny

SINCE OUR last meeting, Danny and his family had moved, and he now attended a different residential school. Danny and his mother drove several hours to meet with me on this hot, muggy, ninety-degree day after deciding they wanted to take a vacation to come meet with me instead of my going to their home state. They arrived a few minutes early for our appointment, straight from their road trip. When we met previously, nine-year-old Danny was a day student at a residential school. Now, however, he stays in the dorm at his new deaf school and gets home every other weekend for a visit with his family.

We agreed to meet at Danny's old school, which was familiar territory for him. The school was empty on this summer evening. As I looked over the spacious campus through the main doors waiting for Danny to arrive, I had visions in my head of the students and staff scurrying about during the busy days of the regular school year. I wondered what Danny would be like now. I remembered him as being a very articulate, happy, delightful, fun-loving child who was positively engaged in his school milieu. One of the striking impressions that Danny left with us from his childhood interviews was that he projected a strong sense that *being deaf is no big deal.* Everything in his life seemed very matter of fact, taken for granted, and he was just plain happy. At the time, he fell right into our interviews, eager to show me his drawings of himself, his school, and his favorite TV characters, the Ninja Turtles.

When Danny and his mom arrived, I greeted them and told Danny I didn't know if he would remember me or our meeting of seven years ago when he was nine, here at the school. He responded that he didn't remember. Taller, yet still slim at sixteen years of age, Danny was wearing a blue T-shirt and jeans and reported he was coming down with a cold.

57

Profoundly deaf from birth, Danny is fluent in ASL. Danny's mother proved to be a very competent signer. She told me that she and Danny's father divorced, she is remarried, and that Danny has faced the challenge of adjusting to a blended family situation with hearing stepsiblings. Danny is not alone in his cohort as a child whose parents have divorced. Four of the seven adolescents in this study have parents who are divorced, and within the last seven years, at least one parent of each of these children has either remarried or has immediate plans to do so.

It was evident in Danny's interviews that he was facing difficult times. In his childhood interview, his outlook was much more optimistic. It was disheartening for me to see that Danny's perception of his future vocational and socioeconomic opportunities, and his self-perception and general outlook, are not as positive as they were in our previous meetings. He is more reticent at this point in his life than he was previously.

Despite his dismal mood, Danny does have multiple strengths and has encouraging things happening in his life. He is intelligent and communicates easily in ASL; he sees his potential for college and a career in computers; he boasts of many friends, involvement in school activities, and a variety of leisure activities and hobbies; he depicts a close and communicatively accessible relationship with both of his parents; he continues to enjoy the company of his deaf peers; and he is content in school and family situations that are linguistically and communicatively accessible. In addition, Danny has a variety of successful coping strategies. Another interesting thing about Danny is that he teaches us that as an adolescent, he and other participants in this study now identify new and more subtle differences that indicate that one is deaf, such as stance, posture, and material goods.

୫ର

As DANNY, Marilyn (our voice-over interpreter and transcriptionist), and I continued toward the interview room, I asked Danny how he liked his new school. His response then and elsewhere in his interviews indicated he was content in his school environment. He said that he played sports, and his team has traveled here to play against his old school. He then sat down in the cushioned chair in front of the black backdrop facing the camera.

I gathered my interview script and sat down in the opposite chair. We began our interview when Marilyn indicated that she was ready with the camera, and although I had sent correspondence to each family and teen about the purpose of the study, I reiterated the purpose of our meeting and what we would be doing:

MS: All right, I've just explained to you why we are meeting, and I do appreciate that you drove all the way here. [*Danny smiles, nods, and signs "yes."*] The last time we sat down and talked, I asked you some questions, I asked you to tell me some stories, and I listened to your answers.

DANNY: What did I say then?

MS: Let's see, at that time, you told me that you got together with friends, and if there were hearing people, what it felt like, if they couldn't sign, what you did to participate, join in, or go off on your own. You told me about Ninja Turtles. [*Danny cringes and rolls his eyes as if saying, "Oh, that . . . "*] You were fascinated with them at the time. That was quite a while ago, and that was quite common for kids your age at that time. [*Danny grins and nods in agreement.*] Now that you're older, I want to know what's different than before, what your ideas and dreams are. Also, people who are interested in learning about deaf people tend to listen to hearing people and their ideas. Deaf children and teenagers don't often get the chance to share their views. So, I want you to have the chance to share with the world what it means to be deaf. Right now, the two of us will be talking, the same as we did before, although I've changed it a little because you are older . . . So, first question, if you were to explain to people what it's like to be deaf, and you were either going to write a book or produce a movie, which of those would you prefer?

DANNY: I'd like to make a movie, because there's more action in movies. I'd like that better.

MS: What would you put in the movie? What kinds of stories you would tell about yourself and your life? What would you want people to know about you?

DANNY: My own story?

I nod encouragingly.

## SCHOOL, FRIENDS, AND SPORTS

Danny begins by telling me about what he considers to be of prime importance:

Well, I'm deaf, I attend the School for the Deaf, and I'm involved in soccer and basketball. I think that's all. Hmmm, I stay in a dorm because I'm pretty far from my family's home. But the dorm's fun; we play every evening. I play video games with my friends. I get together with my friends. It's a lot of fun. We play basketball. We have scrimmages. We play a game called "help," where you find your way through. We get together and have fun watching TV. We play video games. We talk. We get into trouble at night after bedtime; we get up and sneak around and get into trouble. I like that. You know teenagers like to get into trouble. They like to sneak out and have a good time. I like that, I love it.

## THE FUTURE

Danny has a mixture of expectations for his future. He sees college as a possibility, but of significance is his perception that his principal aspiration, to be a professional basketball player, is out of reach for a deaf person. Basketball appears to be his niche at this point in his life, and he enjoys playing with his friends at school. Although deaf people have succeeded in professional sports careers, Danny likely has no knowledge of this. Danny sees a career in computers as an alternative, yet he envisions communication difficulties in an office environment and sees the possibility of working with his father as a solution to this.

MS: What kinds of games do you play with your friends?

DANNY: Basketball mostly. I'm crazy about basketball . . . I want to be a pro basketball player. I'd like that.

MS: That's your dream?

DANNY: Yeah, I'd like to be the first deaf person in professional basketball, but I don't think it's possible . . . Yes, impossible. [*He smiles thoughtfully.*] They make a lot of money. Whew! [*He shrugs.*] I want to work with my father. My father makes good money, and I can talk to him. It'd be helpful; he can sign fluently. I mean, if I had a job where everyone was hearing. So I'd like to get a job with my dad, I'd like to learn more about my dad's job. He works with computers. So there'd be a person with me who could help. I like it. It's good money.

As Danny's mother indicated, his adjustment to his parents' divorce has been difficult for him. He reports that his experiences with that have made him reluctant to marry.

I want to live alone. I don't want a wife. Yeah. I've seen my parents' divorce, and I don't want to get married. Maybe just a girlfriend, that's all. But my sister's had a boyfriend for a really long time. They're perfect. I think they'll get married later. But not me, no, I won't, but she probably will.

In Danny's photo interpretations he reveals that he sees college as a possibility for some deaf people. He also recognizes groups of deaf people in photographs at what he assumes to be Gallaudet University or the National Technical Institute for the Deaf. In response to one photograph in particular, he says, "That's college. She's got a backpack. She's deaf, she'll study art."

Danny's interpretation of another photograph suggests that he believes that when deaf people work together in a hearing environment, they may congregate. Although he does not clearly indicate it, he may see this as an accessible identificational community.

This looks like it's at work, and they took a picture. Maybe it's for the Internet. This is what this job looks like. They're working on a computer or something. They could be hearing or deaf. The five of them could be deaf, others at work could be hearing. They got together, those who are deaf, the five of them at a job, they got together.

## PERCEPTIONS OF SELF AND OTHERS

When I asked Danny about what hearing people think deaf teenagers can do with their futures, his response indicated that he perceived hearing people as wanting deaf people to be like them and as seeing deaf people as inferior and less mature. He has perhaps internalized this attitude because he admitted that, excepting himself, in some respects he shares that perception:

DANNY: You need to do smart things, and we're forced to be like hearing people. Don't do immature things. Must act like hearing people . . . Be mature. Sign in a laid-back way.

MS: Do you mean hearing people think deaf people should act the same as them?

DANNY: Yeah, need to be mature. Not act goofy . . . I think we are intellectually inferior . . . most are than hearing. I think . . . Yeah, I look around at many kids at my school, they're intellectually inferior, but not me; no, but we have many who are. My sisters and brothers, their school, I look around, and I see that many of them are really smart. I know hearing people are smarter than deaf people, but I don't care.

Danny was the only participant who expressed the belief that most deaf people are intellectually inferior. Deaf children and teenagers may see that hearing people have more awareness of or information about the world around them and equate this with intellectual superiority. However, when deaf people have the same access to information and environment, their awareness of their environments and opportunities for growth are the same. Environmental systems have a responsibility for the deaf child's literacy. When multiple environments with which a child interacts are accessible, the likelihood of greater overall literacy is enhanced. Deaf culture curriculums in educational programs for deaf students can counter the myth that deaf people are intellectually inferior. Compounding Danny's perception of deaf people as intellectually inferior is his belief that hearing people are more fortunate than he is, thus his anger:

> DANNY: My mother told me I was born deaf. I don't know how it happened. During the birth, there was a problem. There was something wrong in my mother's pregnancy. Then when I was born, that was what happened, and then later, for my sister things went smoothly and she was born hearing. That's why. Makes me mad. Darn, I wish it didn't happen. [*He shrugs and shakes his head; signs are subdued here.*] She's just lucky.

> MS: Your sister's lucky?

> DANNY: Yeah.

> MS: In what way?

> DANNY: Many things . . . It's awful.

> MS: Would your life be different if you could hear?

> DANNY: I think so.

> MS: What would be different if you could hear? How would it be different?

> DANNY: Well, just more hearing. I could hear things, if someone called me, I could look in their direction, and I could hear them. I could be looking away and still get some information. I could use my hearing.

Sometimes, being deaf, I don't even notice. You have to wave to get my attention. But the best thing is deaf people who use hearing aids. They're lucky.

I note that Danny doesn't use or is not using hearing aids at present.

ॐ

THE NEXT morning, when Danny and I meet again for his picture interpretations, he views a photograph of two boys on the floor, one on the phone, with a board game in front of them. He imagines the following:

DANNY: They're playing the game Sorry. [*He points to a child talking on the telephone without signing.*] It looks like he's talking to his grandparents far away. Maybe in another state. Something happy about his parents or his uncle or family or friends. He's happy. But the deaf kid is not happy because he has to use . . . He wishes he could hear his grandma and grandpa's voice. [*He shrugs.*] He looks like he's not happy. Maybe he lost the game and he's unhappy. [*He imitates the expression on the boy's face in the picture.*] He could be deaf or hearing. If he's hearing, maybe he lost the game. If he's deaf, he wishes he could hear his grandmother's voice on the phone. He's jealous, like, "He's lucky. I have to get up and walk over and type [on the TTY], but hearing [people] can talk on the phone anywhere." Maybe that's his opinion. Not my opinion, no. That he's lucky to be able to use the phone. He's frowning, maybe.

MS: I see. So if it happened that your brother or sister was talking on the phone and you were sitting waiting, what would you feel?

DANNY: I wouldn't see them. I'd be in my room.

MS: That doesn't happen? You never see your brother or sister talking on the phone?

DANNY: Sometimes. But I don't care.

This is the second time that Danny has indicated that hearing people are lucky that they can hear. He stated this earlier when he talked about his sister. In this example, Danny attempted to separate himself from the character in the picture by saying it was just the character's opinion, but this does fit with his earlier account of his sister's better luck.

## DEAF OR HEARING: OVERT INDICATORS

As was common with the other participants, Danny told me how he deter-mined who was deaf and who was hearing in the pictures we used as story prompts.

> Looks like he has a family. [*He puts down the paper to sign more clearly.*] Looks like he has a few children. Maybe he works in a restaurant. Maybe he's the boss, or he is cooking food or cleaning the restaurant. He has nice clothes, it looks like. Something's happening, an interview, it looks like. [*He picks up the picture and looks closely.*] He's hearing; looks like he's not signing. [*He demonstrates the stance of the man in the picture with his hands resting on the arms of his chair and his mouth moving.*] You wouldn't lift your hands to sign, then put them back like that over and over, I think.

Stance, posture, and placement of arms as an indication that someone might be deaf is mentioned by Danny, Mary, and Pat in this study. It did not come up in the previous study when the children were younger. Some of the chil-dren now notice more subtle clues in addition to the obvious things like hearing aids, signing, and TTYs. Danny discusses some of these subtle and obvious indicators of a person's hearing status in the following exchanges. We will also see that he perceives hearing people to be at a socioeconomic advantage, having fancier clothes, homes, and accessories. Danny also indi-cates that he doesn't see deaf people aspiring to the same material goals.

Looking at the next picture, he says, "Of course they're deaf. Several have hearing aids." He points and appears to be counting the number of people in the picture with hearing aids. "Looks like they're signing." He moves the picture down and points to indicate what he sees as he says,

> Hearing aid, signing, gesturing. It looks like maybe it's at Gallaudet. It looks like they're college students plus deaf. At Gallaudet or NTID. Mom and I went to Gallaudet and looked around. [*He pauses while looking closely at the picture, then shakes his head.*] I would say they're talking about what they're learning at Gallaudet. The students, I feel they're just start-ing school. I feel. Talking about what they do in classes.

In the following exchange, Danny once again hints at the "fanciness" of a person's possessions as an indicator of whether or not the person is deaf. He looks at the photograph of a woman and teenage boy sitting at a desk in front of a computer. He examines all the items in the picture and says,

It looks like a fancy house . . . Technology, lots of books. A watch . . . It's fancy, it's nice. Looks like that's a new car. It looks like the mom is help-ing her son with his homework. He's asleep, and she's looking on the computer. Looking for answers for something on the Internet with each other. They're hearing. You don't see many deaf people with fancy watches. Not many wear watches. Not many.

Danny's indication that hearing people have "fancier" material goods is evident once again in the following picture.

The family lives in that house. There's a woman and her husband, and there's a boy and a girl there. It looks like Thanksgiving. It's a nice day. Rich clothes. They have a log house. I think they're hearing. They're not signing; with the corners of their mouths up, they're not signing. With signing, one corner of the mouth is up. Looks like talking. You know. They're hearing.

He studies another photograph for a moment.

DANNY: This looks like she has a nice, good job. Nice clothes. Lives in a nice house, has a family, a baby too. She's a young woman. See these thin heels on her shoes, very thin. [*He leans forward and indicates something on the picture.*] It looks like a city, you know, like New York. She's hearing. Not many deaf women wear these. [*He points to her high-heeled shoes.*] You know. What do you call them? High heels. Not many that I've noticed.

MS: It's interesting. You've said not many deaf people have fancy watches and wear high heels. What's the difference? For deaf and hearing people to have different clothes, why do you think that is?

DANNY [*pauses to think*]: Not many deaf people have good jobs. Some do. They don't need things. Don't want them. Hearing people feel like they want fancy things. Well, [they] don't need them. I'm not sure why, I'm just making this up.

MS: Okay. Thank you, next picture.

DANNY: It looks like that mom really cares about her children. She's tell-ing them to be careful. She's helping them step into the car so they don't fall down. It looks like maybe they're going out to a nice restaurant. They've got nice clothes on. It looks like they have a big house behind there. Looks like her husband's at work. They're hearing, because she's not using her hands. She's holding them, guiding them to the door.

[*He looks at the next picture.*] These three are hearing. Not many deaf kids like science. A few do. Not many like science. Not my friends. It's tough. Lots of big words. My school uses computers in science a little. Biology . . . Next year I'll have chemistry. I like math better. A lot of deaf people like math better.

## PETS, TRAINS, AND VIDEO GAMES

When I asked Danny to tell me about things in his life, he shared memories of fun times at basketball camp with his deaf buddies. He also talked about the memories he has of making train sets with his father when he was younger, which reflects the quality of his relationship with his father.

> I miss my trains. My dad helped me make train sets, and we had this really neat model train. It had trees, landscaping, houses, and all that. I wish I still had my model trains. But they were old and we got rid of them. I have that memory. It was an electric train. It was really big, in a room in the basement. My dad and I made it. It was really big. I used to have a fish tank. I'd watch them swimming around. It was a big one. But I don't have it anymore. We've got a basketball hoop set up, so I practice shooting hoops. I have pets. I like taking care of pets, playing with them. I have pets at home. I like them. I have lots. A whole variety. Lizard, frog, fish, and cats. We used to have birds, but they were a bother, so we got rid of the birds. But I like taking care of animals, and a dog. When I'm at home, I just play video games. I've got lots of different games. They keep adding new technology. It's expensive, and if there's no captioning, I can always buy the book and read it and then I know what to do.

## COMMUNICATION AND BELONGING

Danny talks about communication access and barriers and the effect it has on his emotional life and his sense of attachment or lack thereof at home and school. When he is out in the community, he says,

> Most of the time I write. That's all. Like in restaurants, I'll write down what I want. Or in a store, if I'm looking for something and need help, I'll write down what I need to find.

It became apparent in these interviews with this group of adolescents that smaller families with a single deaf member were often associated with greater involvement, interaction, and communication access to family conversations and activities. Deaf adolescents reported feeling lost, detached, bored, and shunned in larger family gatherings. This was the case at holiday gatherings with extended family and where there were stepparents and stepsiblings in blended family situations after divorced parents had remarried. Frequently, these family members did not have sign language skills. Danny illustrates this for us here:

> DANNY: Well, I suggest that they teach the brothers and sisters more signs. So they can . . . So their deaf brothers and sisters understand what they say. Instead of having to ask, "What did you say? What did you say?" over and over again. Use sign so they don't have to ask. You can just sit back. The same thing happens in hearing families with a deaf person. Like, if everybody's hearing, they can just listen and you don't have to ask. So it's important to sign for their deaf brother or sister. When they sign, I don't have to ask. If they understand more sign, they don't ask me, "What did you say?" I get sick of it. They need to understand more signs. I have to ask what they say. They should sign more.
>
> At Chris's house, I've seen Chris's sister just talk, too. Sometimes Chris will have to ask her, "What did you say?" Just like my brothers and sisters. I'm always asking them to tell me, and they get mad because they have to repeat it; they say it twice. They speak and I ask them what they said, and then they have to sign the same thing. They get sick of it. They say, "Hold up." Or they look away and they just ignore me. It's hard to explain. Yeah, at my father's house there are less people, but at my mom's house there are just so many people around, I don't know where to look. I'm lost. It's overwhelming! At my dad's house it's a lot smaller. There's just the three of us.

> MS: So, there's your father, and who's the third?

> DANNY: My sister. There's a lot more signing there. It's a lot better than at my mom's. My sister and her boyfriend, they've been together a long time. Her boyfriend is real nice to me; he's real friendly. He wants to learn sign. I'm teaching him some. I like him. I stay at the dorm through the week. I go to my mom's or my dad's on weekends. At my old school, I was a day student. Now I stay in the dorm. Home is boring; the dorm is better. I get to have fun with my friends, play with them. At home, the food is better than the dorm, but mostly the dorm's better. It's more fun. Last year, and still this year, I really like it. We play basketball every evening. I go all the time. They have open gym for the dorms to get together and play basketball. I love basketball! My sister is fifteen. I'm one year older than my sister. She's hearing.

MS: And does she sign?

DANNY: No. She knows how, but she doesn't use it.

MS: I see. I remember when we met before, you said if you were in a group of people that were all hearing and you approached them and you were frustrated, your sister would interpret for you. Is that not true anymore?

DANNY: Oh, she knows how to sign. She can.

MS: So would she interpret for you?

DANNY: Sometimes.

MS: So do all your stepbrothers and sisters sign as well?

DANNY: Yeah, some, sometimes they fingerspell.

MS: And your grandmother and grandfather, do they sign?

DANNY: My grandfather does a little and my grandmother a lot. I think the three, the four who've learned most are my father, my mother, my sister, and my grandmother. The four of them know a lot. We sign. The others just know a little.

MS: And on the weekends, when you go home with your mother, your sister, your stepbrothers, and your stepsisters and you eat together, what's that like?

DANNY: We just eat. That's it. Most of the time they talk, so I don't understand. It's boring. I just talk to my mom. That's all. [*He shrugs.*] Oh well. I don't care.

Danny's expression is tense, a forced smile with raised eyebrows. While he says he doesn't care, it does appear to be a significant issue for him and I think he is attempting to mask his real feelings.

My mom, she signs and signs all the time, yeah, but my stepbrothers and sisters don't. They talk. My mom did try to force them to sign, but they'd sign for a while, and then in a while they'd just be talking. It doesn't make me feel bad. I'm used to it. They just talk. I'm used to it.

Danny tells me about the numbers of children in his blended family:

DANNY: I don't like having a big family because there's more trouble. There's more arguing. I like it when it's just the two of us. There's less trouble and arguing. We're more mature. They're just kids.

MS: All right. What do the siblings think about their deaf brother or sister?

DANNY: They . . . I don't know, it's just normal.

I take this to mean that Danny believes his brothers and sisters take him for granted and see nothing deviant about being deaf. While he doesn't perceive them as viewing him negatively, he admittedly is not happy with being left out of communication and projects. He has a sense of aloneness in his family.

DANNY: Our first vacation with my stepbrothers, with my stepfather's family, we went to Sea World. We saw fish and dolphins and that kind of thing. And we went to Texas. And we went to Hawaii. There are some islands. It was beautiful, trees and everything, but hot. It was pretty crowded in the car. I finally got to sit in the back. There was more room, and I could stretch my legs out. I had a Game Boy. Most of the time my stepbrothers, the hearing people, would talk, and I would play my Game Boy. I would be by myself.

MS: That's like what you were telling me before, seven years ago. You said you just took care of things by yourself.

When we finished the interview, we found Danny's mom, who was eager to show us photos of her children and stepchildren. She began telling me about her family and their new life. She said it's been hard for Danny to have to share his room with his stepbrothers, but she thought it was a good life lesson to learn to share space. Danny, meanwhile, was outside exploring the campus of the school. I imagined the memories he must have of his childhood days on the grounds of this school. We bid our farewells and I thanked them for participating. I thought how nice it must have been for Danny and his mom to have this quality time together with all the recent changes in their lives.

&

CONTENTMENT AND JOY seem to describe Danny's life at his residential school and in the dorm with his deaf peers. His stories reveal school as a comfortable and enjoyable place for him. As with most of the other children, sports are an important part of his life. He participates on his school athletic teams and attends summer sports camps.

Danny also reports that his family is important to him. He perceives his hearing family members as accepting of him as a deaf person even though communication is not always accessible, and with this he expresses a sense of disconnect. His parents are divorced, and Danny splits his weekends away from his residential school between both of his parents. He acknowledges that the addition of a stepfather and stepsiblings in his life has complicated communication at home, and he expresses concerns about this (i.e., boredom at the dinner table when others are just talking and not signing). Danny tries to pretend this doesn't bother him, but his body language, tone, and the frequency with which he raises the issue make it clear that it is important to him. But Danny is not alone with this experience; other participants also discuss increased communication barriers and isolation in larger family systems.

Of note in these interviews was Danny's report that he perceives most deaf people as generally inferior intellectually to hearing people (although he sees himself as an exception to this) and not as well off socioeconomically. He identified hearing people in pictures as those with fancier, more expensive clothes and accessories, and he suggests that deaf people do not see such material goods as necessary and may not be able to afford them because hearing people have the better paying jobs. He recognizes differences in body language and attention behaviors between deaf and hearing people that represent the visual or auditory nature of communication and interaction. He also reported that hearing people are lucky that they can hear. While he was the only participant who reported such perceptions of inferiority, the other children spoke of barriers that deaf people face, but they related more positive perceptions of the ability of deaf people to transcend these barriers. Joe and Mary, for example, tell us that deaf people can do anything hearing people can do, and Angie talks a lot about the different avenues that deaf people have to take to achieve the same results as hearing people. Alex, Pat, and Lisa tell us that deaf people can do most things that hearing people do vocationally, but they see barriers imposed upon them in certain professions such as the police, military, and firefighting professions. Danny perceives hearing people as generally having a concept of deaf people as deviant and believes they want deaf people to be more conforming to their expectations.

Danny perceives his vocational potential two ways. He anticipates attending college and enjoys computers, which he stated would be a possibility if he could work with his father when he grows up. He believes that since his father signs, he would be able to help Danny communicate on the job. However, Danny's real dream is to become a professional basketball player. Sadly, however, he doesn't think it is possible for a deaf person. He has no deaf professional athletes as role models. I shared a story with Danny about a deaf woman who plays professional basketball in Europe. He appeared impressed and surprised, and with widened eyes, and a crooked smiled, he shifted his head back and asked, "WNBA?"

At the time of this study, Danny did not see marriage in his future. His parents' divorce and the addition of a stepfather and stepsiblings in his life has been an adjustment for him that he wants to avoid in his future.

In the previous study, themes of overt and covert identity issues arose. Overt identity reflects the deaf person's perceived identity of another person as deaf, hearing, or hard of hearing. The covert identity of the person is the actual deaf, hearing, or hard of hearing identity of the perceived person. The children in the phase I study identified several visible indicators of another's identity, such as their visible use of sign language, TTYs, and hearing aids and alerting devices. In this study, however, more subtle clues such as stance, placement of arms, and evidence of material wealth emerged in Danny's interviews as well as those of other participants.

The teenagers are now dealing with barriers on an increasing number of multiple levels. Independent communication in the community (i.e., restaurants, employment) is one area that the participants are beginning to discuss. Thus, where in the previous study, Danny talked about communication at home, in school, and in play groups, he now talks about his pathways to communication with hearing people in the community when they don't sign and indicates writing as an option in restaurants and working with his father as a solution to communication in the work environment.

# 6

# *Angie*

So, I need to start getting ready.

—Angie

Aɴɢɪᴇ's ᴅᴀʏ to be interviewed arrived, a beautiful, breezy summer afternoon. Angie's father met us at the door with Angie following closely behind. Her mother was still at work. Her father confidently signed with us and showed us to the living room, where he left us to give us the privacy we needed.

Angie had blossomed. Now seventeen, she was ten years old at the time of the phase I study. She greeted us wearing a warm smile and a dark blue T-shirt with Gallaudet University imprinted in gold. She was happy, pleasant, cooperative, and detailed, and she has grown in her depth and ability to focus in these seven years. She was polite and enthusiastic about our meeting. She needed little probing or refocusing from me, and a greater maturity in her perspective was clearly evident. She was articulate, engaged, open, quick to respond, and adept at ASL. An only child, Angie lives with her hearing parents, who use Signed English. She has grown in her insight, and her stories are fluid and connected. She also displayed an ability to consider scenarios from various perspectives. She still possessed the same fun-loving sense of humor that she had when we met before. Although Angie has ADHD, she was noticeably calmer in her demeanor compared to our previous meetings. Profoundly deaf, Angie continues to be mainstreamed with other deaf children in a public school using a total communication philosophy.

Angie's growth over the past seven years can partly be attributed to her insatiable curiosity. Throughout her interview she demonstrates a delightful inquisitiveness about an assortment of topics including history, travel, current events, and information that will allow her to succeed in many areas of her adult life. She expresses interest in such things as personal financial management, parenting, and self-protection. She is consciously proactive and future oriented. She describes loving parents who have provided guidance and education, answering many of her questions and taking her on insightful excursions where she has learned about cultures, history, and geography. Greatly complicating the fulfillment of her curiosity, however, is her awareness of and apparent frustration with access to information in her environment. For example, she explains that while she is grateful that her parents can sign and for what they have taught her, she is dissatisfied with what she perceives as a lack of responsiveness from extended family to her desire to be a part of their conversations. She also points out the absence of captioning in movie theaters and on televisions in the homes of others.

If we define *literacy* as the competencies that one brings to the social world that allow for the achievement of their goals in the world, then Angie's story is strongly instructive. Her drive and inquisitiveness are potent forces that will help her tremendously, but visual access to information and the sign language literacy of others in her environment is needed as well.

She grinned as she told me she read her chapter in my book with fascination and laughter. She described it as interesting and fun to read:

> The story that said I wanted to drive when I was sixteen, I found that and started reading it. I wanted a job at a food store. I think it was related to shopping with my parents. I don't think I'd earn enough. I always do that. I come up with different ideas. My goal before, I wanted to be a teacher, and then I changed, I wanted to write a book. I realize I will probably change my mind again and want to become something else. Whatever.

ℰᴧ

As I begin to explain the purpose of our meeting, Angie is leaning forward, watching attentively and nodding affirmatively to indicate that she understands. I ask her, "You said you wanted to write a book in the future. Suppose you wrote a book about yourself. What would you want to let people know about you?"

## Deaf Life, My Life

Angie has so much to say about her life. She tells us about Deaf culture, communication with her family, sign language literacy, her early life, and the discovery of her being deaf.

I'd let them know about my life, my school, my family. And I would call it "Deaf Life: My Life." And I would explain about what I'm interested in, my activities, what I like, my childhood, getting older, thinking about college, high school, and friends in school. It could be distributed in stores, on the Internet, in magazines.

Angie is now clearly aware of Deaf culture, and she recognizes differences between deaf and hearing people. With this she is ready to teach people who don't share in her knowledge about all of the resources available. She is grateful that her parents sign and wishes that her extended family would learn as well.

I would want them to know about Deaf and Deaf culture, what deaf life is like, the variety of types of deaf people. Most hearing people don't know anything about deaf people. They might have some very limited experiences, but they don't know about sign language. Like in my family, extended family, they know I'm deaf, but they've never learned how to communicate. I would want to show hearing people about Deaf culture. I would want people to be curious about how people who are hearing and people who are deaf are the same and different. Things like using the TTY on the phone, or having a visual alarm to wake up, having a baby cry alert, contacting services for an interpreter if you're going to the doctor, or if you're going someplace where you'll need an interpreter, going into school, being successful. Things like that.

Angie repeats for us her interpretation of the story that her parents have shared with her about their discovery that she was deaf, their emotional reaction, their challenges, and how the three of them adapted together to communication and language. Looking back, Angie perceives herself as a troublemaker as she was attempting to communicate and to learn about her environment.

I was born seventeen years ago. When I was about two and a half, my parents noticed that I wasn't talking and I didn't seem to understand. I would be playing, and they would say my name and I wouldn't look up. So they took me to some different doctors, and the doctors kept saying maybe I could hear. But my parents were feeling frustrated because they were sure I couldn't hear. Then one doctor had some special thing he threw down and mom saw that I didn't look. I just kept looking around. Then my parents were somewhere else and my mom's friend was watching me playing. She clapped her hands behind me several times and I didn't look around. And her friend told my mom she didn't care what the doctors said, I couldn't hear. So they took me to a children's hospital and did some tests, and they said I was ninety decibel profoundly deaf. That means that I can't hear anything. My parents were shocked. They got me hearing aids, and my parents started learning sign language, and I started learning sign language too. They felt pretty nervous, but from then on, everything was fine. My mom told me that story. I was frustrated with what I wanted. For example, if I wanted crackers, I would just gesture, I would just point and my mom wouldn't know what I wanted. There was a little conflict. I remember I was a troublemaker in school. At lunchtime, I threw my milk and my food.

Early on in life, Angie had a sense that she was different from other children her age. And she recalls being ridiculed:

I wanted to be the same as the other kids. I remember I noticed my cousin who is two years younger than me didn't have a hearing aid. I thought that meant he wasn't going to school, that's why he didn't have one. Later I understood. I found out hearing people don't have to wear them. I remember I asked an older neighbor to put on my hearing aid, and she said, "Ow, it hurts my ear."

I remember when I was around five, at school, there was a boy who was an awful bully. One time he hurt me, and someone took me by the arm to my mom, and I was crying. My mom talked to the teacher. I had the last laugh on the bully because he got in trouble.

Kindergarten was the worst. My parents didn't like it because I was using some words. I was doing things like that everywhere. I did it at church, at school, I did some things. I was just a little girl. I didn't understand. I was ignorant. I enjoyed taking markers and writing on myself, on my arm. I loved that. If I were watching TV, I would copy things. I would do things like that. I was young.

I remember my mom was really scared because she thought I swallowed my hearing aid battery. They took me to the hospital for an x-ray, and I was really scared. I asked my mom, and she said, "It won't hurt. Don't cry." I didn't understand, but she told me it wouldn't hurt. They put me on the table and they found out I hadn't swallowed it. I told Mom I was sorry.

Angie sees herself and her family as a success story, having pulled through many challenges and brought them into perspective. She also demonstrates a strong desire to continue to grow and succeed in life. Angie's stories often contain issues of self-protection. She talks about getting into trouble when she was younger and how she has overcome that, avoiding trouble in the present, and she emphasizes her need to continue to grow in her ability to take care of herself and her family in the future.

> My mom and dad taught me, so I've learned a lot of things about the right and wrong way to behave as I've grown up. Sometimes I've made mistakes, gotten in trouble; now I'm fine. Sometimes I like to avoid trouble. I like learning from my parents what's going on with people. There was this man; he was mentally ill; he offered me a beer. My dad told me he was drunk, he didn't know, he wasn't thinking right because his mind's not right. I was walking along and he offered it and I said "No, thank you!" I want to try to help people stop drinking, to get a good life. I try to avoid trouble. Someone will say, "Come here," and I'll say, "No thanks." When someone wants something, sometimes it's hard to say no. I try not to get involved, so there's a conflict. Sometimes it's awkward. For example, if the teacher wants something, sometimes I disagree, but I can't say no. There are things I have to do. If another friend wants me to ride in a car, I might say, "I'd love to, but I don't have my parents' permission."

Angie is becoming more of an independent thinker. She talks with her parents about how to handle things. But she doesn't always agree with their answers. She knows when she disagrees and when it is appropriate to act on those disagreements, she is distinguishing between levels of risk in various situations. Her parents and teachers have served as a supportive resource for her as she learns about self-protection, and she has learned to protect herself and avoid trouble. She knows not to put herself in danger.

Here Angie describes communication with her extended family, her feelings about it, and how she deals with it.

> I was two and a half when my parents found out I was deaf, and they informed my aunt and uncle. They didn't start signing until later, when I was still young. Maybe they didn't teach my aunt and uncle. My cousins can sign some. I'm lucky. One who is a senior is learning signs at school, so communication is easy. With one aunt it's not so good. She knows a little bit, but we mostly write, try to talk, or use body language. For example, with my cousin I can use gestures to show something. [*Here she demonstrates with gestures and classifiers, "I need an ironing board."*] My cousin knows the signs for showering, drinking, and eating, and I might write. We explain things through body language, and we manage to understand.
>
> Every Christmas we visit my mother's family. But I just have this feeling inside, when they don't learn sign language; I think maybe they're

embarrassed to talk to me. They don't want to write or use body language. So, I get my parents and ask them if they don't mind interpreting and they will interpret for me. I try to watch facial expressions. It hurts my self-esteem a little bit if the family is talking, and I don't understand what they say at all. My mom will interpret some, but I keep having to ask, "What are they saying, what are they saying?"

Sometimes, like at Thanksgiving, I think my mom feels bad if she has to leave the table or if I'm in another room. It's not a lot of fun if the family is talking. I just twiddle my thumbs, I just sit and focus on my food. I don't know what to do, how to join in the fun with my family. Sometimes I feel really disheartened. Sometimes I'll ask, "What's wrong?" or "What's funny?" I scream, "What's wrong," and my mother will explain to me and I understand, but it doesn't feel good inside. I wish they could sign. Sometimes my mother will not interpret much because she's concentrating on what she's hearing. So, I'll have to ask if she'd mind interpreting, my dad too.

Angie realizes that there may be some communication variation among families with deaf members and among her friends. She describes how she has experienced these differences.

MS: Have you talked with other deaf teenagers who have similar experiences?

ANGIE: Some of them are hard of hearing and some are deaf. Some of the parents sign, some talk. I know parents who know sign language and other family members don't. Some of my friends talk; some of them sign, and I don't know how my friends feel about people around them who don't sign. I don't know if it hurts their self-esteem. Some can talk, I don't talk well. My three best friends are hard of hearing. They speak well, and they're able to understand better. I have friends who can interpret for me when somebody talks. For example, if we go to a movie without captioning, they understand and they can explain to me what's going on. Sometimes I feel bad depending on hearing or hard of hearing friends to let me know what's going on in a movie. I wish there was more captioning, but we don't have much. But I'll be puzzled about what's going on with the characters in the movie. Sometimes they'll look sad, sometimes they'll look happy, and I'll try to figure it out based on their facial expressions. When I don't understand, I'll ask my friends to explain it to me.

Angie sees the role of communication as being central to her relationships. Even though she sees hearing people who do not know how to communicate with her at first as potentially being shocked and recalls childhood playground stories of rude responses from other children, in her maturity she expresses empathy toward their lack of understanding, and she accepts a responsibility to teach them.

If a quiet deaf girl doesn't know how to make good friends with hearing kids, to say hello, it may be hard for her to talk. She might feel bored, embarrassed, or shy because she's deaf. Sometimes, when I was little, when I went to the playground, I would socialize with a lot of hearing people. I can't remember how I communicated. Sometimes they were playing games like "It," and we would have bike rides that we would share. We had different activities. We played kickball and softball, all kinds of things with hearing. Sometimes the hearing boys would talk and they would yell, and I would gesture, "What? I can't hear you." They would be shocked. It's hard to remember what I used to do. I liked to associate with hearing people, with kids. I was almost never shy. I just socialized, chatted. The hearing kids would tease me by making fun of signing. [*Here Angie's expression is unhappy.*] I'd just look at them. I really don't remember what my feelings were.

Sometimes hearing people are shy. If they're learning signs they can be embarrassed. But I don't get mad, I don't bite, I understand their feelings. I'll teach them signs, I'll help them with fingerspelling and teach them. Sometimes I'll bring in an interpreter, if I'm at school, I'll ask if they mind interpreting. Sometimes hearing people are embarrassed, and that's okay. Deaf people are embarrassed sometimes too, but it's fine. That's normal. After a while, they get used to it.

Sometimes I feel frustrated. It's a boost to my self-esteem if my relatives are watching TV and I ask them to explain and they set up the closed captioning. It's a relief to know what's going on. But at my grandmother's house and some cousins' and my aunt and uncle's house there's no captioning. So I can't understand. My mom and dad know how to sign. My mom knows more; my dad knows some.

An only child, Angie has good communication with her parents. They share a sense of humor, fun activities, and a respect for each other.

We do trips together. I like socializing with my family sometimes. It depends on what we're doing. Sometimes I get bored. My mom has her hobbies and Dad has his. I like to watch TV and get on the Internet with friends. They respect what I want. My mom sometimes complains because I'll copy her behavior. I'll sign back at her the way she does. I'm just having fun. If I'm bored I'll tease her. Sometimes I don't like my parents bothering me, like reminding me that it's time to do homework. I'll say, "Cut it out."

In discussing her family vacations, Angie runs through a list of places where she has traveled with her family.

We've been to lots of places! To the beach, to different restaurants, to different stores in North Carolina, and to Disneyland and rode on rides. We went to a mall and to Washington, D.C., the Kennedy Center, and saw the spaceships one time, and a small amusement park. It was nice. In Michigan, we went to a very small island. I don't know the name of the island, but wow, the people there are really cool. They rode bikes around. I really enjoyed that. There was a boat, and I got splashed all over. [*She names and describes other places.*]

You know New York City? Taxis go so fast. We almost got in a wreck. It's really big. Do you know in New York the hotel near the World Trade Center? The restaurant there, I didn't know what that was. I had no idea. I looked up and I saw that, and [*speaking with wide, serious eyes and raised eyebrows*] I wondered what was in there. I remember that. I have the pictures from when we stayed there. Whew, it's a relief; we're lucky we weren't there during the time, September 11.

Some states, like Hawaii, that was vacation. That was two weeks. It was beautiful countryside. Really fascinating: the beaches, the water, the surf is really strong. You could lie down and it would pull you, or if you tried to walk. The water was very strong . . . It was beautiful! Wonderful! We've been to lots of states!

## COMMUNICATION ACCESS

Moving away from the subject of family, Angie talked about communication at school and with friends. She reveals the inconsistent nature of fluent sign communication in her environment. She is so inquisitive and driven to learning, yet her environment is so inconsistently accessible that she seems anxious and frustrated over how this inhibits her growth.

Angie brings to our attention the geographical distance between deaf adolescents, which impinges upon their socialization. But when she does get together with her friends, she is happily entertained. Her discussion of the dispersion of her deaf peers at school gives us a close look at what a typical school day is like for her.

ANGIE: I went to a public elementary and middle school, then I transferred to my high school, and I go to the Deaf Club, and there are teams, so I do a lot of activities with my friends. When I was young, at my old school, there were a lot of hearing people, and some signed. Then I transferred to another school, and I didn't socialize much with hearing people. I joined a club at school and started making friends. Some of my friends knew some signs. Then I went to high school, and there were some people who knew signs. Now at my current high school there are deaf and hearing people there. A lot of hearing students are learning ASL, so we socialize before and after class.

Other friends from my classes from a long time ago I don't see anymore. There are people who live all over that I haven't seen for a long time. I have hearing friends who sign pretty well. I have some friends who are hard of hearing and some other friends who are deaf who live here. Some sign and some don't know it so well. But we use body language, and we fingerspell, and I teach them some signs. One deaf friend signs and speaks. And another hearing friend signs pretty well. I can understand that friend. Sometimes we have a hard time with fingerspelling, spelling out a long word is hard. And then I have some other friends that know a little bit of sign language that I socialize with. We get along fine.

MS: And are there other deaf students in your school?

ANGIE: Yes. Sometimes we'll be in a group, but often we're spread out, not in a deaf group. First period, there are four of us who are deaf. Second period three of us stay until fourth period, and we keep signing. Then two of us stay. Sometimes we all eat lunch together, and sometimes hearing students who were fluent in sign, seniors, joined us, but they are gone now, so it's just the deaf group at lunch. Fifth period I'm the only one. I'm all by myself for ASL. There are two of us in math, then in gym I'm by myself.

MS: So sometimes you're with other deaf students and sometimes you're by yourself?

ANGIE: Exactly, exactly!

MS: When you're alone, how do you understand what's happening?

ANGIE: Well, in cooking class and gym, I have a friend who's in my work team. Sometimes there's an interpreter who I'll ask to interpret while I talk to my friend. We'll use body language, like for sports, you can show throwing the football or picking it up, showing the goal, that kind of thing. There's a hearing girl, and she knows some signs. She's taking ASL II right now, and we can use body language.

MS: And are the sign language teachers deaf or hearing?

ANGIE: Hearing.

MS: Are there any deaf teachers at your high school?

ANGIE [*with much emphasis, a big zero extending across and beyond her chest with force*]: None!

MS: Okay. Tell me more about your friends. Who are they?

ANGIE: I have many. I have some friends who've been friends since I was very young. One friend who's hard of hearing, she's a sophomore at a different school, and Anna, who's a freshman there. Gina is from another school, and she's hard of hearing, a junior. One friend will graduate. Emily lives in New York now. Tiffany is hearing. Most are deaf and some hearing. There are so many.

During the summer, I'm living here, and most of my friends live in other places. I want to work during the summer. I don't have a job yet, but I do want to work. And I want to go to Mexico really bad with my family. It's very nice there. I've been there before. I'm curious. They have Spanish and Indian things, related to their culture. They have a very big village in that area. I've seen in books and I've looked on the Internet. I'm curious about events there. I remember I studied in school. In Mexico, the Spanish, we studied that, the French, the English, Canada, and French Canadian history. I looked on the Internet. I can get hooked on the Internet real easily, corresponding with my friends on e-mail and getting on Web sites and looking around at things. I have to tell myself to stop. E-mail is wonderful, but there's no facial expression. Sometimes I look at the sentences and I can't tell if they're angry or if it's good news. If I'm with someone, I depend on facial expression. I don't want people to blame me for things that I've said. So I prefer face-to-face conversation.

This summer I want to go swimming with my friends. I have to practice driving. I need to take a driving class, but I put it off until the fall. So I need to start getting ready for my temporary license. I don't have enough time now to take the test because I'm focused on school. That's more important. [*She laughs.*] I remember my dad said I couldn't drive until I was twenty-one. And I said, "Why?" He's been telling me that all along. Then I found out that my dad was just teasing me. My dad always gets scared in the car and I say [*laughing*], "Don't worry, peace, love."

Then mom will say, "Calm down." I need to go really slow, but I have a problem with a heavy foot. Mom said, "Slow down, slow down." One time we almost hit a mailbox at church. Mom said, "Be careful, look over there." Mom said, "Be careful, don't hit the flowers." [*She laughs at the memory.*]

MS: In the summer, will you still have the deaf youth activities?

ANGIE [*nods*]: We continue. Tomorrow, we have a speaker. We'll have that one time. Then we'll have other events, like we'll go roller-skating, bowling, or swimming. Sometimes we'll have a car wash. We have a special club for teenagers. We talk about things related to dating and relationships. It's only for thirteen- to eighteen-year-olds. I like that part best because they're close to my age. I don't go a lot. Sometimes with my schedule I can't.

When I do get together with my friends, we go to the mall; we go to the movies. We have a game where you link arms and you go around. I love that game. We have lots of different activities: swimming, parties, lots of things. Sometimes we'll have overnights and stay up watching funny movies and eating, talking, and laughing. We have the volume up too high and my parents will come in and say, "Turn it down." It's so funny. But we'll put our hands on our mouths to be quiet so my parents won't hear us. I remember I had friends spend the night and my mom was awake and heard us laughing and came and just smiled. Mom said, "Try to keep it quiet," but we were laughing and laughing. I have fun with my friends.

My friends are Deaf and hearing, mostly deaf or hard of hearing. We can communicate. The deaf and hard of hearing people all sign pretty well. Some of the hearing people sign some; fingerspelling, they're okay. They do pretty well.

## Gender and Signing

In discussing her observations of the student composition of her ASL classes, Angie takes note of gender role tendencies and the implications this has for her.

Mostly girls know sign language, very few guys. Last year, freshman year, I went to visit the school. I went into ASL III and sat down. There were women all around and only one man. Now I'm in ASL I, and there are some guys, but mostly women. So it's very different. I think women seem to be the ones who take those classes, but I'm not sure. Women seem to be interpreters and teachers. My teacher told me that. I see a difference. I don't want male interpreters, I'm not comfortable with that. I'd prefer a woman. It depends on the place, like a doctor's or health care. I'd be embarrassed with a man explaining. It's easier to get along with a woman, more comfortable. If a male interpreter interpreted in my class, explaining about health things, I'd feel embarrassed. Like one class, family relations, dating, health, socialization, it's a lot of fun. One time there was a male interpreter who came. I sat and put up with it, but it was embarrassing.

A deaf man going to the doctor might want a male interpreter rather than a female. I think it's better that way. I guess maybe it's tradition, I mean for jobs. For example, most women like teaching young children, men tend to teach middle school, high school, college, or they are principals. My elementary school had mostly women, only a couple of men; at another school the only man was the principal.

Angie's expression is appropriate throughout her interview. She is serious as she talks about communication and school. She smiles as she discusses her favorite things and passions, and she blushes as she talks about her embarrassment such as the prospect of using a male interpreter in health care settings.

## THE FUTURE

MS: In your future, what kind of work do you want to do?

ANGIE: I'd like to travel. I'd like to write a book. I'd like to go to another state, to Colorado. I'd like to see the mountains and know about the history of the state. I'd like to know more about America, the Civil War, what happened here. I'm interested in that. I'd like to write about history. I love travel and history. I love writing. I love writing poetry. I love it.

I'm interested in what's happened in the past. One time a teacher was talking about the Vietnam War. It's a very long story; it was a few years ago. Talking about why we had the Vietnam War, the North and South in Vietnam battling for governance, but I didn't understand. So I started asking my mother, asking other people, "What happened in World War I? What happened?" Now when I hear the news about what's going on between India and Pakistan, I ask the teacher what's happening. She says it's really hard; it's a long story. She hasn't explained it to me. It's been on TV, but I don't really understand what's happening. Lots of events.

She says this with longing. Angie has a real thirst for knowledge, but information access is a problem. She appreciates captioning but misses enough in her environment that it is difficult, even with captioned television news, to put the pieces of current events together.

MS: How do you learn about what's happening?

ANGIE: Well, in school sometimes the teacher will read the newspaper and explain to us so we can understand. What happened with Afghanistan and New York and et cetera. I don't watch the news that much because it's so complicated. At home I do have closed captioning.

I'd like to report that I know a deaf woman who's very famous. Her name is Marlee Matlin. I met her before. [*She laughs as she shares this story.*] Yes. At an event. I'd like reporting, asking her about her movie, and what it felt like being a deaf movie star, signing music, and the deaf president, and other questions. I liked meeting her. I'd like to be a reporter and meet people and write and talk about things. I met I. King Jordan [the president of Gallaudet University] at Gallaudet. I shook hands and said hello and my name.

MS: Are you thinking about going to college?

ANGIE: Sure. There are so many different choices. I would like to go someplace in the south because it's warm—but my favorite sport needs a lot of snow, snowboarding—or near Washington, D.C., or where I can be close to my family.

Examining a picture of a young woman, Angie tells us quite a bit about what she thinks her future might entail.

ANGIE: She's very quiet and her eyes are looking up a little bit. I feel inside she might have dreams and goals that she's considering, maybe one would be to get a job after high school. She looks like she's my age. She's deaf, I'm just guessing. Maybe she's going to graduate from high school and go to college or get a job, have children, get married, live independently. But because she can't hear, she's thinking about things. It looks like she's not understanding. She'll marry a deaf man. Her children might be born hearing and learn when they're young. They would learn sign language and talk and learn. The family would be together.

Most deaf men and women tend to marry each other; some marry someone who's hard of hearing or hearing, but that's very different. Most tend to marry deaf people, and most have hearing children. Some who are deaf or hard of hearing have deaf or hard of hearing children. If a deaf person marries a hearing person, I have no idea about the children. Deaf or hearing or mixed, it's hard to know who the children will be. I know this because sometimes I see it. Sometimes I learn in school, sometimes I learn from friends and their families. I know some deaf, some hearing, some hard of hearing. I know their children are deaf and hearing, mixed. Sometimes I just know.

If deaf parents can't hear their baby cry, they need a flashing light at nighttime. Or if the baby's in another room, they need an alert system to know if the baby's crying, to check if it's hungry or needs a diaper changed, or is cold or hot, or needs mommy or daddy, or a toy. You have to watch over them. Sometimes I hear a baby cooing; I feel its belly. You have to pick it up if you notice the expression. You can't hear crying, and you have to see if it's angry or crying or happy; it depends on the expression of the baby. If the baby is five months or eight months, they'll notice the parents signing, and the baby will start learning some signs. If you sign, they'll learn.

MS: And you said that she [the woman pictured] would be independent.

ANGIE: Well, if she wants to live in an apartment or a condo or a house, she would have to get an interpreter when she looked at the house, to talk to the people, to ask questions. If she decides to live in a house and be independent, she'll have to set up a TTY and a flashing light alert system and warnings for theft and fire or if someone comes in during the night. Or in the day, if there's a storm or tornado, you need a weather alert to go to the basement. You watch captioning on TV to know. She's thinking that she'll get married, about a job, and hoping maybe her life will be better. That she can afford whatever, insurance, a car, house, whatever. Some people can't or can afford whatever—bills, gas, and house bills. There are lots of things. Taxes. If you use a credit card, you have to pay each month, write checks. If you have a job, your check will have deductions. If you put down your Social Security number, it's paid to the government for support or whatever. You have to pay for children's education, even if you don't have children. You have to pay taxes. You have to pay for water, home improvements.

I learned in school and from my mom and dad, from different people. My mom told me about credit cards. My dad told me about that and checks and insurance bills, and gas, water, heat, and electricity for the house, computers, cable, you have to pay. I learned about taxes in school and noticed my parents working on taxes. "What's going on, how does the government know?" My mom explained to me when you work you put down your Social Security number. And I asked how—I asked my teacher how the government knew when I was born. If you're born in a hospital, the hospital has to report to the government, so they remember who you are. And new children, young children, have a number. And you have to pay car insurance, and if there's an accident, they pay some and you pay some.

Hearing people sometimes know about the future, about money, what their plans are for retirement, if they'll get government money or stocks, how they're going to buy that. Deaf people know, but they have to mull it over more. Sometimes hearing people know more about math. They know more in depth about things from the environment. Deaf people know, but they have to think what's best for them. For example, some people who retired bought Enron stock. It's collapsed. They should know better. I felt sorry . . . for them when they lost some money. But some was for their children, and the poor parents felt deflated about that. You need to be aware. Sometimes hearing people think about it but don't do right. They put money in Enron stock and it went down and they're stuck. Deaf people need time to think about things. They can't get information from hearing, like complicated things like stocks. It's really complicated, math and money. It's important to do it the right way. You have to know, if you want to save money: think, watch, and be careful. Hearing people have to be careful, but deaf people can't hear about all those things, so they have to think about it more so they don't have their money go downhill and lose it all. You want to save your money and have a better life when you're older. Some people lose money in the sale of their house. They might move somewhere and not have a job and be stuck. It depends on the person.

Hearing people overhear things, read the paper. I just get puzzled about the stocks and I can't figure it all out. That's very different. Deaf people can read some in newspapers and magazines. It depends. Most deaf men who are older love to read newspapers and magazines and watch TV news. The women not a lot. They like to go out and to take care of children. Hearing people can listen to the radio and learn things in school. Deaf people learn some, they know a little about money, bills, independence. My dad loves to watch cable TV about money, and they have the strip across the bottom with the numbers. It's hard to understand. He's fascinated about stocks. It just puzzles me, I don't understand it. My mom explains it when I ask her what's up with stocks. I'll see on TV the hands coming up. It looks crazy. I feel uncomfortable.

I like things more relaxed, an easy pace. I feel more comfortable with time to think.

Prompted by one of the photographs she examines for me, Angie imagines being a parent of a teenage hearing son. She ponders the dynamics of their relationship, and then, because she is a critical thinker, she considers the opposite scenario.

> She's dreaming, thinking he'll go off to college. "'What do I have to do for myself to live and be independent and to be responsible? What if something happens, I need to know how not to depend on him." Like for a hearing person, if someone knocks on the door at night, going to the mother and saying, "'Wake up."
>
> Or maybe he is deaf and the mom is hearing. He is dreaming about goals for college, graduating from high school, and getting married. Will he have a deaf girlfriend and have hearing children and become a father? How he will take care of babies and know if the baby is crying, hungry, or needs a diaper changed? He'll need to know how to get an interpreter for a hearing priest if they want to get married and how to talk with a doctor if his wife gets pregnant. If you're dating, if your girlfriend is deaf, how will you communicate? Say, at a movie, writing, so you can look and see. That will make things go easy and avoid conflict. He might be dreaming about how to take care of children: contacting the school and bringing an interpreter to talk to the teacher; how to get an interpreter for a job interview or for emergencies if you get hurt or are in the hospital and need to talk to a doctor. He might be imagining what's best for his children's lives. Like my dad thinks about my future, and my mom, too, and what's best for me.

In both scenarios, Angie presents developmental responsibilities that the deaf person would confront. In the first, she sees the deaf mother resisting dependence on her hearing son, and in the second, she sees a deaf son thinking about and preparing for his future. In both she considers how the deaf person would deal with communication in a hearing environment.

> ANGIE: I feel that, when my friends graduate from high school, we'll be spread out all over, in different states. Who knows where? We'll socialize and meet new friends, new sweethearts, and forget about our high school friends. I forgot about friends from elementary school when I transferred to middle school, and friends from middle school when I transferred to high school. When I go to college or get a new job I'll forget someone, I'll meet new friends, a lot of new people, men and women. People from different countries, different states, their cultures, how they live, thinking

about how their lives are different. There are different colleges that we're interested in because of the different majors. Then we'll come back here. But we won't have seen each other, almost never, for several years, since high school. Years later, we'll get out our old yearbooks and think about friends that we haven't seen. It's not easy to keep contact. Maybe they moved, got married, live in another state.

MS: When deaf people go to college, some go to a deaf college like Gallaudet and some go to hearing colleges, right? [*Angie nods.*] So what do deaf people do to succeed in college?

ANGIE: Work hard in high school. If they're successful in high school, then they can go to college. They have to work hard, study hard, do well, not depend on the teacher, be responsible, focus on working hard and taking on more responsibility. Get to class on time, show up every day, get good grades. It might take more than four years. If successful, they can get a good job and have a good life. If you don't work hard, you won't get good grades, you'll go downhill and not be successful. You have to think of your goals and what's important. Don't think about partying and friends. Well, think about friends, but you can see them on the weekends.

At deaf colleges, people get together and sign; hearing people get together and talk. If you have a deaf college, you might have special things like TTYs with flashing lights. Then outside, if an emergency happens outside, someone might sign to someone that the person is hurt. Also, you might have a pole with something you can press for an emergency. If you go to a hearing college, it might be tough. You might have to use body language or ask a friend to interpret for you and have an interpreter for classes, and they might not have many TTYs or flashing light systems. In a deaf college, they would have captioning, but I really have no idea about hearing colleges because I really haven't gone into any. Someone whose daughter was in a hearing college there said there were almost no deaf people there, even though they have a program in deafness. But it's very different. Deaf colleges have more relationships with deaf things. Hearing colleges not so much.

## Deaf and Hearing Perspectives: How We See Each Other

When parents find out their baby is deaf, I think they feel shocked. They're surprised. They don't know what to do. They feel nervous because they don't know what to do. They might be embarrassed or ashamed. So, someone in the Deaf community, deaf people, need to let the parents know about schools for their children. They need to teach them sign language, and then they'll be fine after they get a normal start.

Hearing people get nervous, and they shouldn't worry about it. It's normal. They get nervous and sign lousy. I won't get mad. I'll understand. I'm lousy at speaking. I'm not good at that.

Angie is empathetic toward the experiences of hearing parents who may be embarrassed about their sign language skills because she understands what it is like to have difficulty communicating and has found ways to deal with it.

ANGIE: If people don't understand my speech, I'll write. Sometimes hearing people are nervous, or they're shocked because I'm deaf. Sometimes they'll talk to me, and then they'll say, "Oops, I'm sorry," and then they'll take off, and I'm like, "Wait a minute!" They don't understand. Like at a dentist appointment when I'm laying there and they talk through the masks. I just laugh. It's not a big deal. Like with braces, or pointing at my teeth, or writing. I just sit and don't say anything. At the doctor, my parents interpret sometimes; they usually do.

When I look at hearing people, I feel inside that they're lucky that they can hear more and talk to different people. If there's a baby crying, they put their fingers in their ears and say, "Please stop crying." I don't have to hear it. My cousin's baby cries, and I can't hear the baby cry. My cousin says, "That's not fair." And I'll take my hand and put it on the baby. I can feel the trembling from the crying, but I can't hear it. I've noticed, hearing people seem to hear everything. Like I'll be tapping with a pen, or chewing, or sometimes if I'm walking, I'll be shuffling my feet. People will look at me and I don't understand why. Sometimes I'll be making a noise and hearing people will hear it and say, "Shhh." I'm deaf; I don't understand why it makes a noise.

MS: So you and hearing people have different perspectives on sound?

ANGIE: Yes, I learned in ASL class that deaf and hearing perspectives are very different. Deaf people have a different culture. We tend to be very involved in other people's business, and hearing people don't. They don't like that. For example, in school, if a deaf person is late, you ask, "Why were you late?" And they'll say, "I'm sorry I was late. I was talking to my friend." Hearing people think that's impolite. If they're arriving late, they'll just want to sneak in and not say anything. So what deaf people do, asking people why they're late, would be inappropriate for their culture. There's a lot that's opposite. Like hearing people want cochlear implants for deaf people, and deaf people don't. It's opposite. Because we're afraid we'll lose our Deaf culture. We cherish that culture. Hearing people want to give children implants so they can speak and hear easily. I feel bad for the children. I feel bad inside and nervous about the future.

I'm afraid that maybe we'll lose Deaf culture because of implants. I'd like it to stop, but it's a sticky issue.

Angie discussed her hearing aid. Though she was not wearing it at the time, she states she wears it to school every day.

I hear some with it, like the bell ringing. I can hear voices, and I turn it down if I want to concentrate. Sometimes people just talk. And sometimes also, in terms of different culture, there are some sticky situations. Like a deaf person might not mean to insult a hearing person. They'll look at it differently. So sometimes the hearing person will feel insulted. Hearing people don't understand—like the sign "hearing impaired." Deaf people don't like that. I was talking to my teacher about going to the city public schools, and they kept saying "hearing impaired." It didn't bother me. Then I quit that high school and transferred to another school and learned that deaf people don't like "hearing impaired." I talked to my teacher, and she explained that people don't know about Deaf culture. I thought about that, and I don't like that word, it's not appropriate. I like [*fingerspells*] d-e-a-f better.

Angie picks up another picture and describes it for me, revealing her feelings about her relationship with her family.

Wow. The family in this picture looks happy. I have no idea who's deaf. I feel the girl is deaf, because she looks like she's got a lot of self-esteem that she's involved with her family. They love her, they're all together; they haven't rejected her. They're together enjoying being a family. I'm not sure she's deaf. I don't know exactly who is deaf, but that group seems to be enjoying themselves in the picture.

It's better to be together, like my family is together, that's better. Sometimes in a family it's awkward with a deaf person. They feel like they just want to avoid and be away from everyone because the family can't communicate well, or they're embarrassed or ashamed. Some are good and get together and chat and have fun. Sometimes the family doesn't want to bring them to have fun, because they're shy. But you just have to continue to love deaf children.

Like my parents love me, and I'm deaf. They'll say, "Yes, we love you. You're sweet!" I'm thankful. They'll take me to fun places. On my birthday, my parents took me to the mall for activities. They spoiled me with clothes, so many clothes my father bought, lots of things. I said, "Thank you, Dad." My dad takes me places. I want to go to Mexico, and they said fine. And I told my mom I wanted for the two of us to take a trip to Williamsburg, Virginia, to Busch Gardens. My mom was excited. My family enjoys being together. It doesn't matter if children are deaf or hearing; it's no problem. Families still love them. My family has almost never rejected me. But there's one problem. If the whole family is together in a large group just talking, I just sit there and I don't understand what they're talking about.

When we said our good-byes, Angie promised to visit if she comes to Washington. I told her I would love to see her again in seven years to learn more about how people continue to grow. She said her parents will know where to find her when she is twenty-three.

ANGIE IS very sure of her parents' love for her and their attachment. At the same time, she has a healthy attitude about emancipation. Angie's stories reveal a wonderfully inquisitive, future-oriented teenager who actively explores her interests in current events, history, geography, and information that will help her accomplish her present and future goals. She is aware of current and future environmental barriers to the knowledge she seeks and the visions she has for herself. She has developed many pathways around current barriers and has considered many strategies for defying them in the future. She articulates changing roles and responsibilities in her development toward adulthood. Angie accepts tremendous responsibility for her growth, but her drive for multiple literacies is a major theme in her life as she battles an environment outside of home and school that is largely illiterate in its responsiveness to her.

Angie is attuned to the unique differences among deaf, hard of hearing, and hearing people and their families. She has had exposure to classes in ASL and Deaf culture, and she brings what she has learned from these classes into the interviews.

Like other adolescents in this phase of the study, she gives greater consideration to individual and family variables in her responses. She knows where she is comfortable and uncomfortable in social schemes. She is empathetic toward the experiences of others.

Becoming more of an independent and critical thinker, Angie is able to identify when she disagrees with the ideas of others and to communicate her own opinions, but she is also able to differentiate between situations where it is or is not advantageous to express her views. She is able to recall previous perspectives on issues she considers and to indicate how her perspectives have changed. Meanwhile, she continues to be conscious of safety issues. She loves and respects her family and knows that her parents love and respect her in turn.

# 7

# *Joe*

I've been through a lot of things . . . I work hard.

—Joe

After corresponding with Joe's mother for a couple of weeks to plan our visit, I was eagerly anticipating our meeting. His mother spoke adoringly of Joe and all of his activities and achievements. As Marilyn and I parked in front of Joe's home, we saw Joe and his mother beaming and waving to us from the front porch steps. Joe, now sixteen, has grown to a towering six feet two inches. He greeted us in a red high school football jersey. I told him I remembered he had dreams of playing high school football, and now he is.

Joe was ten years old when we met last. Growing up deaf and black in hearing and predominantly white schools, he related many painful social experiences in our previous interviews, and I had remained concerned for him over the years. Despite this, it became clear that Joe, like his mother, was content with his many accomplishments. They were especially meaningful to him in light of the adversity that he has faced. He understands his mother's esteem for him: "She stands by me through everything . . . Now she's remarried and she has someone for herself and I'm happy for her." He shared with me that he has maintained a 3.6 GPA on top of his busy athletic and extracurricular schedule and that he is looking forward to playing varsity sports next year. Needless to say, I was pleased to learn about his success.

Joe and his mother and stepfather have moved to a new home. All of his siblings, who are hearing, are now away at college or are adults and living on their own. Joe has always been mainstreamed in public school total communication programs. One of the most striking things about this interview was the fact that Joe still has painful experiences in school with hearing peers, but his coping skills and resilient attitude are the key to his survival. His stories ring of responsibility and achievement.

He maintains an outstanding academic record and résumé of extracurricular activities despite these experiences. He tells me, "It's not easy," and he doesn't understand why adolescents do what they do, but he copes with these challenges by "showing them" through sports, academic success, and a generally mature approach. Compatible with his concept of his success to this point in his life, he has high expectations for his future. "I want to go to a Division I school, play football or lacrosse, major in business, and become a business executive." He acknowledges his difficulties but also his strengths.

It was fun to see the warm, loving, and mutually respectful relationship he has with his mother. It was ten thirty Saturday morning, and Joe was finishing up a glass of juice. He looked tired, and his mom reminded him to comb his hair. He chuckled and finished his juice. His mom took a breakfast tray downstairs to give us some privacy.

The story responses that Joe provides based on the pictures I showed him were fairly reserved and brief, and I probed a bit, hoping for elaboration. Although perhaps not evident from this excerpt, Joe was content to stick to what he saw as actual detail; he worked hard to understand the perspective of the person in the picture or what the photographer was hoping to capture, and sometimes, rather than drift into the imaginary, he stayed safely with reality—"Well, they're just models," he told me. This was in contrast to the responses I got from Alex, who was more spontaneous, who freely associated his first impressions with his free-flowing imagination and eagerness to create ASL stories based on the photos. While Joe is sensitive and talked about his feelings and his relationships, his approach to our second interview using projective storytelling prompts with photographs was more rational than creative and illustrated his critical thinking skills as he considered various possible interpretations. He asked if I would be using "psychology." He was very aware and informed, and he understood the purpose of my techniques. He is mature in his thinking and insight. In fact, he even mentioned psychoanalysis in relation to one of the pictures I showed him, and he told me that his sister is majoring in psychology or wants to be a psychologist as he discussed their supportive relationship.

A bright and talented adolescent, Joe has been selected to participate in a study abroad course this summer. "Well, I've been going to a lot of meetings to prepare for my trip to Europe." Joe proceeds to tell me about the organization that is sponsoring his trip, its history and purpose, and how they are still helping youth on an international basis today, saying, "I'm real eager." He knows this is an honor and a highly selective process. This is an opportunity available to talented hearing students that has been extended to deaf students as well.

As he sits down to begin our interview in his living room, Joe is smiling. He seems a little nervous at first, but he's polite, pleasant, and cooperative. In the beginning of the interview Joe fiddled a bit with his hands, rubbing them together when a topic was stressful, exciting, or interesting for him. Later on in the interview, he appeared to become more relaxed.

Joe became deaf as an infant, possibly from a reaction to one of his inoculations. He considers himself hard of hearing, yet he appears to be more immersed in and comfortable with a larger social group of signing deaf youth than he did seven years ago. Joe and his mother both signed in English and spoke at the same time during our interview.

MS: Do you call yourself deaf or hard of hearing?

JOE: I always call myself hard of hearing because I can hear things. If someone calls me I will look at them. So I call myself hard of hearing.

He leans forward here, relaxing his arms on his thighs and folding his hands in front of him.

## SCHOOL

Unfortunately, Joe's secondary school experiences have echoed the persistent social ostracism he faced as a deaf child who is black in a school that is populated by students who are both white and hearing. He boasts a repertoire of responsible and constructive coping strategies that have enabled him to transcend this painful adversity. His personal strengths and talents—specifically his academic performance, athletic skill, self-confidence, maturity, self-discipline, and sense of hope—and the resources of a supportive home environment, teacher, and coach, as well as role models, participation in responsible leadership activities, and friends that he identifies with have all boosted his success. Joe's response to the first general question about himself tells us that he considers his school experiences to be a significant struggle, yet he is proud of how much he has accomplished despite the challenges and how he manages the stress he deals with.

MS: In this movie that we talked about, what would you want them to know about you?

JOE: My personal experiences, what I've gone through. What it's been like for me to try and get friends and communicate with them. Pretty much that. Well, it's hard to explain. I've been through a lot of things. I've had a lot of conflicts because I'm deaf and hard of hearing. You know, hard of hearing . . . This is not to insult the school—education's great, the teachers—but students themselves, it's like, the students themselves give me a hard time all the time. And I ask myself, why do they give me a hard time? Things like that. [*He has turned more in my direction now.*] Like in my class. I don't want to say specific people. I don't want to point out anybody. But most of them, they'll gang up on me, they'll play tricks on me, and I don't like it.

MS: Hearing students?

JOE: Oh yes, hearing students. I don't go to a deaf school, so it's a hearing school. I've had to struggle, try to fight, try to [*signs "stifle"*] hold myself. There's a lot of things. They call me names, and I try to just [*signs "close my eyes"*] keep things closed and not listen to what they say.

MS: So, you explained that to me back when you were ten. And I felt really bad for what you were going through and what you were experiencing then. Has that changed, or has it stayed the same?

JOE: Well, now I'm in high school, most of the kids are mature. I like the high school. Some of them, like the freshmen, new boys, are immature. I'm on the lacrosse team, and I'm trying to be a role model, and they think, "oh, he's deaf, he can't be, he can't do the work, he can't be like us." And I have to show them. I have to fight through. Some people are really jealous of me for some reason. Maybe they're jealous of me because I'm deaf and I'm successful. So, I try to make peace. I'm not against anyone. I'm not mean to anyone; I'm nice. I'm very physical. I'm involved in sports. I'm a good athlete.

MS: Tell me about your friends. Do you have friends who support you even though there are some people who pick on you? Do you have a group of friends that you feel comfortable with? [*Joe nods.*] Tell me about that.

JOE: Okay, well, there are some friends, well, I'll call my good friend Mike. We've been best friends for a long time. He's deaf himself. We both get together and do sports together. We have most classes together. Last year it was the same thing, but this time we have one class apart and we have lunch apart. I force myself with the mainstreaming and other kids. And I have some kids who are willing to learn sign language. They think it's fun. And some people will try and tease me, and I hear some people say, "Stop, he's deaf, what are you picking on him for?"

MS: Hearing friends?

JOE: Yes. Sometimes, me and Mike, my friend Mike, we [*signs "support"*] back each other out. Yes. For a while in middle school, that was a terrible time. But I survived. I'm glad I got out of it! About two years ago is when I got an award for maintaining a 3.62 GPA. I was so proud of myself, and I was glad I was out of middle school.

MS: Three-point-six, that's fantastic!

JOE: Yeah, and with three sports!

MS: That's wonderful!

JOE: That's what my coach said.

MS: Okay. Do you have anything else that you would like to tell people, in your movie, about you?

JOE: Well pretty much, I'm very friendly. [*He turns to face me more.*] I'm very active. I want to do things. I don't want to sit at home. Sometimes, maybe sometimes moody times.

MS: Sometimes you're moody?

JOE: But not a lot. So I'm not like that all the time. I get out with my best friend.

MS: What do you become moody about?

JOE: Sometimes I get angry at myself. Sometimes I have a bad grade. Like on a test I make simple mistakes and mess up. Like one time in geometry I had a C on a test and I was mad. And it was a really simple mistake. I had flipped some answers and I got mad at myself. And that's when I'm moody. Sometimes I get a bad grade, and that causes me to be moody. But other things don't really cause me to be moody.

MS: You like to do well in school.

JOE: Yes, very much, very much.

Joe tells me about a project he is doing for class.

> JOE: I have a ten-page essay due on Monday. I'm almost finished, just a few more changes. It's about Japan and the war, when they invaded us back in history. Really it's for my English class but involves history, world history and American history, and English. They try to connect them. We learned about the French Revolution. We read Charles Dickens, *A Tale of Two Cities*. My mom helps me with my English a little bit, but mostly I do my homework myself. It's hard. I mean there's too many words. And to know how to cite, bibliography, all that, how to write, translations, topic sentences.

> MS: You told me that you had to go through a lot in the public school and that you have a friend that supports you. What else do you do to help yourself get through all that?

> JOE: Continue to get good grades. Become active in sports. Like in football, that really helps. I wanted to join football because I thought it would be fun because you get to hit people. Because I'm big. And now I'm continuing in football because it helps me to get out some of my anger. You hit, but mostly it's a game. And lacrosse, too—it helps let out all the anger because you swing with the stick. You let it all out when you play. And I'm pretty skilled because I want to release bad. I have some teammates that support me and some classmates that support me because I help them. So that's a good reflection back. There's a lot of things. Friends can help a lot. Some don't.

Joe's interpretation of one of the photographs I present to him provides further evidence of his unpleasant experiences with hearing students at school. In addition, he appears to see this as a common experience of deaf students in school. He also tells us how he determines who is deaf and who is hearing.

> JOE: I know that most of them are deaf, because some of them have hearing aids and they're chatting. Maybe they have some issue or topic that they want to talk about with an adult. Maybe they have some kind of issue.

> MS: What kind of issue?

> JOE [*pauses*]: I'm not really sure. But it looks like they have an issue.

MS: You said some of them are deaf because they have hearing aids. Are some . . .

JOE [*looking at the picture*]: And some look like they're signing. They may be having problems with other students. If there's a problem with how people act toward them, teasing them. Something like that.

MS: Okay. So that's a common experience for deaf teenagers?

JOE: Yes.

MS: Is there anything else that you wanted to add about school?

JOE: In school, overall, in general . . . it's kind of hard to look back. But in elementary school, it was like, the kids teasing about anything. You'd have to get "hands off" quick before they'd go, "'Oh, he's bothering me" or something like that, before they suspect something or accuse you of something or try to blame you of something. I didn't want to get in trouble, and I'm the one they call. They go, "Oh, he did it." And I'd say, "What did I do?" And I didn't have an interpreter then. And that's why in elementary I tried to just back off a little. And I joined two clubs; one was student council, and the other was peer mediators. So I could back it off and wear the shirt [for peer mediation] and they can't bother me.

Being a peer mediator is a terrific way for Joe to remove himself from the role of a victim and scapegoat, and it is also a wonderful leadership opportunity.

MS: You backed off and . . .

JOE: I backed off and they can't bother me and they can't accuse me of anything because I'm responsible. I'm supposed to be monitoring and solving problems. So I think it was a pretty good idea because one of my teachers said, "Why don't you try peer mediation?" I decided that was a pretty good idea to try to solve, help people instead of causing problems or being accused of things.

Here Joe pauses thoughtfully, his left hand on his chin and the other on his right thigh.

MS: That's very mature. [*Joe grins.*] Good! You have some really healthy ways of dealing with things.

JOE: Yeah.

MS: That's really good. In the movie, what stories would you tell about your friends?

JOE: About my friends? [*I nod.*] Well, um . . . About my friends. Some are nice; some are good; some are supportive; some are not. Some are immature. Some are nothing at all. That's really in general, a concept.

Not unlike hearing adolescents, Joe's peer group includes students he gets along with and some who he does not. He sees himself as a role model to some of them, and some are role models for him.

MS: So, there's a lot of variety among your friends.

JOE: Yeah. Too much. Some I call friends; some I don't. Some just like a role model or some look up at me. So, there's many different definitions.

MS: Who are your role models?

JOE: Mine? Last year I had a football player I looked up to. I followed him. He was a good guy, and he attends State University. He doesn't play football for State. He just goes there. And he also played lacrosse, defense. Yes. He said he was going to play lacrosse at State, but he didn't. I think next year he would. But I really look up at him.

MS: You said some people look up to you also.

JOE: Oh yeah. Like some of the freshmen or some of the sophomores who maybe struggle with their grades. And I would, like, try to help them and be friendly with them. So I would try to help them. Try and get socialized.

He shrugs. This is another one of Joe's positive coping strategies.

## FAMILY

In Joe's family, there are separations. His parents are divorced. His older siblings have moved away now. It is apparent that Joe has a close relationship with his mother. He also shares touching stories about the supportive relationship he has with a sister who signs and a competitive relationship with one of his brothers. With the exception of Lisa, being closer to family members who sign was a theme for the other teens as well. The better the communication competencies or matching of communication modes of the family members, the closer the relationship appeared to be.

MS: And what stories would you tell about your family?

JOE: My family? Well, they're great! My mom, she's always been with me for all my life. And my sister tries to help me. She's almost like my psychologist.

MS: How is that?

JOE: She's always trying to help me. Sometimes, if I'm moody and if I . . . I explained that one day I had detention because one boy accused me. He said I threw paper. I did have paper, but he threw the paper, and he accused me, and the teacher gave both of us detention. So I had all these feelings, and my sister was trying to calm me down. She said, "'What's wrong? What's wrong?" And she was, like, trying mediation with me. And I expressed my story, and she said, "Oh well, things happen." And she was, like, trying to solve the problem. She was telling me, like, "Talk to the teacher, talk to the teacher." And that helped, but I still had detention anyway.

MS: Sounds like you have a very supportive sister.

JOE: Yeah. She's living in Boston now.

MS: Was she visiting you when that happened? How did the two of you communicate when that happened?

JOE: Oh, my sister understands sign.

During this exchange about his family and his sister, Joe is relaxed, calm and attentive.

MS: Was she here visiting you when she talked to you?

JOE: That was, like, Christmas break. But that was a long time ago.

MS: And she signs?

JOE: Yes, she signs and understands. But now she pretty much forgets some signs. But when I sign, she understands. But I understand her orally.

MS: Do other people in your family sign?

JOE: Just my mom. And used to be my sister. My brother is stubborn.

MS: Anything else about your family that you want us to know?

JOE: I would say that for many years my mom's been helping, and I really love her. She was there for me. And I would say that my stepfather married her recently, and I'm really glad because mom was able to relax and have someone to support her. [*He smiles.*] Well, all mothers do love their sons, I guess.

MS: Okay. Generally speaking, not just for you, how do you think parents . . . what do you think parents think about their deaf children?

JOE [*laughs*]: I would say generally my perspective is many parents and mine, I would say that the parents try to support the kids as much as they can. And try to see how much they can succeed just like hearing kids can. And see how much they can succeed and what they can do to change their future. And I would say that it's a hard job.

While it is common to find parents and teenagers struggling with conflicts related to separation and individuation, Joe's relationship with his mother is warm, respectful, and mutually supportive. It appears to be a source of strength for both of them. It does not appear to be conflict laden. They respect each other's boundaries and support each other's growth.

MS: Okay. And with deaf kids or teenagers, when they have brothers and sisters, what do their brothers and sisters think of the deaf kid in the family?

JOE [*laughs when he realizes my general question is really about his situation in particular*]: My older brother, he didn't really believe that I could do things, but I did. He thought I couldn't play soccer as well as him, but I did. That was when we were young. He was kind of young. One time he tried to compare skills. We played a game on separate fields. He scored three goals and I scored four. It was really fun. And my brother was like, okay, fine. And most every night we play soccer with each other. And I would say my brother, kind of, his viewpoint was to try to be somebody for me to look up to. He was trying to be a role model, like, be someone that can do what he can do, to succeed. His perspective of me was that I was deaf, like I need someone. I would say like that. And from the other perspective of a brother, I would say generally, sometimes a hearing brother or sister has a temper about the deaf brother or sister. Because some friends that I have that are deaf, he has a younger brother, and he doesn't want him to hang out around them, his hearing friends, so he's just alone most of the time. Maybe he's embarrassed because he's deaf, or ashamed or something.

MS: Do you think that's a general feeling that brothers and sisters have about their deaf brothers and sisters?

JOE: Maybe. Maybe some didn't care. I mean, some didn't care; my sister didn't care. She brought me to her community college when she was in California. She moved to Boston, but she took me there and said [*emphatically*], "This is my brother and he's deaf. Don't bother him." [*He puts his head back and laughs.*] Yeah. It was really fun. I got to see the college. It was really cool. Seems like she wants to major in psychology and she received a scholarship.

MS: I remember the last time you told me that your sister helps you, talks with you about things.

JOE: Yes . . . I kind of helped her pick out what she wanted to be.

His relationship with his sister is one of mutual respect and support.

MS: Good. So the two of you help each other?

JOE [*nods*]: Yes. We help each other out with my other sister . . . I don't know what her career is because she keeps changing it.

Joe looks at the next picture I gave him and smiles.

JOE: This might be family members sitting and discussing business issues, finances maybe. They're probably deaf because of the sign "okay" or maybe "two." [*He laughs.*] There's one person signing "okay" or "two."

MS: Does your family have meetings from time to time to discuss family issues?

JOE: Sometimes.

MS: What kinds of things do you talk about?

JOE: Well, what we're doing. What to bring for camping, to get a camper.

MS: Does your family involve you in decisions related to the family?

JOE: Not all the time. Sometimes they just inform me.

Effective communication in families goes beyond the compatibility of the mode of communication. It also involves the participation of deaf family members in family decisions. This level of communication participation in the family unit can go a long way toward the development of interpersonal, interfamilial communication skills, self-determination, decision-making skills, self-respect, and self-confidence. Joe's examples below show us that with this level of communication, the deaf family member is a participant rather than just a passive observer in family activities and interactions.

JOE: In this picture, now, well, none of them seems to sign. I guess they're hearing.

MS: If the whole family is gathered, if there's an all-deaf family, or an all-hearing family, or if it's a mix of deaf and hearing, would there be any differences in these families?

JOE: Well, an all-deaf family, all members, most of the members would be signing, using gestures, and an all-hearing family would be talking. I don't know, or moving their mouths lots more. And they would be busy eating, too, eating more than deaf. It's like signing and eating. They have more of a chance to eat than deaf people do.

In the last sentence, Joe is referring to the need for deaf people to maintain eye contact and have their hands free to communicate, which hearing people conversing with each other do not need.

MS: Okay. Now suppose only one member of that family were deaf. What would that be like for them?

JOE: Really looking around and eating. They'd probably just sit there and watch what the other family members are doing. Observing. They could participate if they know what the topic is. They might ask the other family members, "What are you talking about?" If this was a deaf family, he'd possibly, maybe, feel more in with the deaf family. But with hearing, he might have to work his way through it and get the attention.

## COPING STRATEGIES

Joe is an assertive young man with a healthy array of coping skills. When he recognizes that he is being left out of communication he knows he can use the situation to his advantage. He asserts himself as well. This assertiveness is an important skill and relates to overcoming the passive observer role that is frequently imposed upon deaf and hard of hearing people in situations that are not accessible to them.

JOE: Well, I would say maybe this person [in the picture] is talking on the phone with one friend, and he's playing a game with another friend. But he's more focused on the phone friend.

MS: Does that happen to you sometimes when you get together with your hearing friends?

JOE: Yeah, it probably happens. But they don't take as long. Sometimes if they talk to a friend, but I have some advantage, I could win the game, or I might feel a little bit left out.

MS: Suppose you get together with hearing friends and all the hearing people start talking, what happens for you?

JOE: I might feel a little bit left out and I would try to work my way into the conversation.

MS: How would you do that?

JOE: Get their attention. I need to talk. Say, "Hey."

## THE FUTURE

As Joe tells us about his brother, he reveals his plans for his own future. He wants to attend a large university where he can play sports, get a degree in business, and position himself for a job as a business executive. He also reveals a variety of potential career options for deaf adults.

JOE: I want to follow him because he's at a Division I college. I want to attend a Division I college because it's good education and good sports. I want to go to any of them, Virginia or others, and study business and play lacrosse and football. Now I'm taking harder classes next year, but I feel confident that I can do well. I'm taking higher algebra . . . and American studies.

MS: Anything else that you want to tell me about your future?

JOE: I would like . . . I would hope to be able to get a good job. A top executive manager . . . like way up top, you know, like at the top of a company. Like, and I also look up to my best friend, his brother, his old-est brother. He attended State, and now he is a top executive manager for, in Chicago, for like a big company. I can't remember the name. It's like a long name, but I would really like to be what he does. It sounds like a lot of fun. I know it's a lot of work, obviously, but it's something that I would like to do, that I would like to learn how to do. Math is really my strong area.

MS: Wow, I'm impressed. Great!

When Joe examines a photo of three characters dressed in costumes he reveals the following opinion about the vocational potential of deaf people:

JOE: This picture looks like three kids. One wants to be a scientist, another an inventor, another a traveler . . . oh, maybe he's in business. They're pretending about their futures. The traveler, like Crocodile Dundee, this guy I saw on TV, who wrestles with crocodiles all the time. The guy who goes around to different parts of the world, he videotapes the animals and he does some wrestling with crocodiles.

MS: A zoologist.

JOE: Yeah . . . Or just, kind of like a . . . something . . . Anth——. . . Like, he finds old ruins. Like an anthropologist maybe?

MS: Could deaf people do those jobs?

JOE [*quickly*]: Yes. Deaf people could.

MS: I remember last time we met, when you were ten, you said you wanted to be a cartoonist.

JOE: Oh yeah. I remember. Yeah.

MS: You remember that. Did you say before that you knew a deaf cartoonist?

JOE: Yes. He did, um, what was that cartoon called? I watched it sometimes. Oh, "Doug." He also helped one guy to present his ideas to Disney, and they liked it.

MS: That artist was deaf?

JOE: I think he was more like helping the actual artist. But he, well . . . One lady from church, she introduced him to another artist. And talked to me about his aid, helped him, helped him, like process changing, the art, his colors. He would like draw it, tracing maybe from books. So he knew how to help, the technology, what to do.

MS: Do you still draw?

JOE: Not so much. Well, seems like drawing took up a lot of my time. I put it aside. I draw once in a while.

Although not all examples are illustrated in this chapter, Joe determines whether or not individuals in the photographs are deaf or hearing based on the visual evidence he observes, such as hearing aids, the use of sign language, and the appearance of talking. Even though this picture was an exception in that he could not pinpoint why he thought the girl in the photo was deaf, it is important to recognize that he understands that deaf people have the potential to become doctors.

It looks like a girl. Maybe in college. In college in California, because the tag says California, so I'd guess. Oh boy. Maybe, I would have to guess maybe psychology field, or to become a doctor. She's probably deaf, because . . . I would have to say because . . . I'm gonna have to assume she is.

## COMMUNICATION

Joe laughs as he considers what he might want to say about communication in his movie. He talks about how sometimes he has a hard time understanding people when they aren't making eye contact with him and how he tries to make himself understood by hearing people as well. He looks up thoughtfully and tilts his head from side to side as if trying to decide what to share.

Well, I would say sometimes communication is hard. Because some people aren't really trying to listen to me, and some people are trying to understand me. And sometimes I have lazy speech, obviously, or sometimes I will try to show gestures. Or I will try to, if they don't really understand, I will try to repeat often, or write it down. Because most of the time they will understand what they're saying after the third or the second attempt. Sometimes they will try to talk to me, like today, I'm practicing, and a freshman caught me and asked me if he was still on the JV roster, because we have a lot of players . . . And only about half of them can't travel. And I'm on it because I was right behind varsity. So he was just, like, asking me, and I'm like, "What?" because he just popped up the question and I wasn't really on the task. I was paying attention to the drill. And he was asking me, and I was like, "What? What?" Then

I understood and I was like, "Oh, yes you are." He surprised me. I was, like, "I'm doing a drill."

MS: So, that makes it hard, when somebody asks something out of the blue.

JOE: Yeah, right. Like, "What?" Right. Something like that is hard to understand. But something like on topic, like they ask me, "Is there homework in health?" or something, and I say yes. I would say that with adults, they try to pay attention more and try to speak slower and not try to treat me like I'm mentally retarded, but . . . [*He is calm and seems relaxed.*] They don't try to treat me like that, but they'll try and speak slow, and if they talk fast, I'm like, "Yeah?" I will look and be able to make eye contact with kids, they look all around and away from me, and there's never one place. There's never one place. Like you see little kids, they move their heads around. It's hard to understand them when they're not looking at me. And people my age, they're like halfway between. They'll be like, sometimes, not paying attention, or like, "Okay," or they try and listen. So I would say teenagers are about halfway in between.

Joe realizes also that there are differences in communication preferences among deaf and hard of hearing people.

JOE: Some deaf people, when I go to the Deaf Youth Club and some kids are really, like, against, refuse to talk for some reason. When we went to an ice cream store, one guy did not want to talk, or try to communicate, or write with the clerk, the person on the counter. He did not want to, and he just gave money to the leader. The leader, the adult leader, who is in charge of the group, he's responsible for us. He gave him the money, to tell him what he wants, signed. And the leader went up and got it and gave it to him. But for some reason I asked him why, and he said he's just really against it, he had a bad experience; that one, he said, because of a bad experience. He had a bad experience being around hearing people, a bad experience communicating.

MS: And that's different from your experience, or is it similar?

JOE: Yes. Well, it's really different. Each one is different. Because I'm around them every day for ten months each year. [*He smiles.*] So I just really blend in. Now I'm really experienced. If someone tries to insult me I'm like, yeah, sure. I insult them back.

MS: So sometimes deaf people are concerned about communication with hearing people, but you don't worry about it so much?

JOE: Not really.

But then Joe tells us about his attempts at cross-cultural communication in Puerto Rico.

JOE: Well, I went to a family vacation with my real father. We went on a cruise, and it was a lot of fun. It was a cruise. We went to Bahamas and Bermuda and an island. I'm not sure what island, but it was an island. It was the third, uh, Virgin Islands. So those three and we went on a cruise and it was really cool. I could see a different culture in Puerto Rico, and then I had to speak a different language, Spanish. And my brother tried to help because he took Spanish in college. He's not very good, but he took a class. It was required foreign language. So, when I went there with my family, it was fun because I tried to say, "No hablo Español." [*He voices this while he signs "No speak Spanish."*] Español, meaning "I don't speak Spanish." "No hablo Español." That guy didn't understand what I was saying. I repeated it again; he was like, "Oh, oh, I understand, you want English."

MS: He could speak English?

JOE: A little bit, yeah.

MS: So the two of you were able to work it out?

JOE: Yeah. It was kind of hard because of his accent. I was watching closely, I wasn't sure, and I said, "Can you say it again?" And then he showed me on the . . . on the price tag thing, the price, and it was funny because I was trying to say his language, and then he tried to say in our language, and then finally we worked out with showing gestures and showing the numbers.

MS: That's a real challenge to be deaf and to have two different languages happening that you have to deal with.

JOE [*sits back and smiles*]: Yeah. I will be more challenged when I go to Europe because I will be staying there for three weeks. I will stay with a "home stay family," people that live there, and they will assign a family that I will stay with. Oh, and I'm not allowed to have an interpreter because they're not responsible for interpreters overseas. If it was like around the United States, they would send an interpreter with me, but

I don't know if the family signs. We will go meet different cultures and peoples, and we will meet them and see their culture and the European people and meet the culture and learn the history behind it. You know, there's a lot of history. There will be many things. We will go to see the sites.

He is smiling as he shares his plans for this trip. He seems relaxed, leaning back in the chair.

## PERCEPTIONS OF SELF AND OTHERS

MS: GENERALLY, WHAT DO HEARING PEOPLE THINK ABOUT DEAF PEOPLE?

JOE: Hearing people? I would say some haven't met one or experienced one. That person who hasn't, I would say they would probably think lowly of the deaf person. Yeah, if they haven't experienced. Like I had a teacher who really thought I couldn't do anything; she thought she had to instruct me again, and again, and again. I'm like, "I'm already doing it right." It was a cooking class. I bake really good, you know, you can ask Mom. So I was cooking, and she was yelling at me because she said you're supposed to be in this order and I'm already ahead. And she said, "No, you have to be slower." [*He sits back.*] But I'm doing it right. Now she understands, but the first day it was like . . . I can't really explain it, but she didn't really think I would succeed.

MS: And you think people begin with low expectations of a deaf person? Until they get to know you, and then their attitude changes?

JOE: Right.

MS: You've shown them.

JOE: Yep! [*He laughs.*]

MS: That's good. What do you think deaf people think of hearing people?

JOE: My perspective, I don't think I have a bad opinion about hearing people. Some people I look down on, not their grades, but their ability and willingness. And some people I look up to and think they have good success because of their willingness and abilities. I really don't have an opinion about hearing people because some I look up to. I stereotype each person until I know them or I can see their abilities if they're bad or low.

## Friends

As Joe moves further into the interview, away from telling us about his school experiences and into this association with deaf and hard of hearing peers, he seems to become more relaxed.

JOE: When I get together with my friends, mostly we go . . . like every . . . most every Saturday, I go with the deaf, my friends, and we go out and we will do things like with the Deaf youth [Club], and we will do things there. We will have guest speakers who are deaf talking about their experiences. Like a deaf man and another man, I can't remember, he was deaf and just turned blind. He was a scientist with a team. He was part of a team. His work relates to computers. He's in charge of computers. He used to be a scientist trying to cure cancer, but now he can't see and he's deaf. So he has a hard time, and he tries to type. It was really cool. So we see different people. Like people who are successful like this other deaf man, who is successful. He's like the top administrator.

MS: What's it like for you when you get together with your deaf friends?

JOE: Oh, I get to learn more sign language, ASL, and be more flexible, flexible speaking. I don't have to speak, but I just sign. So, I become more comfortable with sign. But later I can talk, so I've become more comfortable with talking, and with signing. I last longer with signing. With talking, I'll stop more.

MS: Where do you feel most comfortable—with your deaf friends, or with your hearing friends, or with a combination of both? What situation is ideal for you?

JOE: I would say a combination of both, so I could gesture and talk.

MS: So if they're all in one group of people?

JOE: Yes.

MS: Would those hearing people sign? Would that be most comfortable for you?

JOE: Well, I have my best friend and some other deaf, and we will get together with my other deaf friend and his soccer team members, who are hearing and some sign, but I just read lips, and I was talking to them, and they say, "You can talk, oh whew!" And I felt it would help for me to talk, and they would help me a lot. And it was kind of fun. And I would sign and try to talk, or I would just talk.

MS: And do your deaf friends understand your hearing friends and vice versa?

JOE: Yes. They know some sign. Like using the alphabet.

MS: I see. Okay. Do you tend to go visit your friends? [*Joe nods.*] Do your friends live close by?

JOE: I have two friends over there [*points*], and one lives around my old area. I drive now. I have my license. I drive on weekends but for school, no, because I take the bus. Because of parking. There's so many kids who drive. I'm stuck, I can't. My friends who live nearby are hearing. They're my team members from school. They play with me. I go over there to play; they have a field with a goal post over there, so we go and shoot. They own it. I go over and play.

MS: Neat. I remember when we met before, you were telling me, there was a guy living near you, and you said, "He's deaf like me. He talks." Is that the friend who's over in the old neighborhood?

JOE: Yes.

MS: You've been friends growing up; that's a long time.

JOE: He's in most of my classes, except that I have photography and he has another class. And I have lunch separately. That's the only separate one. I just took him to Deaf . . . it's called Youth Club. We talk about teen issues and things. Last night I just drove him there. I enjoy that. Lots of kids go, I would say roughly about twenty-five.

MS: And they're from different mainstream programs? From the residential school?

JOE: I wish I could see more students from the residential school, but I haven't seen that much. But I see, like, mainstream schools. Like some people from the different schools. We have three or four of ours who go. One from another school.

MS: Neat. And so you talk about different teenage issues?

JOE: Well, we pick one topic each night. Last night [*smiling and perhaps embarrassed*] about bad words. But we keep things confidential.

Yes, I had a friend, Chris, for a long time. And one, he moved. He moved out to . . . I'm not sure where. I think he moved to California. His name's Kevin. He's deaf, too . . . And they would come to my house and we would play, especially on snow days. That was fun. [*Joe smiles as he remembers this.*] I remember one time; we had a snowball fight. And I remember we had two days . . . or like five days, I think it was like five days of snow days. Because we had a huge snow. I'm not sure when. But I remember we built a fort. And that was cool. We started out big, making big balls that came up. That was cool. Other kids, I think they had a wall. They made a wall. But we made like a big circle. That was fun. And then we were throwing snowballs from both sides.

MS: Thank you for your time. It's really good for me to see how well you're doing. I'm impressed. And I'm happy for you that things are working out so well.

JOE [*smiles*]: Yeah. [*He leans forward thoughtfully.*] I work hard.

As we close, Joe and I exchange e-mail addresses so that we can stay in touch about the interviews. I told him that if he was willing, I would like to contact him again in seven years and interview all of the participants again to see what their perspectives are then. He asked if I was going to write another book, and I said that it was beginning to look like this might lead to another one and further study into the development of deaf and hard of hearing people. Joe talked about the psychological theories he was familiar with. His mom reappeared and reacted with a look of wondrous disbelief when Joe grinned and said, "I'll be twenty-three in seven years."

෧ඁ

WHILE JOE continues to experience much adversity in his predominantly white hearing public school, he is mature beyond his years in his coping strategies. When he perceives others as being unaccepting, having lower expectations of him, or being jealous, he defies and transcends their negativity by trying to "make peace," appropriately using sports as a physical outlet for stress, quietly and patiently demonstrating his competence, working hard, asserting himself, adopting leadership positions, and turning to supportive and accessible relationships. He refuses to internalize the attitude of his aggressors or allow himself to be oppressed, and he keeps his sense of humor. He maintains a realistically positive perception of his abilities and qualities and has hopeful expectations of his future that include attending a Division I college where he can play sports and major in business to become a business executive. Joe noted broad career choices available to deaf adults, including anthropology, psychology, cartoon art, and medicine.

Like Angie, Joe does not have deaf role models in his mainstreamed public school setting. He speaks positively of the peer and role model interaction experiences afforded by a local community-based deaf youth group, where deaf adults are frequent speakers. While open to relationships with both deaf and hearing people, Joe finds his social and communicative interaction with deaf signing peers in the deaf youth group and with his best friend, who is also deaf, to be a refreshing reprieve from the daily challenges presented at his hearing school. Here he sees himself as a participant in interaction, as opposed to feeling like an outside observer among hearing people. He recognizes that each deaf and hard of hearing person has unique social, communication, family, and educational experiences; he also recognizes where he fits in the scheme of things.

Joe has an especially positive, mutually caring, and respectful relationship with his mother. He believes that most deaf people have parents who are generally supportive of them. He also speaks fondly of a reciprocally supportive relationship with a hearing sister who is now away at college. One of Joe's stories was of overcoming what he felt was a brother's underestimation of his competencies. It is clear that Joe values reciprocal relationships; he doesn't want to be kept at the receiving end of relationships, where people have often tried to place him. He wants others to recognize and accept from him the strengths, qualities, and competencies that he brings to his relationships.

# 8

## *Alex*

I'm proud of myself. I'm proud of being deaf . . . My goal is to live far away with trees all around and a pond. I want a cabin, a big one that I'll make myself!

—Alex

I ARRIVED at Alex's home a bit early on a cold, damp March evening. Fourteen-year-old Alex greeted me warmly at the door of his family's modest townhouse. Alex was seven when we first met, and he has grown considerably since our last interview. He is now at eye level with me. He was very polite, responsive, and cooperative. He seemed eager for our interview and nicely offered to help us set up the camcorder. After greeting us, Alex's mother and siblings retreated to another level of the house to give us privacy.

Alex is profoundly deaf from birth and a proficient user of ASL. He attends a residential school for deaf students but commutes daily from his home where he lives with his hearing mother and siblings. Alex reported he was a bit shy about using the camera and was sensitive to protecting information about his family.

❧

GIVEN THE choice between a book or a movie as a medium for teaching others about deaf teenagers, Alex, like most of the children in this study, chose the movie. This turned out to be a good choice for Alex. He told me how much he enjoys his ASL classes at school, and it became apparent that he was well practiced at signing stories for an audience. Alex let his imagination soar, and although he said he was shy, he performed exuberantly for the camera as he created stories about the story-prompting photographs.

114

## COMMUNICATION ACCESS

Alex's initial response to the following question revealed that his concern about being treated as an equal is of primary importance to him.

MS: Okay. So if you were making a movie about yourself, what would you want people to know about you?

ALEX: Well, I'm deaf, and I have rights to things. That deaf people are the same as hearing people, to know my rights and know about me. [*Alex is the only participant who mentions "rights."*] I have a right to be equal, not hearing people doing more, to join in, to participate just like everybody else does. I'm not less than they are. I should be able to join in any activities. I should be permitted to speak up as they do, with someone to interpret for me, and I could use sign language.

MS: So does it sometimes happen that hearing people don't want to give you those rights?

ALEX: Yes.

MS: Can you tell me a story about that?

Alex's example illustrates that at this point in his adolescent life, as he ventures out in the community where he has the opportunity and responsibility to communicate independently in public places, he finds he is brushed aside and receives rude and unequal treatment in his interactions.

ALEX: Well, it's hard to remember. Maybe, for example, in a fast-food restaurant, and the staff people come up to me, if I try to fingerspell, and I have to stand to the side. Everybody else goes in line in front of me, and they pay and get their food. And I have to wait. That's rude. Then an assistant comes to take care of my order. That's rude. I feel belittled if that happens. It's not right. There was one woman who knew I was deaf. She'd seen me, and I go there all the time with my sister who's hearing, my older sister, to this fast-food place, and she'd interpret for me. There was this one woman who just walked away and left me. I had gone there by myself four or five times. She just ignored me, and her job is to listen to what people want, and I have my rights, but she just walked away.

MS: What else would you want people to know about you?

Alex: I don't know. I'm proud of myself. I'm proud of being deaf. I don't wear a hearing aid or try to be hearing. I accept my culture. I can speak up for myself. Let me be equal to everyone.

## School and Friends

Following Alex's stories about the unpleasant experiences he has with hearing people in communicatively inaccessible interaction, he changes topics to share with us how much he enjoys his activities in a contrasting deaf mileau. He participates on his school baseball and wrestling teams and attends summer camps with other deaf students.

Alex: I enjoy going to school and hanging around with my friends. I enjoy sports and doing things with my brother. I like baseball, and my favorite is wrestling. For wrestling last February we went to New York. I flew with my team. We were competing against other schools. A New York deaf school, and . . . Texas, Iowa, MSSD [Model Secondary School for the Deaf], Indiana, that's five, and we make six. There were two more that I can't remember. I won three or four times and lost eight or nine. It was my first time, as a freshman. I was kind of awkward and unsure with all of it, so I won maybe three and lost nine or ten.

I've gone to a lot of deaf camps. It's a lot of fun. I've been to Illinois and South Dakota most. Do you know the South Dakota Festival? I've done things with the Baptist Church, which is here. I've gone to Chicago, which was a long drive. I've been to a lot of different camps, and I've had a lot of fun with that.

Here, as Alex tells me about summer camp, he is beginning to relax more. He loosens his left leg and drops it down a bit.

I stay for a week at each camp. Some people are hard of hearing, some hearing, but mostly it's deaf. It's fun. We communicate easily; I communicate with everyone. We do a lot of sports, baseball, softball, where you throw the ball and run, archery, and rock climbing. There's a really big climbing wall that you go up. Two people have to go up, and they have to help each other. It's really hard and it's fun. You have different teams competing against each other to get to the top. There are twelve different levels, and they're as far apart as my waist to my chin or more. You take turns moving to the next level. And there are no ropes; you're not allowed to touch the lines. You have to just climb. It's hard. And we have swimming, and we play around; we just have fun.

A trip to New York City for Alex brought recollections of the tragic events of September 11, 2001. Needless to say, deaf adolescents were not immune to the effects of terrorist activities against the United States. Alex was exposed to the media coverage and had information from his family's communications about a New York City relative who was there when it took place.

> When my team went to New York, we saw where the World Trade Center had been, the ruins. And we saw the Statue of Liberty. It was neat. We saw where the two towers went down. There was a wall and a high wooden area where you could go and you could look down. You could see vehicles and where people might have been sleeping or working. There were so many people going through, and it was very crowded. And we saw where people had written on the wall the names of people who had died. And we looked at that as we went by. There were so many. There were lists and lists of names of people who had died, and people had written them. One person in my family was hurt, but she's fine. My aunt. I saw her. She's alive, safe, in a safe place. She worked in the tower, I think on the thirtieth floor, but she walked down and escaped, then later there were problems. She's fine now.

It is not uncommon for deaf students to change schools perhaps more frequently than hearing students do. Educational programs for deaf students are often referred to or defined by the communication mode used, such as total communication, oral/aural, bilingual-bicultural (ASL and English language), by the student composition (hearing schools or deaf schools), by whether or not they are residential or day schools, and by the level of mainstreaming in hearing schools (partially mainstreamed or fully mainstreamed). Since our previous interviews, Alex had switched to a hearing school where he was partially mainstreamed with an interpreter. This was not a satisfactory experience for him, and he then transferred back to his residential school for deaf students. His preference is to be at this residential school, where he has a reference group of deaf peers he identifies with and where he can participate in sports.

MS: What would you tell people about your school?

ALEX: Well, the residential school is a good place. It's for deaf people, and because there are deaf people around, we can communicate. We have fun in the dorms. The dorms are for people who live far away; they sleep there. I go to the dorms after school, and I have a lot of fun playing there.

I don't sleep there; I just go until about seven thirty, and then I go back every day. I go for tutoring from six thirty to seven thirty. I also have sports, baseball. We started baseball just three days ago. There are a lot of people who know sign language. There are a few deaf people, hard of hearing students. Most of the teachers are hearing.

Here Alex is relaxing more. He scoots back into the couch and relaxes against the back of it. While he is positioned more comfortably, he also crosses his arms momentarily at this point. However, this is the last time in the interview that his arms are crossed. He unfolds them as he responds to my next question.

MS: Your mom told me that you transferred to another school a while ago, two or three years ago?

ALEX: Two years ago.

MS: What was that like for you?

ALEX [*with a crooked smile on his face*]: It was tough. In the classes, everything went really fast [*his smile fades*] and I had to focus because the interpreter, interpreting is behind. After someone talks, then the interpreter signs it. So you're always catching up. And it was all in English. It was the public school group, and most of the other kids were hard of hearing, not deaf. So they were talking and using English. I was the only one who was really deaf. Then I met one other person, a gal, who was deaf, too, and one guy. It was fun talking with them. But there were just the three of us. They were fun, but mostly it was hard. Communication was hard, and there were about five hundred people I couldn't communicate with and only two or three I could. I like gym and cafeteria. Gym is best.

MS: Which do you like better, the residential school or public school?

ALEX: I like the residential school better, but I think the education is better at the public school. With the residential school it's easy to communicate, and it's a lot more fun, with more activities than school. The other school, the public school, was more focused on English, and the signing was slow. It was hard. I had to focus on the interpreter, and they were behind. It's a lot better with a deaf teacher; it's direct. I can use my eyes. With an interpreter, I had to look at the interpreter all day. I couldn't look at the teacher or other things. The deaf school is probably better because I have more friends there. I can communicate. In every class, when we change classes, it's a lot of fun. I can talk to them. We play in the dorms. We talk a lot. We play computer games. It's a lot of fun, because they can sign like me. I fit in better. It's a better match for me, because I have friends. I have so many friends. I have Kevin, and Matthew, and TJ (he's got a long last name), and Abel, and a girl, Megan, do you know Megan? Oh, I have many friends. There are some other girls, too. There's Katie, Tiffany something—it's a hard name. Umm, who else? Muriel and Sean, and Katrina, and many others.

Social interaction is an important part of everyone's education. Through this interaction we develop interpersonal skills and absorb incidental learning.

MS: Wow, you do have a lot of friends. You're very lucky. Are they all from the residential school, those friends you listed?

ALEX: Yes.

MS: Are any from the public school?

ALEX: Yes, one. Tyler. We did a lot of things together, and then I quit and went back to the residential school. Then he followed me afterwards. So he's now at the residential school. We see each other in the morning, before class. We're on the same bus. We see each other every day now. And he lives near me, not very far.

The importance of the residential school and all that it represents to Alex and what he perceives as a lack of communication in the families of many deaf people is depicted in the following creative story from his observation of a photograph of a teenaged girl.

Looks like a girl. She's maybe sixteen, seventeen, eighteen, somewhere in there . . . Well, the girl lives far away, in the country, with hills. It's dry and kind of hilly. She has a family, and she walks with them. Her father died, so her mother's a widow, so she lives alone. They've lived there for many years. Later she decides she wants to go to school. Her mother starts looking for a school. She finds the deaf school, the residential school. So they agree on that. They drive there, and they have to drive a long way. They finally arrive at the residential school.

They go in, and they see the school, and it's really neat because everyone is communicating. She's deaf, and her mother and the rest of her family don't sign well, only a little bit, and understand a little bit. She mostly uses gestures and writing to communicate with her mother. So she finally meets another deaf person for the first time. She sees them communicate, and she's so excited. She goes running in with her mother, and they go into the office and talk with the person in charge. She says she wants to join the school, and they say fine and agree, and they talk about classes. She thanks them and everything is ready. She's very excited.

The next morning, after sleeping all night, she's excited, and they drive and arrive there. She decides to stay in the dorm during the week, and on the weekend she'll go back home. Her mom says that's okay. It's a long drive, and they arrive in the morning, at seven o'clock. She is really tired. She goes into the cafeteria and sits down and eats. She's communicating with many new people, telling them her name, telling everyone her name. Let's say her name is Kate. So she's talking with people and introducing herself, telling them where she's from, and she's very excited. Then the bell rings and everyone lines up and files out of the cafeteria and goes to school and into their classes. She meets her first deaf teacher, Charisse, her first teacher. She can communicate, and it's really neat! It's the first time she's met a deaf teacher. She's surprised and excited. She goes to all her classes, and lunch, and dinner, and the dorm. She goes into the dorm, and she meets a deaf girl there. They talk about sleeping in the dorm. They chat and laugh and have fun.

Alex painted a very positive perception of his residential school as a happy, "neat," fun place for deaf adolescents to be. While the mother of the girl in the story above doesn't sign well, Alex appears to be aware that his own mother is an exceptional signer. It's interesting to note that for Alex it is the communication that makes the experience of the residential school so "neat."

MS: Thank you. [*I start to get our next photograph when Alex gets my attention.*]

ALEX: My ASL class, at the residential school, I go every day to ASL and I'm always telling ASL stories that are good and dramatic. That's important.

MS: You're an expert. [*I picture Alex standing in front of his class at school where he feels very much at home with himself and his language, sharing long and impromptu stories in ASL. He seems to sense this is his niche.*]

ALEX: Thank you.

FAMILY

> MS: In that movie, where we're telling people about you, what would you tell them about your family?

> ALEX: Well, my family, not really, um . . . that's private.

Alex shook his head and told me that he was sensitive about sharing his perspectives of his family. He agreed to talk about this if the interpreter did not voice for him on the videotape. We also agreed that I would do my best to protect their anonymity in my writing and would get his permission before publishing anything.

He shared with me the names, ages, and other identifying information about his family members. He tells me his family history and everyone's whereabouts, how often he sees them, and how much he loves them. He talks about the many activities he enjoys with his parents and what he learns from them and the skills they have and how "neat" they are.

Alex is remarkably descriptive and quite animated in his stories as he relates information about his surroundings and family relationships. He smiles, makes good eye contact, and goes on and on about his family relationships, pets, activities, and future plans with different family members. He is quite excited about many of these activities and plans. Clearly, his family is very important to him. He talks about decisions that family members are faced with, such as college and living arrangements, and how important technology is for communication when family members are apart. He talks about how his younger siblings are growing and learning language. But of importance to Alex is the fact that his younger brother is beginning to learn sign language.

> So cute, he doesn't sign yet. He's just learning. He can sign "ball" and "more." He says "more" a lot! I think in a month he'll be fingerspelling. Then there's my other little brother. He's so cute, and he's learning a lot, he understands a lot. He can talk too. He can both talk and sign. My mother teaches him to talk and I teach him to sign.

He also tells me he has two older siblings. Here it is interesting that Alex's expression changes throughout this sentence. He starts with a matter-of-fact expression as he says, "My family is all hearing"; then he begins a semi-smile as he says "except one is hard of hearing," and he completes his sentence with a full smile as he says, "and me, I'm deaf."

MS: Wow, you've told me a lot about your family. Family seems really important to you. Thank you for sharing that information.

ALEX: You're welcome.

## COMMUNICATION

Alex has already told us that communication at school is more important to him than his perception of the quality of a school's education. He has also shared with us that he believes he fits in with a group of signing peers and clearly feels excited about and stimulated in that environment. Furthermore, he takes pride in his ASL storytelling skills and values the signing competency of his hearing family members. He reports less conflict in signing relationships than in relationships with others who do not sign. He feels left out when he is in the company of a large family group where people do not sign. He misses the company of his older sister who used to interpret for him in social settings.

ALEX: Oh, it's very important to communicate. To talk to people one-on-one. If hearing people have trouble understanding me, there's a conflict. I can't understand when they talk; I can't hear what they're saying. It's very important to learn to communicate. They should learn to sign to communicate in ASL. English is important to communicate. I try to use writing, and there's signing in ASL to communicate well.

MS: You remember when we met a long time ago, you told me sometimes you would go out and play and there would be hearing people around, and that your sister would help you and . . .

ALEX: Interpret. When she's gone, I'm stuck by myself. I use gestures. I miss her.

MS: Now when there are hearing people around, what do you do?

ALEX: I write. In my family, we have all hearing. I'm the only one who's deaf. The only one. It's just me. Sometimes my mom invites lots of family, and I'm the only deaf person. I get bored and space out. I just hurry and eat and leave. I play video games on TV or on the computer. That's my favorite.

MS: Oh, I want to ask you one more thing. You take ASL classes at the residential school?

ALEX: One.

MS: You're taking ASL 1? [*Alex nods.*] And you enjoy that?

ALEX: Yes. It's a lot of fun.

MS: Do all the students have to take that?

ALEX: No, they don't have to . . . The ASL teacher wanted that, but the principal said no.

MS: You're an expert at ASL storytelling.

ALEX: Thank you. Because in class today and yesterday and two days ago we made up hand shape stories. Like . . . [*He demonstrates a story using only the "V" hand shape, the "1" hand shape and then the "5" hand shape.*] We make up stories with those words. I had the most of all the people. It's funny, making things up.

MS: I wanted to ask you, around hearing kids, how do you feel?

ALEX: I just try my best to join in. I study the situation to see what I need to do and I act things out, write, I try my best to gesture.

*The Future*

MS: What can you tell me about your future?

ALEX: I haven't decided yet, it's a long explanation, I need to make good decisions. When I'm fifteen and a half, I'm going to get my license early, so when I'm sixteen I can get my license. I'll hold onto it, keep it in a safe place, and I'll start practicing and testing with my mom helping. When I'm sixteen, when I finally get a car, I can drive back and forth to school. No more bus. I can drive myself there and home. When I'm seventeen or eighteen and I graduate from school, I'll go to college. I want . . . my goal is to go to RIT [Rochester Institute of Technology]. It's a huge school. They have twelve different colleges on-site there. I think I'd like to study electrical technology. That's my goal. That's what I want."

MS: With electrical technology, what would you do? What kind of work?

ALEX: I'd learn about computers and how computers work, electrical connections. Technology. I'd make new robots. I like that. Also right now I'm interested in the science project I have right now. I'm looking for a circuit board. I'm figuring that out, it's hard. There's the green board, and there are all these wires. It's complicated, like in that video recorder. There's that kind of machinery in there. I'm learning that now. I love it.

MS: And then, where would you work? Here? Far away?

ALEX: I forgot to tell you. I haven't decided if I'll work, if . . . It depends on if I'm able to pass college. Maybe three or six years. Four—I think it's four years. I'd prefer full time. Finish my four-year degree. Get an advanced degree. Then work with computers or where they have rocket science. Do you know the name? They use gases they pour. Do you know?

MS: Chemist?

ALEX: Yes. They find things. Animals—funny, tiny animals they look at with a microscope . . . That's what I want. If I find that they have good money, if I do the calculations and it's good money, I might go. My goal is to live far away with trees all around and a pond, a man-made pond. A big one, with trees all around, and privacy. I want a cabin, a big one, that I'll make myself!

MS: It seems you really enjoy being outside.

ALEX: Yes, of course, I love it, and I want to live near the water. I want to have a fence and a high porch where I can look out and see the water and trees. It will be private. I imagine it as beautiful. Yes. That's what I want. That's my goal, and I want to have a garage and a car or a motorcycle, either one. I feel I'd rather have a motorcycle. That would be better, because of going up hills. I love motorcycles.

MS: When we met back when you were seven, you told me you were going to be a police officer.

ALEX: That's right. [*He covers his face with his hands.*] Or either a scientist or the army. But I can't. The army doesn't permit deaf people. So I'm stuck.

Although Alex has not yet found a way to make a career for himself as either with the police or in the army, he does have options. Deaf people are making inroads to professions that were previously inaccessible. There are now EMS workers, doctors, and security officers who are deaf. His dream of being a scientist or engineer has already been realized by many deaf adults.

## PERCEPTIONS OF HEARING AND DEAF PEOPLE

ALEX: I was born deaf, it's that simple, no reason. I was just born and I was deaf. It's what God gave me. [*He shrugs.*] What can I say?

MS: In general, when parents have children who are deaf, how do the parents feel?

ALEX: Well, there are a lot of different reasons. They might be scared. They might never have seen a deaf person before. They'd be scared about how we'd communicate. They might send them to a foster home. They might not like them or think they're "not my type" or reject them. I don't know. Different reasons. I'm really lucky that my mom accepted me.

MS: And your mom signs.

ALEX: Yes . . . My mom found out I was deaf, and she talked to the doctor. I went to my very first speech therapist. We learned to sign and read books, and we met deaf people. Then my mom decided to become an interpreter. She got better and better. She taught me. My first signs were "ball" and "milk." I learned and learned, and now I'm better than my mom even though I started later than her. My mom worked real hard. She wanted to know more about Deaf culture and understand Deaf culture.

MS: If deaf people have brothers and sisters, what do their brothers and sisters think about them?

ALEX: I really can't say. My opinion is, most deaf kids' brothers and sisters might not like them or they might ignore them. They might talk and not sign, and the deaf kids might not understand them. Or they might forget about them. Sometimes that happens with me. Often they will forget to sign, and I'll remind them and say, "Please sign," and they'll say, "Sorry." Then they'll sign for a while and then forget again. But I teach them and they improve.

Alex indicates that not all siblings of deaf adolescents will approve of their deaf brother or sister, and they may not be consistently inclusive in their communication. This reflects the reality of many adolescents (as

Angie said) that family members have to be reminded to sign or to include them, and this doesn't feel good to Alex. But Alex sees that his self-advocacy efforts have helped the situation and in turn his feelings about himself.

MS: If kids are ignored, how does that make them feel?

Alex: Belittled. You have to say, "Come on," and if they say no, then the parents will punish them.

MS: And can that make things change?

Alex: Yes. A little. Things can improve. My siblings improved. One improved more. At first my mom was teaching them, and one really wanted to learn, and my dad learned a little. Now it's better. They are learning more and have improved. They know a lot more signs. My mother knows it all.

In Alex's family, parental support, language and cultural modeling have been important to his relations with his siblings.

Alex: It helps me feel better about myself that they all know signs. [*He smiles.*]

MS: Okay. Now, what do hearing people think of deaf people?

MS: They think it's cool, and they're curious, and they're real interested. They think, wow, I've never seen a deaf person before. Sometimes they stare at me. But I don't mind. I just keep signing and stay focused.

## Self-Advocacy

While Alex has depicted his residential school experience as a positive and exciting place, in the following scenario he teaches us that, not unlike hearing students in hearing schools, deaf students in residential schools also have their social cliques, challenges, and even bullying. But Alex is self-directed in his approach to problem solving.

There's a table, and there are people seated and standing around, looking down at it. They've been accepted into a club, their own group; others are rejected. It's rude. They just want to be by themselves, communicate among themselves, use their own language, make up their own religion. They reject other people at school, which makes those people feel dejected. They stay to themselves and have fun and play and talk. Someone comes up and asks what's going on, and they tell him to get lost and shove him away. He's depressed, and he walks away. They laugh and go off together. The group is called the Green Gang. It's a weird name. So they go off by themselves, laughing, and go to another place.

Later the boy that they pushed down is walking along, feeling glum, and he's thinking about how he can make friends. He's all alone, hurt, discouraged, and he goes home to his mother. His mom asks how he is, and he says not so good, so she asks him what's wrong. He doesn't want to talk about it, so he goes into his room and puts his head on his hands and thinks about what he can do. He gets an idea of maybe looking for friends and getting a group together that's larger, that will beat the other group. So he writes something out, gets his idea figured out, comes up with ideas for rules and the name of the group and such.

The next morning when he wakes up, he realizes he forgot his homework, so he hurries to write that. It's time for the bus, so he has to grab his homework and hat and coat. He remembers the paper and checks his pocket. It's there. He goes out to the bus, and it's pulling up. He takes his baseball gloves. He runs out and gets on the bus. He says hello, then he goes and sits down. The others are all hearing and they're talking. He's bored, so he gets out his paper and he starts getting more ideas, so he adds those. There are people insulting him as he walks, and he just brushes that aside. There are people talking with friends, just some people. He goes in and looks at the paper and thinks more about how to make friends. He walks up to a boy who's sitting alone with his hands on a table, and he asks what's wrong. The boy scoots over, and he sits down and they talk and talk and start to be friends, and there's more and more talking and understanding. Then at lunch, they talk a lot, and they're friends. They keep meeting and being together.

Later the two of them together meet a girl and talk to her. They talk, and now there are three of them. Then they meet more and keep adding more. Every day they add more, until there are eight. They're excited and talking and having fun together. They sit together in the morning and at dinner and laugh and chat. Until again the gang comes walking up to one of them, and they stand all around him. They're staring at him, and he tells them to go away, that this is his place. So he looks at them, and then his group comes up behind him and overwhelms the other group.

Alex is practical, and when he experienced boredom in an inaccessible situation with hearing students on the bus, he took advantage of the quiet time and his internal motivation and focused his energy on strategizing solutions in his preferred social group, that of his deaf classmates. This is a good coping story that shows his autonomy, his ability to problem solve in social interactions, to build a social support group where he feels attached and empowered.

MS: Has that happened to you at your residential school before?

Alex: Yes.

MS: When people said, "Go away," what happened? Did you feel bad?

Alex: Not now. I'm fine now. They're all my friends now.

Though not apparent initially, this next story is about young deaf people and some of Alex's own experiences. The story reveals that Alex is aware of new responsibilities that come with changing bodies and social relations and he is developing ways of coping. The story also shows Alex and his friends in a struggle to communicate in the community with hearing people, how they then return to the comfort and enjoyment of their own group and language, and then how once again they are faced with the hearing-centered expectations of others when they return to a hearing environment.

Alex: This next picture, there's a man standing there giving information. He's got his hand up leaning against something. There are three students looking at him, taking in what he says. And the man is a teacher. He's standing and teaching, lecturing. He's talking about pregnancy, that a man needs to help if a woman gets pregnant, and what to do. The students have lots of questions about what to do to help when a woman is pregnant, how to help her, whether to send her to a hospital. He says it's best to send her to a hospital and help her stay calm when she's pregnant. Then another woman asks if, when she gets to the hospital, should she push, and what to do if the water breaks. Things you should tell the doctor and discuss with the doctor. Then one woman asks what she should do if a friend is pregnant. And the teacher says just go to the hospital, like he told the man. She thanks him. Then the bell rings, and it's time to leave for the next class. The teacher tells them that for their homework they have to figure out what to do if someone is pregnant, find out more information. He tells them they can use the Internet or books or ask someone in their family.

The three of them leave together. They walk along and go into a restaurant where they sit for a short time, about a half hour after the bell. This is college. They get in line and move up, and the one talks and orders. They write it down. The manager comes over and picks it up and looks at it and says, "Oh, you're deaf." So, she puts in the order, and tells them how much, and points to show where the amount comes up on the display, say $18.30. The woman checks the food to make sure it is right. Then they talk and laugh and eat. They have fun talking about pregnancy, their family heritage—talking and having fun. After school they sit and chat and have fun and laugh. They tell jokes and eat. They watch football games on TV and cheer. They like State University and the pro team games. It's fun.

MS: That was a good story. I want to go back to the beginning of that story. Is that like the residential school? Do they have classes that teach about pregnancy and what to do?

ALEX: Not so much. Sometimes.

ℰᴂ

ALEX IS learning and thinking about responsibilities he will have and situations he will face in the future. He is imaginative and creative and has many internal and social resources to draw from as he faces new situations in life and moves toward independence. He knows where he fits in and where he can find support. Alex has good coping skills and a group of supportive peers whose company he enjoys. He knows that he is loved and respected by his family, and he loves and respects them in return. His stories have happy endings and depict a sense of competency in problem solving, hopefulness about the future, and pleasurable activities. His mother's role is one of guidance that he knows he can turn to if needed, even as he becomes increasingly autonomous and competent.

Alex is the youngest of the participants in the study. Although not certain of his career pursuits, he has ideas about careers that interest him. He discusses the possibility of attending college and imagines living in a beautiful place close to nature. He is practical, has a sense of pride in himself, and is aware of his legal rights. Alex sees his residential school as a positive and comfortable place where he is involved in activities and has many friends. One of the many strengths evident in the interview was his ability to autonomously overcome adolescent social rejection by creating a group of his own and eventually blending in. He clearly enjoys the opportunity to share ASL stories about his lifeworld and projected a sense of competence in doing so. It appears that, in addition to Alex's ASL classes at his residential school, he may also have curriculum content on Deaf culture from which he is learning about his legal rights and the culture and language of Deaf people.

To Alex the residential school is a positive, comfortable, and fun place to be, where he is involved in a variety of activities and has many friends. His attempt at mainstreaming proved to be incompatible with his social-emotional, educational, and communication needs. He clearly loves, respects, and enjoys his family. He recognizes an ongoing attempt to achieve balance in communication and inclusion in family relations, which is sometimes a challenge, but he sees his mother's support and his own resourcefulness as the key to their success with this.

Recognizing that he has rights, Alex realizes that people in the community may not always respect his rights, and he acknowledges his responsibility to educate others and advocate for himself. Like the other teenagers, he is now beginning to confront more community access issues as he ventures farther and more independently into his social environment.

# 9

# *Pat*

Yeah, I could be president! I'd like to. Yeah, I don't know, maybe I could be a deaf president, I could, but they wouldn't understand me because they don't know sign language.

—Pat

ADMITTING THAT their home is difficult to find, Pat's parents suggested we meet at a local restaurant and they would lead me to their house. Upon arrival, I recognized their car in the parking lot from the description they had given me. Sitting comfortably in the front seat was a young man in a baseball cap resting his foot on the dashboard. I said, "Hi, are you Pat?"

He responded, "Yes," and opened the door to get out, took off his ball cap, straightened out his hair so I could get a good look at him, smiled really big, and said, "That's me." I commented that he had grown, and beaming proudly, he said, "Yes." Pat told me he had transferred to a different school and is very happy there. He will be a junior in the fall.

His mother came out to meet us. As we were saying our hellos, I told her that I really did plan to wear the blue-green dress I told her I would be wearing to help her recognize me, but that wardrobe piece didn't work out. She laughed, and we agreed that I would follow her in my car to their home.

We drove through an extraordinarily small, yet quaint, town that appeared to be all of two blocks long, with a cattle feed business seeming to be the only store in town. Then we drove over more country roads, past farms, over hills, and on a one-lane highway lined with trees and fields. Pulling into their driveway, we approached a lovely, medium-sized brick Cape Cod cottage back on a hill in a beautiful remote country setting overlooking rolling pastures. An inviting deck and swimming pool adorned the back yard.

A variety of pets scampered around as we pulled into the paved drive, confirming Pat's mother's friendly warning that we would need to watch our step. Pat politely helped carry our camera equipment into the house. As we approached the door, an excited little dog jumped up for our attention. Pat and his mom were proud to tell us that the dog was due to have puppies in August.

This warm and welcoming family has a well-kept home that seems like a fun place to live. Mom and Dad seem to love their home, but Pat told me repeatedly that he is bored during the summer with nothing to do, no friends close by, and no one to talk with. He spends his time alone, feeds the animals, watches TV, and plays video games. His boredom and loneliness were a recurrent theme throughout the interview. He perceived the lack of expendable family finances and his rural location as factors contributing to his social isolation.

ॐ

IN THIS INTERVIEW, Pat shared that he switched to a different residential school for the deaf a few years ago because he was a victim of bullying at his previous residential school. Needless to say, he was unhappy there and the school was not able to satisfactorily resolve the problem. His new school is even farther away from home than the previous one, but he reports he is much more content. He stays at the school during the week and commutes home on weekends.

Noticing my digital pager Pat said, "I like your pager, I wish I had one. You know W-a-l-M-a-r-t? The store? It's all over. They have many. I want to buy one, but Mom said we don't have any money. You can read the small words. I have to wait. It's a good thing!"

I said, "I remember when we met before. You were ten years old at that time, and we met at your school, and your hair was a little bit different, and you were very exuberant, and you seemed very happy back then. It's great seeing you again. It's been seven years, and you have grown!"

## MY LIFE

Pat and I discussed the process of our interview, and as with most of the other participants, he chose making a movie as the imaginary way that he would tell others about himself. Pat seemed fascinated with the idea of making a movie. Additional probing was required along with this projective storytelling prompt to help Pat tell us more about himself.

MS: Okay . . . so what is something important about *you* that you want people to know?

PAT: Well, I would tell them that I am interested in working with computers and making a movie that way, with different design approaches, and someone would take care of the acting, and I would take care of the production on the computer. But the computer is broken, the memory is full, and the whole system crashed, so it's being fixed now, and mom doesn't have the money to get it from the repair shop, so . . . I have to wait awhile."

MS: So, you want to use the computer to make the designs and the pictures for the movie, and if you were a character in the movie, what would you be doing?

PAT: Well, I would figure that about seven people would be working on this, and one person would be the producer, one person would be taking the pictures, and there would be aliens walking around, and you could see through them, and with the characters, you could see them walking past each other and through each other. That is what interests me. I think it's fascinating.

MS: Okay; now, I want you to think about real life. What is something important about you that says who you are? If you had a chance to say, "This is who I am and this is my life."

PAT: Well, I pretty much do the same ol' thing. After I first get up, I get something to eat. Sometimes I sit in my room and watch TV, I have a remote so I surf the channels and watch TV for awhile, until about noon, then eat again, and then go feed the animals. That's about it. That's what I do every day. My mom works, and if I do my all my chores, I get money. I save the money I earn from doing jobs around here so I can go to the store and buy games. I have a video game box and buy the games. I have video games, the machine for that. So I have to save all my money, then I will get to bring the game home. I have another one: Playstation 2? The black box? The new one? I have that in my room. I play all the different games with that *and* I can play the video games and also play them with DVD. You know what a DVD is? Well I play that. I really like it, it's like a movie inside the game.

These interviews took place during the summer months, and Pat was away from his school and his friends. Pat is bored and isolated without a satisfactory social outlet.

Pat: I just stay here every day, at home. Sometimes I stay here by myself. It gets a little bit boring. My mom and dad go to work. I'm just here. I get bored. My mom tells me I have to stay here day in and day out during the week—Monday, Tuesday, Wednesday, Thursday, Friday—while she's at work. It gets boring. Mom and Dad get out to work. It's boring for me. I want to go out, see my deaf friends; I haven't seen them for a long time, so every day I'm just here, bored. I watch TV. Sometimes I get a headache, then I go take some aspirin, because I'm just sitting here, so bored! I'm bored. All day I watch TV. I get headaches. I'm bored. I'm by myself all day. I asked my mom, I said, "I'm bored here all day by myself. I don't have any deaf friends to talk to. I don't have anyone to sign to." My family is all hearing, and one of my relatives, a little boy, he doesn't know how to sign very well, and that's kinda hard for me, too, so I just feel really lonely, and that's what my summer has been like. I got to go out some; sometimes on weekends I get to go out, sometimes I'm here. It gets really boring. I get really tired, so I sit, I rest, and I ask if I can go places and I'm told no. I have to stay here. It's boring, I'm here alone. I want to drive, I want to drive somewhere, I ask mom when, and she says I can't, so I'm kind of stuck.

MS: What you just said, about being home during the summer, feeling lonely, far apart from your friends . . . I know that must be tough.

Pat: Yeah, I have friends in another town, I want to see them, I miss them, but I don't see them anymore, and I have friends at my school, but they live so far, I mean, four or five hours away. It would be a long drive.

MS: During the week, during the school year, you sleep there, at the school?

Pat: Yes, I stay at a dorm; I live in a dorm there. I stay for two weeks at a time, then every other Friday, my mom drives down to pick me up. It's a four-hour drive. Then we get here, and then on Sunday evening, well, morning, usually at like one forty-five in the morning, I wake up, get in the car, and sleep on the drive back to school. Then I take all my luggage in, and I'm there first thing in the morning, even when it's dark. My dad drives. On Fridays, my mom picks me up. A bus would be expensive. We can't afford that, so . . . In my state, there is one place, Bakersville, near here, yeah. There are some deaf there, but I don't get to see them. I feel stuck; there are some, a few. It's hard. I get lonely.

MS: What about camp for deaf kids? Do you go to anything like that?

PAT: No, no, I don't. I can't really afford it. Those kinds of things are expensive. Mom always says, "No, no, we gotta save money." Now, tomorrow, I have to go to the doctor to get my braces off. I don't know for sure, but I'll get my braces off my teeth! Tomorrow. I'll have to wait and see. *Yes!* Finally! I'll be happy!

MS: I can understand! Okay. Now . . . your everyday life here at home, you were telling me you don't really have anyone to interact with.

PAT: You're right! I want to, but I live out here in farm country! I'm kinda bored! I don't have a bike; I used to, a small one, but the tire's flat and I don't have a new one. My mom and dad don't want to see me get hurt. They're worried about my safety, so I just stay home; that's another thing I just kinda put up with. I just stay home. I *do* cook: I cook eggs, hotdogs, sausage; I can cook my own food, and I do enjoy doing that. It turns out pretty good. Yeah, I'll start to cook something, then watch TV. You know I get bored, so I try to find things to do. Our pool is empty now. Tomorrow a big truck will come and fill it with water. We already called the man who is going to do that, and that will be tomorrow. Mom and Dad said that when the truck brings the water, the water will be very, very cold, and then I'll have to wait, bide my time for a few days until the water warms up.

MS: Oh, I see another cat!

PAT: Oh yeah, we have many cats!

MS: The one you just showed me is her kitten?

PAT: Two of them we bought: my mom bought one and my grandma bought one, then she didn't want it and gave it to us, so we have many cats that are here on the property. We have dogs, rabbits, roosters. I feed all of them. We have ducks and geese. I don't feed them, though. They just eat the grass. [*Pat tells me how many cats, dogs, chickens, and rabbits he has.*] And, of course, I told you the one dog is pregnant, so we'll have to see how many puppies she has, but we'll probably sell some of them or give them away because we have so many dogs and animals here! I stay here all day where it's cool. It's really hot out there, and it's nice to be cool in here.

## THE FUTURE

Pat is captivated by the idea of making a movie, but the mention of school brings him back to his social isolation, the distance from his peers, and his concerns about his vocational potential. The ideal images he has of his future are thwarted in many directions.

> MS: Now we're pretending here that you're going to make a movie. And is there something you want to tell people about your school?

> PAT: If I was going to make a movie, I would be real imaginative! I would fix and make all kinds of things—for a big screen, you know? And the movie projected onto the screen, and a place for the tapes, it'd be really cool, and it'd be nice, that's what I'm interested in, using my imagination. I'm here at home, not doing much, but I do know that I want a job. But I can't have a job. I have to wait until I'm eighteen. I really want to be a policeman, but I can't. I'm deaf.

> MS: I was looking at my notes from when we talked before, years ago, and I remember then that you said you wanted to be a police officer. And you still want to be a policeman?

> PAT: Yeah, I do. But I can't. Darn. No, I'm deaf, I can't. It'll be hard to get a job. I have to be skilled. Some jobs you can use sign, but I don't know. I can't be a fireman or work for an ambulance because I'm deaf. I think it'd be really hard for me. I don't know what to do. I feel really stuck. I want to have a job. A job that I like to go to. I would love to work making movies. Before I had a job and I made such a small amount of money. I didn't like that. I want to have a job where I can earn a little income. I'll work hard, but I have to be patient.

> MS: Do you know of other deaf people who have graduated high school, where they work?

> PAT: No, I don't know.

> MS: What about at your school? Some of the teachers are deaf?

> PAT: Yeah, some are deaf, some are hearing, and they all sign. I'll graduate in 2004. Wow, I'm getting older! Yep, two more years . . . Then I'll be done with school, I'll be home, I'll get to rest, but I have to find a job; I don't know how to drive yet. I'd be really bored if I was alone. I sometimes see myself just walking around. Or just signing to myself in the mirror, making up stories, especially if I was bored. Umm, I don't know what I would do.

> MS: You're not sure about your future?

PAT: No, cuz while I'm here, I just stand in front of the mirror and talk to myself, so . . . Sometimes I stand in front of the mirror, and I'm signing to myself. I try to improve and learn, just kinda using my imagination, by myself. I'm not really sure. I'll just be the same. I wanted to go into the army, and my mom called the army and asked if I could join, and they said no because I'm deaf, so I can't do that. I would love to be in uniform and be called to war. [*I nod in understanding.*] I want to be able to help people or kids that are hurt, like police officers—military police. That's what I want to do, but I can't. It's really hard for me because I'm deaf. I feel stuck. What can I do?

MS: Deaf people *can* do what?

PAT: I don't know what I want to do or what kind of work . . . making movies, or maybe work in a museum, that's what I would want to do . . . No deaf people work at our museum. Well, if not a museum, then a fast-food restaurant . . . I don't know, I couldn't take the orders, maybe, but I'd be able to make hamburgers and could sweep and clean, et cetera.

MS: Well, I think it's important for you to meet other deaf people who have already started working in different places.

PAT: There aren't any around here, so I don't know what jobs, and I'm kinda stuck here. I don't think I'm gonna go to college; I'm not sure. With school and work, it's hard, and I'm not very smart, so I don't think so.

We went back to the picture that had prompted all of this.

MS: So, you think this deaf man works for a newspaper?

PAT: Oh, he might be hearing. Some deaf work as artists, things like that, maybe work for a magazine or a book.

MS: I recall that the last time we met, you were a very good artist. Have you considered art for your future?

PAT: Yeah, I know, but you know, you sit and draw . . . Sometimes I do that. But I'm not as good as I used to be. I'm not that good anymore. I play video games. I don't draw as much.

MS: Well that's something to think about.

PAT: Maybe for cartoons, Mickey Mouse and those kinds of things, draw those kinds of characters . . . I'm not sure how to spell that word, but sometimes art is a little hard. [*He examines another picture of a man sitting in a chair.*] I think he's hear . . . no, I think he's deaf. He's deaf. I don't know for sure. The way he is sitting, I don't know. Maybe he is sitting down, watching TV, maybe he is watching something with closed captioning. I think he has a job.

MS: What kind of job?

Pat's response to my question indicates that he doesn't know much about living on one's own or what is involved in the workday. He needs role models and vocational support to help him identify possibilities for himself.

PAT: I don't know. I don't know what his life is like, where he lives, or what kind of a job he has. After he finished his [daytime] job, he would have to go home, maybe finish some work, write some things, put it in the mail, for his work. After he was home for awhile, he'd have to go back to work. He probably has to work every day: Monday, Tuesday, Wednesday, Thursday, Friday. On Friday, he'd walk home and open his mail, the check, to get his money, a lot of money. He'd get a raise! He'd have about $3,500. I don't know. He would get his check mailed to him from his work. I think that when he got done with work, he would have all kinds of things to do. He would have to turn in his timecard, he'd have to pay bills, like the phone, electric (the light bill), maybe twenty-two dollars for that, maybe seventy dollars for the phone bill. So he'd have to write out all the checks for those and put some money in the bank, so that's what he would do. His home, it depends. He might be bored staying home, sitting, watching TV, whatever.

MS: Are there any other people at his home?

PAT: No, no one. Well, a family, but they'd all be gone. They'd be out somewhere. Three people: a mom, a dad, and me—that's all.

Pat identifies with the man in the photograph. He imagines this man's life as similar to his own.

MS: Okay, thank you. [*I show him the next picture.*]

PAT: I think these people are deaf. I think maybe they're at school. School's hard. I think they go to college. Yeah, you have to learn a lot. You have to study, have a lot of work to do. For classes, like science, there is a lot of writing you have to do, a lot of classes. A *lot* of homework. I think it is a group of deaf people, just talking. I think they're in college so they can get a job and earn good money! So they can earn a good living!

MS: Okay. They'll study hard in college, then get a job. What kind of job will they have?

Pat: I think a movie store, a theater, a *big* one, someone might have the job of cleaning the theater, sweeping the floors, cleaning up; another person would sell the tickets . . . other jobs. The boy could become a doctor, one could be studying to be a teacher, and if that person studied and learned and passed their tests, they could be a doctor. They could get a job that would pay a lot of money and work in emergencies, if someone got hurt or would need stitches and surgery . . . that kind of job.

MS: That person who would be a doctor, is he deaf or hearing?

Pat: No, deaf people can't be doctors. They can clean, or be a nurse, study for that, or cleaning. [*Pat points to someone in another picture.*] I think the teacher is hearing because he is signing the letter *K*, and the students don't understand him, and he is trying to tell them *K* so they can practice. They're learning sign language; he's teaching.

MS: Okay. I'm wondering, can deaf people teach sign language?

Pat: I don't know. I have no idea.

Pat is clearly disappointed and frustrated with the feedback he is getting from his environment about what vocations deaf people pursue (physicians, armed services, first responders, politicians), but he is beginning to conceptualize some possibilities, such as working in the movie business, museums, and restaurants, as well as doing art and custodial work. While there are deaf and hard of hearing physicians, employees in the various branches of the military, politicians, and first responders, Pat is faced with finding a career plan that matches his capabilities. He and his family are going to need resources and guidance as he designs his career.

## School

Pat left his old school because of bullying. Deaf and hard of hearing children and adolescents are not exempt from school bullies. Bullying can take many forms and can be inflicted by peers who are deaf or hard of hearing as well as hearing. The victimization of deaf and hard of hearing students by school bullies is only now coming to the attention of the professional community. While Pat's trauma is evident in this passage, it also reflects his resilience as he has adapted to his new school environment.

MS: When you were at the other school, were any of the people that worked with you deaf?

PAT: I don't go there anymore. I quit. The boys were awful! Yes. It was stupid. They were bullies. I was very upset. I didn't like the dorms. I missed home. I just felt sick to my stomach and felt pressured. I just wanted to go home. At my new school, it's much better.

MS: So you're happier there?

PAT: Oh yeah! The old school was just awful! It was very upsetting for me. At the new school, there was only a few. At the old school there were many, *many*! You know? At my school now there is just a few. *And*, I play soccer. Well, I tried out for the team and joined. I wasn't that good, so I quit. Then I tried basketball and stuck with that! But still, we weren't a winning team. We'd have one game, and lose, then go to another game, and lose, and just kept losing! In fact we played against my old school and we lost!

MS: Basketball was fun for you?

PAT: Yeah. I just hope in the future I can get a job; I'd like to play basketball. For basketball I got a varsity letter, a big *D* for my letterman's jacket, and I got a star to put on the sleeve of my jacket, but I've looked for it and I can't find it! You want me to show you the *D*? I'll go get it!" [*Pat leaves the room and returns to show me his letter.*] I don't have the jacket yet; we can't afford it, but, yeah, hopefully!

MS: Wow, that's very nice! You should be proud of that! So you play basketball and you played a little bit of soccer?

PAT: Yeah, I played basketball, and I quit soccer, and I did play baseball. I joined the team; then there weren't enough players to join, so the team folded. The same thing happened with football. Some kids wanted to play, but not enough did, so that team folded. So now all that's left is soccer and basketball! So, even if I want to play other sports, I can't. I'm going into eleventh grade. I haven't passed my driver's test yet. There's a class at school that I took, so I've learned about driving. I took the test a while ago, but I haven't gotten my license; I studied but haven't taken the written test. My mom says I can't yet. She worries about me! I'm her "baby" and she wants to see me live a long time. [*He smiles.*] I keep telling Mom, "I'm old enough. I'll be fine." But she wants me to stay alive to be safe! She worries about car accidents or about me getting killed. You know, so many kids die in car accidents . . . wow.

We returned to the topic of school.

PAT: Hmmmm, well, I go to school. I have classes. I walk to class. I have science, gym, math, English. Oh, what else do I have? I have computer class. I have all different classes.

MS: Okay, so you have all different courses that you take.

PAT: Many different ones, I can't think of more. The first floor is only art. Maybe I'm wrong. No, that's right, and the high school kids go there only for art, that's it! Another wing is the high school. Tenth, eleventh, and twelfth grade only. The south wing is for the infants and little kids. And some [rooms] are for kids who have trouble understanding or other disabilities, then the others are babies and toddlers.

MS: Sounds like a big place! So all day, you're in class, learning, taking notes, and then after that you have soccer. Do you go to your dorm and study, have dinner? What kinds of things do you do in the evenings?

PAT: Well, when school is done, we go back to the dorm. We usually have a meeting, talk about the things we have to do, you know, our chores . . . In the morning I go down for breakfast, then back to my room, and I have to clean up by seven thirty. Then after school, we go back to the dorm and talk about our chores and check to see if we cleaned everything right—the rooms are inspected. It's kind of a pain! It's our duty to keep everything very, very clean.

MS: Now, in the dorm, do you play?

PAT: For high school, the upper classes—juniors and seniors and sopho-mores—but not the freshmen. We sit in the dorms, we eat. Sometimes I get pop, watch TV, play video games. Sometimes we go over to the girls' dorm and talk to them. The staff decides who we get to interact with. Sometimes I ask them if I can go out or not, and they say, "Fine, go ahead." I do my homework when supper is done. Usually six to eight or seven to nine p.m. and go to bed usually by ten o'clock. Juniors by eleven o'clock, seniors by eleven thirty; depends on what year you're in. There are different rules.

## Friends

Pat misses his friends this summer and is unhappy with his distance from them. His boredom and loneliness are so predominant at this point in his life that, sadly and poignantly, he resorts to playing solitary board games. He feels good about himself when he is in the company of his friends. He describes being overjoyed and surprised when he meets other deaf people that he doesn't know.

MS: So tell me about your friends.

PAT: Well, I want to see my friends, I want them to come see me, but they live too far . . . so I just stay home, by myself, bored to death. I don't even know where some of them live.

MS: Are your friends hearing, deaf?

PAT: Oh, they're deaf! But some kids from school are hard of hearing and they know sign language, but mostly deaf.

MS: Do you remember before, when we sat down and talked, you weren't sure if you were deaf or hard of hearing?

PAT: I'm *deaf!*

MS: What is the difference between deaf and hard of hearing?

PAT: Deaf and hard of hearing are different because someone who is hard of hearing knows some sign but lipreads and speaks; I use my voice sometimes, but I don't want to.

I think the people in this picture are deaf because they're having a conversation in sign language and making eye contact. They're signing to each other and having fun. When you do that, your self-esteem is good inside. If the family is hearing at home, you sit and feel bored inside. You just sit and get bored and frustrated and easily agitated. You feel stuck inside and complain. I want to go out and see my friends, but there aren't any deaf people close to here. They all live far away. You want to be close to deaf people, you want to see them, but you're not sure where. They all live far away. I'm stuck here in this town. I have friends, but I'm stuck, it's not near where I live. So, they're just talking in that picture. I want to get out, but . . . I know one thing I would like, I want to enjoy myself with deaf people and play. You know *Lord of the Rings*?

MS: Yes.

PAT: You know it? Yeah, there's a board game where you can throw dice and play. You can buy it for fifty dollars. It's neat, I like to play. My friend and I at school, we played. You have little pieces, and you roll the dice, like suppose a seven, then you move the seven spaces. You try to get the other guy. You battle, and roll again, and move again. Like, suppose I roll a three, and he rolls a one, then I take his man, I beat him and he dies. We take turns. I had fun. I enjoyed playing that. I miss that! My one friend, he already graduated from school in 2002. My deaf friend. I'm feeling down and disappointed because he's gone and I'll be alone. He's from Missouri; he's not here anymore to be my deaf friend. Some leave and they move away. I have many friends like that. I want to see, I really miss them. I'm disappointed, but I'm stuck by myself too far away.

MS: Your friend who graduated. He went back to his home state. That's a disappointment for you. What will your friend do now?

PAT: Well, my one friend, I have many friends who will graduate in 2003, and move away, and I will graduate in 2004. I will feel my circle of friends shrinking. I'm the only one staying in the dorm; the 2004 class, I'm the only one. Others commute every day.

MS: You'll miss your friends?

PAT: Yeah. Well, it's kind of hard because mom and dad work Monday through Friday. Dad works a lot. My mom, she works for her job. So, I'm stuck and just have to put up with it. I want to go out to the store, but I can't because Dad says no. I can't. He's tired. I understand that and I have to be patient. So what do I do? I play video games and feed the animals and stuff like that. You know, I want to be able to play Lord of the Rings, the board game, so sometimes I play by myself. I set up my side, the good side, then the other side, the bad side, I roll for myself, like I roll five and move five spaces. Then I roll for the other side. Suppose he gets three, so I move three spaces, then I roll again. I do both by myself, you know. One has to move two more spaces, and the other one doesn't move that many, so that first one wins. I play that by myself because I'm all alone.

MS: You switch back and forth taking turns for both sides?

PAT: Yeah, sometimes I play both sides when I'm bored and alone.

MS: Yeah, it would be nice to have some friends to play with.

PAT: Yeah. Oh well . . . I get to see older deaf people and sign with them at church, at the deaf church, but I don't get to go to church every day.

MS: Does your church have an interpreter?

Pat: No, it's a hearing church and I just watch, but I don't understand; my mom pays attention, but I'm really bored. There's no interpreter. No interpreter at all! Now, the deaf church, they sign, but my mom, she gets tired, and busy, and sometimes sleeps in, and I want to go to that one, but we don't. So I don't get to see the people there. We'd have to drive really far to go to those places. I would like to be in a town where there are many deaf people!

Pat told me two highlights of his vacation with his family—seeing the ocean and meeting a deaf couple that he could communicate with:

In S.C. there were a few things; I sat around, then I went to the mall— they have an outside mall—I walked around there. It's really, really neat! I was at the mall and I saw these two people—a man and woman, and they were *deaf*! They were signing! I started signing to them and asked if they were deaf and so talked to them! I met new friends in S.C.! That was really great! This man that I met, he signed a little bit differently. But I got to talk to him for a little bit. Then I was talking to the wife and their two friends came along, and I didn't meet them cuz the four of them left after that. Then we drove back from S.C. It was a long drive to get home! But it was interesting, it was nice.

## Family

Pat reports a disconnect between himself and family members who either do not sign or do not sign well enough for a free-flowing conversation. This is similar to the other teens in this study.

Pat: Well, my family is all hearing. Some of them have a hard time sign-ing; they haven't learned enough. My brothers and sisters, they're older; one's thirty-five, one is twenty-three, or twenty-two. The other I don't even know how old she is. Thirty-three? They have children. The one has two, my brother has two, my sister has two, my other sister has two. That's all!

MS: And do they know sign language? Your brothers, sisters, their kids?

Pat: Yeah, but I wish they could sign like a deaf person or wish they were deaf. I want them to all sign. I want friends. I mean, I sit there and they watch a movie and I can't understand. I'm stuck. My two sisters, they've learned a little bit from a book and from my mom. They don't really know it very well, because I was always really little. My grandparents sign a little bit. They have a hard time, too. But they try.

MS: And do you understand each other when you are together?

PAT: Just a little bit. If I don't understand, I'm just kinda lonely and uncomfortable. I just sit there. I don't understand what they're saying; I feel kinda stuck. I go watch TV. If another person comes up to me and tries to talk to me, I'll point to my ear and say, "I'm deaf," and then they know. So, that's what I do.

MS: Do your mother and father both sign?

PAT: Mom, yeah. My father signs a little bit; it's hard for him, but he tries. My brothers and sisters, it's hard for them to learn—they fingerspell a lot. I'm patient about it. We get together in November for Thanksgiving, and for Christmas everyone comes over, that kind of thing. I feel good inside when we are together eating and interacting, but sometimes, when they're talking, I'm left out. I feel kind of stuck because Mom and Dad and the family talks, and I'm the only deaf one, so I just sit there. I feel a little bit stuck, a little bit bored. I ask them to sign and tell them I don't understand them, and they sign and then I understand. Yeah, it's hard for me.

Like the other adolescents in this study, Pat perceives his parents and siblings as having a strong sense of positive regard for him.

PAT: When my mom had me, I was a little baby, and my mom was praying, "Please, I want my deaf baby." She wanted *me*, and I was born, and my mom cried, and she was happy when she saw me. Then as I grew, I began to learn to walk and started to play, and I guess I was kind of a bad baby sometimes. It was funny. I would throw things, and I threw something at my mom once. She told me, "Shame on you," and I cried. I was born deaf; my mom told me that she prayed for a *deaf* baby, and there I was! [*Pat says this with much certainty and a big smile.*] Mom loved the baby! Hugged the baby! She liked the baby, and Dad, oh, he liked having a deaf baby; he loved the baby. It's okay, it's all right.

MS: Good. Okay. Now, if there were brothers and sisters who saw this new baby who was deaf, what would they think?

PAT: They didn't come to the hospital cuz they were working, but when they saw the deaf baby, they thought, oh how cute! The mom told them he was deaf, and she named him Patrick. They would love the deaf baby! They would think he was cute!

MS: Okay. Now, how would other hearing people view that deaf baby?

MS: They don't know, people don't know. But when my mom went to work, she took me to the babysitter's house. I can't think of their names; you've never met them. Two of them are deaf, and one is hearing, and Mom took me to them, and they watched me, took care of me. This person who could hear cared for me, and the other was deaf. This was while my mom worked. Then I grew, and they cared for me and loved me, and then I got older and didn't go there any more, and I missed them! I didn't see them, the deaf kid, for a long time, and recently, I finally got to see them. We hugged; I was happy to see them!

## Activities

Pat told us he enjoys his involvement in sports activities at his school: baseball, football, basketball, and soccer. He likes his video games and takes care of his pets, but he has also been involved in the school's theater productions. In response to a picture prompt, he said, "I think it's a play; they have costumes. Maybe they're creating a play so the parents can all come and watch this play and smile at their children and be proud. If they're deaf, no one would understand. They'd hire a person called an interpreter to sign so they can understand. It would be easy."

MS: Are there plays at your school every now and then?

PAT: Oh yeah, they have plays.

MS: Have you ever been in one of the plays? Have you acted?

PAT: No, no; I would rather just be one of the people that goes to watch the play; it would be hard for me to be in it and follow the script and everything. I don't always understand all the words, I don't always get it, and I'd be nervous, so I don't get into the plays. I just watch. I've worked the curtains before; I stand backstage, holding the ropes, and wait for the man to signal me, then I open the curtains and close them. We keep really busy and have to wear all black so we blend in to the dark. In one play, they needed someone to stand behind a tree and hold it up, so I did that, and I had to stand there so if it started to fall over, I could grab it. No one could see me because I was behind the tree, and then the curtains closed and I let go of the tree and it fell! Everyone heard it hit the stage. So, I had to get it out of there!

## CURRENT EVENTS

Deaf adolescents are not immune to the realities of the world around us. Regardless of whether or not closed captioning is available to our deaf youth, media images of the events of September 11, 2001, still hit home, and Pat was no exception. He reaches for the next picture and puts the last one in the pile with those already completed.

> PAT: Oh, that man is trying to think of what he can draw. He is creating a drawing for magazines, books, and newspapers so that when people get up in the morning, they open the newspaper and see the comics. Then after reading that, you can turn the pages and see the big spread in the paper about what happened the day before, on September 11 in New York, about the planes hitting the buildings and the explosions and the awful things that happened on that awful day. And it will say, "Look what happened." There'll be pictures about that. It was a bad day.

> MS: You told me yesterday that you were at school and the TV was on and you saw on TV what happened and everyone was shocked.

> PAT: Yes, we were all glued to the TV; we couldn't believe it. There were four planes that crashed that day. Two hit the twin towers, one came this way, and then the other came around this way, and then after the planes hit, a little later the buildings crumbled. Then one hit the military building in Washington, D.C. Then another crashed in the woods. It was really bad. Yeah, people were going on vacation, you know, and got up in the morning and got on the plane to go and didn't realize it would happen. One man was on vacation, and he came on the plane and then the three bad men boarded the plane and one held a knife at the man's neck and they were talking about how to bomb the plane, how to make it blow up. But they got on the plane just like everyone else, like everything was normal; no one suspected anything. That country, you know the name, the man with the beard, his name was Osbi—something. The bad man who put money out to fund the attacks, to buy weapons against America. He gave the attackers money to go to New York in America, and we weren't aware of it, and they can't find him. You know the plane takes off, and the people on the plane, they worked for that man, and we didn't know they maybe had a knife. Yeah, right, but you know it seems like all the people who hate America, do you know why they do? Because

of poverty. Iraq and different places hate America, they don't like us. But Great Britain is our friend. We're allies, our friends, like family. Yeah, there are other countries that don't like us. I mean, they want to win the war, they want to try to take America for themselves. I think some of them want our land because they're poor and they want to start a war because they don't have any money and money is important for all people, all cities and places.

MS: Yes, I hope our president continues to improve relations with other countries.

Pat raises his hand enthusiastically with a smile.

PAT: Yeah, I could be president! I'd like to. Yeah, I don't know, maybe I could be, you know, be a deaf president, I could, but they wouldn't understand me because they don't know sign language. Other people who don't know sign language wouldn't know how to communicate with me. They wouldn't put up with that.

There are other countries, Russia, England, France, these officials all get together and talk about how to be more friendly, how to stop the war, how to cooperate more, and how to make the world a better place because WWII was awful. We don't want to see a WWIII. Many people would die. I don't want to see WWIII. That would be awful.

MS: Yes, it's awful to think about that.

PAT: Yeah, and God said He will come back and pick who's good and who's bad and who loves Him and He will discover who doesn't love Him, and if they don't love Him, He won't pick them.

[*We look at the next picture.*] Okay. There's a mom and someone else working. They've lost the baby and the police are trying to find the baby and Mom is worried, saying, "Where's my baby?" Mom's showing the police a picture. The police find the baby and they bring the baby back to Mom. That's why the baby's smiling and Mom's smiling and Mom's really relieved to get the baby back. I've seen things on TV where two kids are kidnapped. One's really small, a girl, and the other girl was fourteen. They were taken; it was awful.

MS: You've seen that on TV recently?

PAT: Yeah, bad things, you know, where people just take kids and people are looking for them and can't find them. They called the FBI and they're looking and can't find the girls. Maybe someone wants the parents to pay ransom for the children. I don't know.

MS: You see this on TV without closed captioning?

PAT: No, I don't have closed captioning. There's no captioning on my TV. I play games with my Playstation 2 and I put DVD movies in. I go find what I want and some have captioning so I can watch on the DVD. My TV doesn't have closed captioning.

## PERCEPTIONS OF DEAF AND HEARING PEOPLE

As Pat looks at a picture of a group of people he again recognizes what he considers evidence that the people in the photographs are deaf or hearing. But sometimes Pat isn't able to put his finger on just what the indicators are. In the situation he describes below it appears that his intuition gave it away.

PAT: I think they're deaf. I think they're all deaf. A group of friends and they're all smiling and they're happy to be together and they're having fun. They're all deaf, they're smiling.

MS: If you look at a person and you see one person who is hearing and the other person is deaf, what's different about them?

PAT: Well, you know, like I told you, when I was on vacation, my mom and brother and sister and her two kids, we were walking outside a mall, and there were two deaf people, like I told you. One was just like that man. He was an older deaf person; but I don't know, deaf people are more, just more . . . light. I don't know how to describe it. Like older deaf people, these older deaf people . . . I was just sitting there looking around, and I looked over and this deaf man looked at me and he had a funny expression on his face and he waved, and I waved back and I said, "Are you deaf?" and he said, "Yeah, are you?" and he came up to meet me and we started chatting in sign language. My mom and sister came up and they were signing, too, and said, "Hi, nice to meet you," and we talked for a little bit and my mom said, "Come on, we have to go." So, we had to leave, but that man, his wife was deaf, too, and he had a friend who was deaf, and you know, other people could talk, but I met these deaf people. I don't know how I knew, I just had a sense. I saw the man looking at me and he asked if I was deaf and I said, "Yeah, are you?" and we found we were both deaf and we just started talking and I met this new person and that was great!

MS: Did you see them signing? Or was he just looking at you?

PAT: I was just looking around at all the people and, no, I don't know. We just looked at each other and I thought he was deaf, and when he asked me if I was deaf, I said, "Yeah."

MS: So, you were surprised and they weren't signing or anything?

PAT: No, we were out of state, and it surprised me to meet a deaf person out of state.

PERHAPS THE most obvious recurring theme apparent from Pat's interviews at this point in his life is the expression of boredom, loneliness, and feeling "stuck." He reported he felt stuck socially living far away from other adolescents he can communicate and socialize with, stuck alone in his house with no means of transportation or communication while his parents worked, stuck with financial barriers prohibiting his family from sending him to summer camps or purchasing electronic equipment that could put him touch with others, and stuck vocationally with barriers preventing him from achieving his dream of becoming a policeman, fireman, soldier, rescue worker, or president.

Pat is thinking about his future—how to budget his money and how to save and pay for rent and other bills. He looks forward to learning to drive. Vocationally, Pat's goals have not changed over the past seven years. He reported that when he has asked about these professions, he has been told that deaf people cannot join any of them, thus he is disillusioned about his future. He knows that college is a possibility for some deaf people but does not see that as a possibility for himself. Pat is struggling to find career ideas. He suggested doing custodial work, possibly working in a museum, working in a fast-food restaurant, or doing art work, but he needs help finding the right fit and the right path. He is uncertain about the types of jobs available to deaf adults who do not attend college. Aside from custodial and maintenance staff, the deaf adult role models he has at the residential schools all have college degrees and professional positions. He is in need of guidance on options available to him if college is out of the question. Researchers in the field may find themselves in a position where they are called upon to share their expertise and serve as a resource. After our interview, Pat and I talked with his mom, and we discussed vocational and youth socialization resources.

While many teenagers today, deaf teens included, are immersed in a culture of electronic media for communication, entertainment, and information,

Pat does not reap the same benefits from this. His family's lack of money and his admitted difficulties with reading—both of which are necessary for taking advantage of e-mail, instant messaging, TTYs, captioned television and movies, and Web-based information—create a barrier for him. Thus, electronic telecommunications have not helped to fill the social and communication gaps that he talked about here. At the time of these interviews, video relay interpreting and video communications equipment were emerging on the market but were not widely available in the mainstream for families with deaf children and adolescents. Although not a substitute for day-to-day, face-to-face socialization and interaction, this would have been a welcome addition to Pat's life. Technology grants from corporations and businesses to individuals and families will be an important resource.

Pat's life is filled when he is at his residential school, where he has deaf friends and activities; the summer months, by contrast, bring an emptiness and detachment to his life. At school, Pat experiences a sense of belonging, comfort, and attachment, though, like Alex, Pat makes us aware that bullying is present even in healthy identificational communities such as the deaf community. Schools and deaf community resource centers need to find ways to prevent and address this issue.

A very kind and pleasant young man, Pat was delighted to have company and appeared to savor our meetings. Pat is an exceptionally patient young man who longs for opportunities for socialization and work. He loves and respects his family, and his stories about his childhood and his perceptions of his parents' view of him, particularly his mother's, reveal that he believes he is loved and wanted and that his being deaf makes no difference in that love.

Helping me pack my camera and carry it to the car, Pat posed an abundance of questions to me. We stood and chatted for a while. He began to talk again about September 11, 2001, and the World Trade Center and asked if I saw the planes hit the Pentagon. Most of the participants brought this issue into their interviews or afterwards off camera. They were affected by it and aware of the onset and existence of terrorism and the current political atmosphere.

# 10

## *Lisa*

Hearing people should know hearing impaired can talk and try not to be shy to talk to the deaf.

—Lisa

MARILYN AND I rang the doorbell and waited. Lisa's father opened the door and greeted us as a smiling Lisa appeared at his side. I remembered what a challenge it was for ten-year-old Lisa to warm up to us when we visited her seven years ago and noticed how at ease she seemed this time around. Lisa did not remember our previous meeting.

Her father showed us to a cozy, well-lit family room. Marilyn continued to set up the equipment as I reviewed the purpose of the project and our plans with Lisa. Although Lisa knows sign language, her primary means of communicating is through speech and lipreading. Just after our meeting seven years ago, Lisa transferred from her local elementary school, where she used a total communication approach, to a residential school that follows the oral approach.

Lisa communicated using her voice with me, and I read her lips. I signed in English as I voiced slowly when I spoke to her. I told Lisa that I wanted to be sure that we were communicating in a way that was effective for both of us. I asked if it would work for her if we continued the way we had been communicating up to that point, and she agreed. I told her that the interpreter would be available to help us if need be. She seemed to understand me very well and always responded appropriately to my questions. I wanted to respect her communication needs and preferences and to be able to understand and be understood as well. Throughout our interviews, she supplemented her speech with subtle lap-level gestures and occasional signs and fingerspelling for my benefit. It wasn't until I reviewed our videotaped interviews that it became apparent to me the extent to which Lisa was doing this. When I didn't understand her after a first or second try, she raised her hands higher to chest level to fingerspell or sign a missed word for me. To illustrate the communication process that Lisa and I shared, I begin this chapter by indicating in most places what was supplemented with signs and fingerspelling. Though often indicated, her gestures were more frequent than can be seen below. Lisa and I watched each other attentively with eye contact throughout the interview.

In an attempt to show how difficult it was for Lisa and me to communicate, I have transcribed the first set of excerpts rigorously, including my echoes, my requests for clarification from her and the interpreter, and her use of gestures and signs. As can be seen from the number of times I needed to ask Lisa for clarification, I believe she understood me more than I did her. I didn't know how much Lisa depended on her hearing aids or how much she was depending on my signs. As I did seven years ago, I frequently echo Lisa's responses for two reasons—first, to confirm that I have understood her correctly and to give her the opportunity to clarify, and second, to verify with Marilyn, our voice-over interpreter, that we are both understanding the same thing. Our interviews may mirror Lisa's communication with other deaf and hard of hearing people.

I realized later, as I reviewed the tapes and transcripts of these interviews, that Lisa and I were so focused on understanding each other word for word that my ability to mentally process and track content was adversely affected. Thus, I missed opportunities to probe for further information. One of Lisa's strengths in this interview, however, was her presentation of her yearbook and photo albums to provide me with a better understanding of her school experiences.

❦

LISA WAS SEVENTEEN years old at the time of this interview. She smiled throughout most of the interview and projected a general sense of well-being and happiness. Lisa warmed to our sessions much more quickly than she did seven years ago. She has continued to be involved in a number of activities. She reported that she has been conditioning for swimming and planned to try out for her high school team in the fall. She relaxed a bit as we proceeded. She was very cooperative, cordial, and pleasant throughout the interview.

MS: Okay? Fine. I know you're not signing now; you just use your speech.

LISA [*nods*]: I talk.

MS: And that's what's most comfortable for you?

Lisa: Yes.

MS: It's okay with you if I sign myself?

Lisa: Yes.

MS: Because that's what I do every day and that's how I'm most comfortable. So will that work out?

Lisa: Yes, that's okay.

MS: And if I have trouble lipreading, then Marilyn can help us. Okay?

Lisa: Okay.

MS: Okay. So, if you could either write a book or make a movie about deaf teenagers, which would you prefer?

Lisa was listening intently with her eyes fixed on me and sitting very still.

Lisa: Maybe a book.

MS: A book? Okay. In that book, I would like for you to tell people a story about yourself. What would you tell people about yourself?

Lisa [*shrugs slightly, glances away for a second and then back*]: That I'm hearing impaired.

MS: That you are hearing impaired and . . .

Lisa [*takes a long pause, shrugs slightly a few times, and opens her hands, which have been folded on her lap, in a gesture of nothingness*]: I can't think of anything.

While other participants in the study refer to themselves as deaf or hard of hearing, Lisa uses the term hearing impaired to describe herself and the population of deaf and hard of hearing people.

MS: Can you tell people what you do every day?

Lisa: Right now I have . . . [*pauses, looks away and then back at me*] condition.

She realizes I do not understand what she is vocalizing. I watch intensely as she orally spells out c-o-n-d-i-t-i-o-n. I still do not understand, so Lisa switches to fingerspelling: "c-o-n-d-i-t-i-o-n."

MS: Conditioning? Oh, I see.

LISA: Every Tuesday and Friday morning.

MS: You have conditioning for what?

LISA: For swimming. I have to do a lot of running. [*She closes her fists and lifts her arms a bit in a gesture of running.*]

MS: For what?

LISA: For swimming.

Unsure, I begin to sign "swimming" and look for clarification to the interpreter, who confirms my understanding.

MS: So you're conditioning for swimming.

LISA: Warm ups. [*She flashes her hand in a cooling gesture.*] A lot of running and weightlifting and swimming laps.

MS: Running, weightlifting, and laps. To warm up for swimming?

LISA [*nods*]: Yes, but I don't know if I'll make the team. [*She moves her hands back and forth in an "either way" gesture.*]

MS: You don't know if you'll make the team. Which team?

LISA: At my high school. And one day a week, I work at a store.

MS: You work?

LISA: At [*she tells me the name of the store*]. I work as cashier. One day a week because I have conditioning and tutoring.

MS: You have conditioning and ——?

LISA: Tutoring.

MS: You have conditioning and tutoring. What's your tutoring for?

LISA: To finish my math.

MS: To finish your math.

Lisa: Algebra.

MS: Algebra. We talked about math the last time, too. You were telling me that in third grade you were learning multiplication and division. [*Lisa laughs.*] And now you're learning algebra. You've come a long way.

## School

Lisa tells me that she has completed her program of study at her oral residential school and she will switch to a hearing public high school this coming fall where she will be partially mainstreamed.

MS: And you have been going to Fall Beach School, is that right?

Fall Beach is the oral residential school she has attended for the past several years.

Lisa: Yes, but I'm finished. [*She gently signs "finished" at her lap level.*]

MS: You finished. Did you graduate?

Lisa: Yes.

MS: Great. And now you're going to a new high school.

Lisa: Yes.

MS: And you'll be mainstreamed?

Lisa [*gestures "so-so"*]: Sort of. But not really mainstreamed. [*I am confused about what she means, and she responds to my puzzled expression.*] Not really much mainstreamed.

MS: Not really mainstreamed? [*Lisa nods.*] What will it be like?

Lisa: Some classes I won't have an interpreter, a sign language interpreter.

Not understanding, I look questioningly, and Lisa repeats this, subtly signing "interpreter" and "sign."

MS: You will have an interpreter?

Lisa [*gestures "so-so"*]: Maybe not.

MS: Maybe not.

Lisa: I'll be with the deaf class or the hearing class.

Here Lisa supplements this for me by signing "group" at her lap level on the left side and then spatially moving to the right, gesturing "push away" and then "group" on the right side to indicate being without deaf classmates at other times.

Lisa: I'll have both sometimes. [*She points back and forth from one side to the other.*]

MS: So sometimes you'll be in a deaf class, and sometimes you'll be in a hearing class. Back and forth?

Lisa: Yeah.

MS: Okay. Tell me about Fall Beach School. What was it like there?

Lisa: It's for oral only. [*She signs only at her lap.*]

MS: It's for oral kids?

Lisa: And you have lower [*signs "low"*] school, meaning younger kids, meaning they could be six to thirteen years old. Middle school is for thirteen to seventeen. They're a good school. They help the children speak up.

MS: It's a good school that helps students speak up. And they have a school for little kids up to about twelve years old, and then they have a middle school up to age seventeen?

Lisa: Seventeen.

MS: You know, I never went to a school for deaf children where everyone just talked. Tell me what you do there, how people communicate.

Lisa: At school, we have classes, like reading, English, math, science, and government.

Like other children in the study, Lisa's interview gives us a glimpse into her daily life, and her individuality. It is striking how different each child's life is and how different their communication and personalities can be, yet there are so many similarities.

MS: You have classes for reading, English, math, science, and ——?

Lisa: Government.

MS: Government.

Lisa: And we have gym.

MS [*looking at the interpreter for confirmation*]: Gym?

Lisa: And we have speech lab.

MS: Speech lab.

Lisa: Speech lab. So some children have to go down to talk in speech. Good language. Good speech. And the teacher faces to the children to talk.

The interpreter and I did not understand the last part of the sentence.

MS: The teacher ——?

Lisa: Faces to the children. [*Lisa adds a gesture to indicate "face to face." It becomes clear to Lisa that we still do not understand, so she uses a shoulder level gesture.*] Face to the children.

MS: Oh, face to face. [*Lisa copies my sign.*] And talks?

Lisa: Yes. Sometimes the teachers turn around while they talk to the board, in the back. [*She demonstrates writing on the board.*]

MS: Sometimes teachers ——?

Lisa: Sometimes teachers talk while they write on the board [*again demonstrating writing*].

MS: And they face the board, not facing the students?

Lisa: Yeah. Teach them for high school.

MS: So they talk while they face the board, talk and write, and then they turn and talk some more?

LISA: And they have activities.

MS: Activities.

LISA: They have art and yearbook.

MS [*not understanding what she said*]: Art, and ——?

LISA [*signs*]: "Bookstore."

MS: Bookstore.

LISA: They have newspapers, and they have yearbook. [*I indicate that I don't understand, and she signs "book" and says, "yearbook."*]

MS: Book? Oh, yearbook. Uh huh." [*I nod.*]

LISA: And they have biking.

Lisa repeats this with a gesture that I don't understand, so she fingerspells, "b-i-k-i-n-g."

LISA: I love to go biking. And [*shrugs*] I live in the dorm.

MS: In the dorm.

LISA: We have housemothers and housefathers. They're nice. They talk with the kids. If anyone gets hurt, we have an infirmary.

MS: You have ——?

LISA: Infirmary.

MS [*puzzled, looking to the interpreter*]: Oh, an infirmary.

LISA: To get medicine or other things.

MS: And you like it there?

LISA: I like it.

## FRIENDS

I want to know more about Lisa's life at Fall Beach School.

MS: Tell me about your friends at school there.

LISA: I have a lot of friends there. Some of them are from Florida [*points downward*] and Maine. Most of them have hearing aids, implants. [*She points behind her ear.*]

MS: Some of them have cochlear implants. Do you have a cochlear implant? [*Lisa looks puzzled.*] Do you have an implant?

LISA [*shakes her head*]: Some of them were younger [*gestures*], some got them a few years ago [*gestures*]. They speak different than when younger. They speak good.

MS: They speak well? [*Lisa nods.*] And did you say that they speak differently?

LISA: When they first came to my school . . .

MS [*not understanding*]: They speak differently?

LISA: Yeah, not the same as I talk.

MS: Not the same?

LISA: Yeah. I speak.

MS: What do you mean?

LISA: Like, when they first came, they talked too quietly, now, they talk now, more than the first time.

MS: So you mean when you first went into your school, your speech was not as good as when you finished?

LISA: Yes.

MS: Your speech improved while you were there?

LISA: Yes. [*changing the topic*] My friends and I have a good time together.

MS: Good. That's important.

LISA: Yes. And sometimes we play soccer. And I made nominated for All-American Swim Team.

MS: You made ——?

LISA: Nominate.

MS: You were nominated for ——?

LISA: All Deaf American Swim Team.

MS: You were nominated for the All Deaf American Team!

LISA: Yeah.

MS: That's exciting.

LISA: Yeah.

MS: So you are on the swim team at your school?

LISA: Yes. For five years. [*She signs "5."*] This year, we did great; we won ten.

MS: When we met a long time ago you were swimming. I remember you had practice during the summer. And you still do. So you've been swimming all your life.

LISA: Yes. It's my favorite sport.

MS: Is it? Great. Now, your school team, who do you play against? Other high schools?

LISA: We play some against high schools, some against middle schools.

MS: Some high schools, some middle schools.

LISA: And one team is a deaf team. We don't like that team.

MS: You don't like that team. That's your rival?

LISA: [*She nods and tells the name and location of the school.*] We don't like each other because that team, that school is only for signs. [*When she sees I don't understand, she signs, "Only signing."*]

Clearly, this is different from the rivalries common among hearing schools. Lisa's school rivalry with the other deaf school is not just a matter of team loyalty but rivalry based on different communication philosophies.

MS: Only signing. And you don't.

LISA: Yes. And sometimes we fight with each other.

MS: You fight with each other. Do you have other teams at your school? Other sports?

MS: They have basketball, gymnastics, and soccer. That's all.

MS: Okay. Do you have any stories, funny stories or sad stories, or any kind of stories you want to share about school?

Lisa: I have too many stories, I don't know. I have a lot of memories from my [oral residential] school. [*She considers what to share, then shrugs.*] I can't think of any.

MS: Do you have any stories that you want to share about your friends?

Lisa: There's one or two of my friends; we always talk at night, past our bedtime. We're talking and talking. We talk a lot. All of a sudden, our housemother came and yelled at us. We're supposed to be in bed. So my friend was laughing because we were fooling around in the [common] room. We're not supposed to do that. So the houseparent told us to go back to our rooms. So we did. But the houseparent went back to her room. But we came back again to meet. And then we talked and talked a long time.

MS: What kinds of things do you talk about with your friends?

Lisa: Sometimes we talk about problems. We talk about school stuff. Make up foolish talk about funny stories.

MS: Okay. You said you talk about problems. What kinds of problems do deaf teenagers have?

Lisa: Sometimes we have problems with teachers. Sometimes problems with other friends, sometimes a problem at home.

MS: Okay. Thank you. Do you have other stories you want to share about your friends?

Lisa: I can't think of one now.

MS: Okay. Who are your friends? Do you have friends here and friends away at your school out of state?

Lisa: I have thousands of friends. But one of my friends lives in another city three hours from here. His name is David. My best friend, I have two [*signs the number 2*] best friends. Her name is Gina. She lives in

Texas. And there's Alysha. [*She repeats and fingerspells each name for me as she tells me about her friends.*] She lives in Vermont. And Robby, and Ryan, and Nebyat, and Cassidy, and more.

MS: That's a lot of friends. So your friends live all over the country, right?

LISA: Three of them in another country. We keep in touch on e-mail or AOL. [*I miss part of this, so she fingerspells.*] E-mail or AIM or AOL. And I have some friends who are teachers and housemothers.

MS: Do you keep in touch with them during the summer too?

LISA: Yep.

MS: Good. Do you have friends here in town from your old school?

LISA: A few. I haven't seen them for a long time.

MS: What about kids in the neighborhood? I remember when we talked before, there was a girl who lived close by. You used to go over to her house.

LISA: Over there. She's not there.

MS: She's not there anymore. She moved? [*Lisa nods.*] Do you have other friends in the neighborhood that you play with [*Lisa shakes her head.*] during the summer?

LISA: No.

MS: What else do you do with your friends? [*Lisa shrugs and shakes head.*] That's about it?

LISA: Yeah.

At the end of our first visit, as we were preparing to leave, Lisa's father said that Lisa has been working on a scrapbook from school and suggested that she show it to me. Lisa went up to get it and set it on the kitchen table for me to see. It was a carefully prepared, bright, colorful scrapbook with many photos of school friends, activities, parties, and sporting and dramatic events. Lisa had told me her swimming team had had a winning season, and from the scrapbook I could also tell that she had participated in several dramatic productions at her school. Her photo album was a positive testimony to her activities and life at her residential school. There were many photos of school trips that she had taken, and she explained to me that when students stayed at school on the weekends they often went away for weekend trips. They traveled to many historical, fun, and educational places.

Lisa's photo album also included pictures of her prom. Lisa didn't mention any boyfriends or dating. Interestingly enough, I think that subject didn't come up with a lot of the adolescents as I expected it would.

೪ಎ

AT THE START of our second visit, Lisa's father reported he was going upstairs until we were finished. Lisa disappeared from the room for a moment after I told her that Marilyn would still be coming. I assumed she went to tell her father that so he would know to send her into the family room for us. I didn't know if she had a doorbell light, so I assumed she would want her father to be alert for the doorbell. When Marilyn arrived, Lisa and I were not aware that she was at the door, and her father showed her to our meeting place.

Lisa showed me another scrapbook on the coffee table in front of us. I opened the book and saw many neatly inscribed mementos written to Lisa from friends and teachers at her school. It was clear that she had many close relationships with people who cared about her there. As I turned the pages, I asked her to tell me about the people in the pictures who were important to her. She told me about her teachers, houseparents, friends, and classmates. She showed me pictures of herself on her school swimming team, in the drama club, and on the gymnastics team and yearbook staff, and other photos of her in group hugs with friends and with classmates. Each of the seniors had a paragraph on the back of their picture with their memories of their school years. The adolescents in these pictures were well-dressed, and they appeared to be happy.

I have never been to Lisa's school. During the phase I study, I had the opportunity to visit some of the participants' schools. I was able to observe classes in Mary's and Alex's current schools but not in the other participants' schools. So, while my experiences with each of their schools were different, Lisa's was the most unknown to me. Having never visited or observed an oral residential school, I had the most questions for her about what her days were like there. The fact that she shared her photo albums was helpful to me in picturing her life away at school.

MS [*looking through yearbook*]: Oh wow, lots of friends. Many comments . . . from teachers also.

LISA: Yeah, that's my housemother.

MS: She has many nice things to say about you.

LISA: She misses me so much. I've known her for five years. That's a group that made the yearbook, these are seniors.

MS: Want to tell me about any of these people? Anyone special that you want me to know about?

LISA: I know her. I used to be in her homeroom. Sometimes I was a trouble-maker. I won't listen. I wouldn't pay attention. And I always gave them a bad attitude. I don't pay attention, teachers talking. I don't listen to what they say. I don't like to learn. Not before, but now it's okay, but I still don't want to go to school. [*Lisa indicates a picture in the book.*] Mr. Sibley, he's my coach for swimming and drama club. He always said I'm his favorite girl.

I flip through her book, examining the contents of each page. I look up at her as I turn pages to see if there is anything she wants to share with me as I look through it. Lisa points at the book.

LISA: That's Mrs. Groves, hearing. She loved to talk to me, she always feels comfortable with me, and she always wanted to take me with her, to go over to her house or anywhere she wanted to go.

MS: And the preschool there has both deaf children and hearing children?

LISA: Yes. There's a lot of deaf, but I don't know how many. [*She shrugs and points at a picture in the book.*] Her name is Mackenzie. She loves me, too. Both want me to be their sister.

MS [*continuing to look through the book*]: These are the seniors?

LISA: Yes. [*She points at her picture.*] That's me.

Upper-level students at Lisa's oral residential school graduate in ninth or tenth grade. They then transfer to mainstream settings for the remainder of their high school years. Lisa will be a sophomore in the fall at her local high school.

LISA: Sort of. But some students go to ninth or tenth in high school. But some go to eighth or ninth. We are graduated; we're called seniors this year. All of us are gone.

MS: They're all gone. How do you feel about that?

LISA: Sad.

MS [*pointing to a picture in the book*]: Is this you? [*Lisa nods.*] And this is your friend Kirsten? [*She nods.*] And who's that?

LISA: Carmela.

MS: Carmela. There's three girls, and all those boys.

LISA: Eleven boys.

MS: And this is your senior picture. [*I see from her pictures that she is involved in a variety of activities.*] Drama club, yearbook club, newspaper club, swimming, biking, Web site design, photo club, gymnastics. Wow. You're very active!

LISA: There's more I listed, but they didn't have room.

She watches intently as I read a passage she wrote about her experience at her school, her sadness about leaving, and her reflections on what she considers a "great school" that has helped her with her speech and attitude. She thanked the staff at the school, talked about the friends she had made, the things she had learned, and how she would like to be remembered for the things she loves and as someone who enjoyed teasing people.

MS: That's very nice. What other activities were you involved in?

LISA: Art, and, um, cooking . . . I don't remember what else.

MS: That's wonderful. Sounds like you accomplished a lot there. That's something to be proud of.

LISA: Yeah.

MS: Tell me about your Web site design. Did you do that for your school?

LISA [*nods*]: We made a Web site for our newspaper. We are finished. So people can read it all across the school campus. I can't check it here. It doesn't work. It's only for local use.

MS: Tell me about which of those people are special to you. Carmela is your friend?

LISA: Some of those. Him, him . . . [*She points to several pictures and tells me her friends' names.*] All my classmates.

MS: And is this you also?

LISA [*nods*]: In gym.

MS: I'm looking for other pictures of you. Is this you?

LISA [*nods, points at another picture*]: I'm on a snowboard.

MS: And swimming.

LISA: All school rooms have phonic ears [a listening device that deaf and hard of hearing children often use in the classroom]. Younger students have suspenders around their backs [to hold the phonic ear system]. The older and middle school students have a string around their necks instead.

MS: I see. Were you involved in this? [*Lisa nods as I point to the writing club.*] So you write poems?

LISA: Yes.

Lisa points to the book to indicate her involvement in the annual winter and spring performances. She tells me about her characters, the themes of each show, and the positive audience reaction.

LISA: They laughed. That's my housemother, my dorm, Christmas dinner.

I thank her for sharing her photos with me.

MS: Is there anything else you'd like to share with me about school or friends?

LISA: I can't . . . I don't know.

MS: What other things happen in your life that are important to you that you think hearing people should know about?

LISA: Hearing people should know hearing . . . can talk.

I am not sure what she is saying. I lean forward, puzzled.

MS: Hearing people should know . . . [*I look to the interpreter who understood her to say "parents."*] Hearing parents can talk?

Lisa: Hearing impaired.

MS: Oh, hearing impaired [people] can talk.

Lisa: And try not to be shy to talk to the deaf . . . understand.

MS: And try not to be shy?

Lisa: Hearing impaired that don't understand.

MS: People who don't understand?

Lisa: Hearing impaired don't know what you're talking about.

MS: Hearing impaired people don't know what you're talking about.

Lisa: Don't know what you're talking about. You ask questions, some people say, "Never mind." Hearing impaired don't like that.

MS: Hearing impaired people don't like that. They don't like it when people say, "'Never mind"?

Lisa is saying that hearing people sometimes shy away from talking to deaf and hard of hearing people or brush them off when they don't understand. She is becoming more relaxed as our interview progresses. She loosens up a bit, bringing one leg up on the sofa and letting her smile fade into a more relaxed conversational expression.

From here on, I will eliminate most of my repetition, clarifications, and indications of Lisa's use of subtle lap-level gestures and supplementary signs as we proceed through the interview.

## Communication

MS: Okay. And what do deaf people think of hearing people?

After a long pause, Lisa shrugs.

Lisa: I think I'm fine with hearing people. But some people have trouble with hearing people. Not communicating. Making friends. I'm fine with it. I don't know.

Lisa's response to this question and others pertaining to the dynamics of communication interactions with others indicates she just takes her relationships with nonsigning hearing people for granted. She believes she is loved by her family. She acknowledges her siblings are supportive. At the same time, she acknowledges struggles in communication and in meeting and making friends, and she admits to sometimes feeling "lost" or bored.

MS: How do you make friends with hearing people?

LISA: Talk with them and . . . Or I'm part of a club. Or my sister's friends, if they have a sister or brother, we can meet each other.

MS: What do you do when you get together?

LISA: Talk. Hang out.

MS: How do parents feel about deaf children and teenagers?

LISA: I think they feel fine. I think they have no problem with me.

MS: Is that true for all parents of deaf children?

LISA: Some other parents have tough times. Some don't know how to take care of [a deaf child].

MS: Okay. Deaf kids have brothers and sisters. How do those brothers and sisters feel about the deaf kids?

LISA: They feel fine. They love me.

MS: They love you. Okay. And is that true for all families?

LISA: Sometimes, I think. But I don't know.

MS: Okay. What would you like to tell people about your family?

LISA: I have two sisters. One of them is not here anymore. She lives in Alabama. She will be married, and my other sister is here, and my mom, my dad are here. They try to help me because I'm hearing impaired. They try learning how to know me, talk to me, and know very well about me.

Lisa tells me where her sisters are going to or have gone to college. She tells me about the oldest sister's major and her place of employment, but she isn't sure of her other sister's major.

Lisa examines a picture of a family sitting around at dinner.

Lisa: The boy is trying to sneak out, to open the window, while his family is not paying attention to him. So they won't know what happens next to him. It looks sort of like my family, talking.

MS: When your family and relatives get together and people are talking, are you able to follow the conversation?

Lisa: Sometimes. Sometimes I'm not with them. I'm at another table with my other cousins. I have a lot of cousins.

MS: How do you follow the conversation?

Lisa: By lipreading.

MS: Do you get lost sometimes? [*Lisa nods.*] You do. Then what happens?

Lisa: I go ask them what happened, what are they talking about.

MS: And they help you?

Lisa: Yes.

MS: How do you feel in a big group with many cousins and relatives?

Lisa: Fine.

While Lisa indicates that she feels "fine" in large groups of family members where communication is more challenging, the passages below reveal a sense of confusion and feeling "lost" in situations where she doesn't have access to the communication around her. Her approach to this is to assert herself and ask what people are talking about through speech and lipreading.

## Perceptions of Deaf and Hearing People

We move on to another picture.

Lisa: The boy, two boys, are playing games. But another boy heard the phone ring. He is talking on the phone during the game, and another boy is waiting for him to finish [the phone call]. So he became bored. I would say hearing [the boy on the phone]. This one's deaf [the one who is waiting].

MS: Does that happen to you? [*Lisa is nodding.*] When hearing people are talking and you don't know what they're talking about, do you become bored sometimes?

Lisa: Sometimes.

In Lisa's interpretation of another photograph, she points to a boy she identifies as deaf.

Lisa: Because it looks like he doesn't know what he's doing.

MS: So these two are hearing?

Lisa: Yes, they know what to do. Because the boy who's deaf doesn't understand. [*She looks at another photograph.*] This woman, maybe she will go to some store. I would say deaf, because she might not know where places are and try to talk to other people, but she's too shy. She might have a business job.

In the following excerpt, Lisa acknowledges the value of sign language.

Lisa: There's a woman telling a girl what to do, and the girl is trying to understand why things happen to her, so the woman is helping her. The girl is deaf, but the woman's probably hearing, because she was signing.

MS: So a hearing person would sign, and the deaf person would not sign?

Lisa: They would sign but don't understand talk.

MS: Not understand talking. Okay. She would not understand what the woman was talking about if she didn't sign?

Lisa: Yes.

## The Future

MS: What about you? Do you know what you want to do in the future?

Lisa: I want to be a . . .

MS: You want to be ——?

Lisa: A [*fingerspells*] vet.

MS: A vet. That's a wonderful goal. Do you know where you will go to school for that?

Lisa tells me the name of one college she is considering, then shrugs and shakes her head,

LISA: Maybe. I don't know other places.

MS: That would be wonderful. You must like animals.

LISA: Yes.

MS: What other things do you imagine for yourself in the future?

LISA: I don't know; I can only imagine about the vet.

Lisa looks at a photograph of a man she believes is deaf.

LISA: His face looks, he has no idea what [the man is] talking about. Maybe he's applying for a job, maybe business. [*She looks at another picture.*] And this man is drawing for a comic book, and he wants to be an artist. He wants to draw. I would say deaf; I'm not sure why.

MS: Some of your friends from school, what do they want to do in the future? What kinds of jobs do they want?

LISA: Some want to help people. Talk about feelings, psychology, and some of them want to be in business, but they don't know what kind. Some of them want to be vets, and some of them want to be singers.

Singing is a highly unique aspiration for a deaf adolescent. None of the other students mentioned this.

When we left Lisa's home, her father told me that the decision to send Lisa away to school was the hardest but best decision they have made for her. As Marilyn and I stood out on the curb for a moment after packing up the car to discuss our next steps, the garage door suddenly opened and Lisa pulled out in the car with her dad in the passenger seat. Yes, she was driving. I drew a big smile and looked at her and said, "Driving!" She grinned, and as they passed us in the car, her dad said, "Watch out!" And I thought, "Yes, watch out"—there she goes off on her journey through life with so much to explore and accomplish!

❧

LISA IS ONE of four adolescents in the study who attended a residential school for the deaf, but she is the only one whose school relied on the oral communication approach. The other three residential school students attended bilingual programs that utilize English and American Sign Language. Lisa frequently referred to herself and other deaf and hard of hearing people as "hearing impaired," a term that the other participants did not use. These differences in terms reflect the different hearing or deaf cultural orientation and philosophies of the respective schools. The school that Lisa has attended for the past seven years used oral and auditory approaches that focused on speech, lipreading, and auditory listening skills. Lisa's stories reveal that she has adopted and integrated these same values into her daily life. She believes it is important for hearing people to know that she and her peers can talk. However, a common theme she shares with the other teens is her disdain at being brushed off or left out by hearing people, and she acknowledged the value of sign language.

Like the other three residential school participants, Lisa had primarily happy stories to share about her experiences in her educational and dormitory environment with her friends and peers and with other teenagers that she identifies with. Though she seems very happy socially, she admits that she doesn't like school and learning. She was involved in a variety of extracurricular activities and had a wide circle of friends. Her expression of these experiences was joyful and positive. Telecommunications and Internet technology provide a means for her to stay in touch with her peers when she is away from them.

While vocational objectives did not arise in our phase I interviews, Lisa now has plans to attend college and hopes to become a veterinarian. She revealed that she has faith in the future and the many varied career possibilities open to deaf adults.

Lisa continues to believe her parents have a positive view of her and sees them as nurturing. She acknowledges that some parents have a tough time in their adjustment to their deaf child, but she doesn't seem to see this in her family. She shared stories of enjoyable family activities but expressed a sense of confusion and feeling "lost" in communication with larger family groups. While Lisa continued to report that she is "fine" in the company of hearing others, she once again reported boredom in inaccessible communication situations. She acknowledges the need to be assertive in these situations but appears to see herself as shy, so assertiveness may sometimes be difficult for her. One difference between Lisa and the other participants in this study is that the other students acknowledge they are most comfortable with deaf peers who can sign, while for Lisa it is important to have a peer group with whom she identifies.

Her identification of deaf and hearing people in the pictures I showed her reveals that in addition to the deaf/hearing identity indicators she discussed seven years ago (i.e., hearing aids and talking), she now identifies more subtle indicators such as the meanings of the facial expressions (e.g., "looks like he doesn't know what is going on" and "talking").

An accomplished and competitive athlete, Lisa is disciplined and committed to the sports she participates in. She has a part-time job in an environment that involves much interaction and communication with hearing people.

# 11
# How They Have Grown!

All truths are easy to understand once they are discovered; the point is to discover them.

—Galileo Galilei

In THIS book, Angie, Alex, Danny, Joe, Lisa, Mary, and Pat have shared many aspects of their lifeworlds with us. Their individual chapters brought each of their unique adolescent experiences and diverse existences to light. To reiterate a message of *Inner Lives of Deaf Children*, no two deaf people are alike. The population of deaf and hard of hearing people is diverse. In fact, we can see from the stories, backgrounds, and experiences of the informants in this study that the collection of individual characteristics each possesses contributes to their narratives and the distinct interpretations of their experiences in various situations in life.

We have seen the joys and triumphs, the trials and tribulations, and the strengths and limitations of each of the adolescent participants in this study. Yet, while this is a diverse group of participants, they share many similarities. These similarities are presented in this chapter as the common themes that emerged from this research. The themes that emerged from the participants' interviews in phase I of this study were presented in *Inner Lives of Deaf Children* (2001). These childhood themes will be briefly revisited here, and comparisons will be made to their adolescent perspectives.[1]

In approaching my analysis of these phase II adolescent interviews, I wanted to be careful not to automatically assign my interpretations of

---

1. The reader is referred to Sheridan (2001), *Inner Lives of Deaf Children*, for an in-depth discussion of these childhood themes.

the participants' data into the categories emerging from the phase I study (i.e., *Images*: attachment and domesticated others, alienation and disparate others, infinity, covert and overt identity, images of communication; and *Pathways*). Using computer software designed for the analysis of qualitative research, I carefully examined and reexamined the data and found that the themes emerging in the adolescent study were unavoidably falling into the same categories identified in the phase I study. This meant that as a group, the adolescents continued to present and emphasize images of their lifeworlds, themselves, and others related to *attachment* (attachment and domesticated others, alienation and disparate others, infinity, overt and covert identity, images of communication, and pathways).

Although *strengths* was not originally identified as a theme in phase I, *Inner Lives of Deaf Children* did emphasize the many strengths that the children presented in that study. Since qualitative research is constantly open to interpretation, it is fair at this point to say a category of *strengths* also existed in the phase I study. To confirm that I was not biased in my assignment of the new data to the old categories, I met with my peer debriefers, who agreed that the previous categories were fitting. I was also able to identify differences between the informants' perspectives in the phase I and phase II studies.

The following themes emerged from the phase II study:

Strengths
Images
- Attachment and domesticated others (including parental regard and friendships)
- Alienation and disparate others (including boredom in inaccessible relationships, layers of alienation)
- Infinity (continuing education and vocational choices, socioeconomic potential, intimacy, deaf constancy, and independence)
- Covert and overt identity
- Images of communication
Pathways
Generic issues of adolescence

Each of these themes is described in the following sections.

## STRENGTHS

*Inner Lives of Deaf Children* discussed the social constructions of deaf people represented in clinical, cultural, and bicultural models. The traditional social perception of deaf people as deviating from a hearing norm has been a constant presence in the lives of deaf and hard of hearing people, and it has created many oppressive barriers to full participation in society. The importance of highlighting and recognizing the strengths that emerged in this research cannot be overstated. These strengths have important implications for research, policy, and program planning. In keeping with a strengths and empowerment perspective (Saleebey, 2005), I believe it is important to begin this presentation of research findings with a discussion of the countless strengths that these deaf adolescents displayed in their interviews.

These are outgoing, articulate, assertive, talented, resilient, and social teenagers who have much faith in themselves and, with few exceptions, in their futures. They believe they are loved by their parents and friends, and although they acknowledge communication barriers, they express strongly affectionate relations with their families. They have many strong positive and comfortable relationships at home, with friends, and with peers at school. They have many enjoyable experiences with family, friends, and schoolmates, as well as a sense of humor and a variety of recreational activities. They recognize and acknowledge their challenges, and they are creative and defiant in transcending social barriers. They are involved in a variety of extracurricular school activities, particularly athletics. They articulate their feelings; they know where they fit in, who to go to for support, what they like and don't like, what their options are in many situations, and how to ask for support and resources. Many of them appreciate culture and history. They are adaptive and are able to educate others about communication, Deaf culture, and ways of communicating and interacting with them. They recognize diversity among deaf and hard of hearing people, their families, and educational programs. They are autonomous in that they are able to make many decisions for themselves and can solve problems as they confront barriers. Primarily, they see themselves as being independent, educated, socially active, and working and contributing members of society in their futures. At the same time, they acknowledge realistic limitations.

While many of the strengths the children indicated in phase I have carried over into their adolescence, some differences became evident in the adolescent study, including the following:

1. The adolescents are involved in a variety of extracurricular school activities that were not a part of their lives in the earlier study. These will be addressed in the Pathways section.
2. As children, the informants taught hearing others in their lives to sign; as adolescents they are teaching others in their lives to sign, and they are teaching others about Deaf culture and the realities and meanings of being deaf.
3. In adolescence, they also take it upon themselves to teach hearing others how best to bridge their cultural and communication differences to achieve more successful interaction.
4. As children, the informants moved back and forth between their taken-for-granted deaf and hearing play relationships; as adolescents, they are more aware of a preferred social identification and social network. They focus their social energies on relationships with others who are like them in their communication and culture preferences. In these *self-same* relationships (that is, "deaf like me"), they now report feeling ease, depth, and comfort in communication and social relations. In particular, ease of communication was of great importance to them and allowed for greater depth in their relationships.

The interviews also revealed some undertones and indications of what some of the teens see as the challenges that deaf people face in their lifeworlds. Angie's interviews were ripe with an energetic and optimistic desire to learn, grow, and move toward a successful emancipation and adult life. She indicated that deaf people have to work harder and use different resources to find needed information and to access the same services and environmental events that are more readily available to hearing people (e.g., information on taxes, medical care, emergency response, communications). Danny and Mary both shared their perception that deaf people generally do not have an equitable distribution of wealth and material goods. Mary stated that deaf people struggle more with English, and Danny indicated that hearing people might generally be more intelligent, an opinion that has been socially perpetuated but is not supported by research (see Braden, 1994). Pat, as an exception, saw his vocational options as more limited than the other participants did. Regardless, all of the teens presented multiple strengths in their perceptions of themselves and other deaf people that far outweighed what they saw as their limitations. Examples of these strengths can be found throughout this chapter.

## IMAGES

### Attachment and Domesticated Others

In both phase I and phase II studies, the participants shared stories that revealed their feelings about their relationships with others, especially their parents and friends. Their comments as adolescents contain similarities to and differences from the information they shared when they were younger.

All of the participants told me stories about situations where they felt a sense of attachment or belonging. In both studies the informants indicated a greater sense of attachment in relationships that were linguistically matched or communicatively accessible. However, in the phase II study, the adolescents expressed a stronger, deeper, and more direct sense of attachment in these self-same relationships.

In phase I the children said that they had comfortable relationships with people regardless of whether the other person was deaf or hearing. These other people in their lives were identified as *domesticated others*. While it was apparent that communication access was more important to the children in phase I than whether or not the other person was deaf or hearing, the children also indicated the most comfort in relations with deaf peers. They were involved in enjoyable play activities, and play was an important aspect of their lives with both hearing and deaf children.

In the phase II study, the ease and depth of communication became more important than just accessibility to communication, and it is clear that this ease and depth facilitates bonding, comfort, and identification with others like themselves. The adolescents reported feeling more comfortable with deaf peers they identify with or see as similar in communication and language. They adapt to communication differences but make references to having more fun in relationships with deaf teenagers. In other words, as children, the theme is *it's not whether you are deaf or hearing, but how you communicate*, while in adolescence the theme became *I am more comfortable when you are deaf like me and we experience ease and depth in communication.*

These adolescents actively choose domesticated others who share their language, communication method, and culture.

The following quotations illustrate the adolescent stage of attachment in relationships with domesticated others.

> Alex [*talking about his brief experience with mainstreaming*]: They were hard of hearing, not deaf, so they were talking and using English. I was the only one who was really deaf. Then I met one other girl and one other guy who were deaf, too, but there were just three of us. They were fun. [In the residential school] it's easy to communicate and a lot more fun. I have so many friends.

> Mary: Before, when I was little, it was fun, I didn't mind because we played. It didn't matter. The older I get, the more I want to socialize with peers who are deaf like me and can talk and talk and talk with me. I like that. [*She imagines how an adolescent deaf girl would feel in her hearing school and how that would be different in a residential school.*] She probably wouldn't be very enthusiastic about participating in sports after school because it's hard to communicate with hearing peers. [If she transferred to a deaf school she'd be] more enthusiastic about talking . . . I'd talk and chat and socialize more.

*Parental Regard.* In both childhood and adolescence, the participants were overwhelmingly certain of their parents' love, positive regard, and affection for them. This is an important finding because anecdotal and published information assumes that deaf children and adolescents most often feel their hearing parents do not love or accept them. At the same time, there is some evidence at both stages that the participants see their hearing parents as needing to adjust and believe that their parents would worry about them. Stories of enjoyable family activities are expressed at both phases.

> Joe: My family? Well, they're great! My mom, she's always been with me for all my life. For many years my mom's been helping and I really love her! She was there for me. I would say generally, many parents and mine try to support the kids as much as they can and show how well they can do. It's a hard job.

> Angie: My family enjoys being together. It doesn't matter if children are deaf or hearing. It's no problem. Families still love them.

*Friendships.* In both the phase I and phase II studies, the informants delighted in their stories about their many friends and the activities they participated in together. Yet, as indicated before, it is important to note that they recognize greater comfort, depth, enjoyment, and ease in relationships with peers they identify as like themselves.

ALEX: Friends come up and talk and laugh, waiting for the same bus, saying funny things and laughing. They sit down near each other where they can all see each other and go on laughing and talking.

LISA: My friends and I have a good time together. I have thousands of friends.

MARY: We got together and had a lot of fun. We went out to dinner and went dancing until eleven o'clock or twelve o'clock. Then I went to a friend's house and stayed overnight there. We partied most of the night, partied and enjoyed. It was really fun.

DANNY: Well, we play. We get together and have fun watching TV. We play video games. We talk. We get into trouble at night after bedtime. We get up and sneak around and get into trouble. I like that. Teenagers like to sneak out and have a good time. I like that.

JOE: My good friend, we've been best friends for a long time. He's deaf himself. We both get together and do sports together.

## Alienation and Disparate Others

While the children and adolescents report many positive experiences with comfortable relationships, they also, like all individuals, have uncomfortable relationships and experiences in life. Some of these relationships and experiences were evident in these interviews and often included *disparate others*, or individuals that the participant perceives as different. In the adolescent interviews these differences sometimes included deaf or hard of hearing peers.

*Boredom in Inaccessible Relationships.* The children in phase I of the study repeatedly reported boredom in inaccessible situations. This continued in phase II; however, the adolescents reported more instances in more areas of their lives. In phase I, the informants' stories about boredom focused on play relationships with hearing peers where communication was inaccessible. In phase II, the adolescents placed greater emphasis on the boredom and disconnect they experienced in extended and blended family communication and on communication and experiences in community situations. They also discussed hearing peers.

ALEX: Sometimes my mom invites lots of family, and I'm the only deaf person. I get bored and space out.

DANNY: Most of the time, they talk, and I don't understand. It's boring.

PAT: It's a hearing church, and I just watch but don't understand. But I'm really bored. No interpreter at all!

LISA: Talking on the phone and another boy is waiting for him to finish and he's bored.

*Layers of Alienation.* In childhood, the children talked about potential discomfort, rejection, mistreatment, or inaccessibility in play relations with hearing children. Awareness of this type of alienation took new forms in adolescence. They moved from this one layer to several additional layers in adolescence, including a disconnection and alienation in interactions with hearing extended and blended family members, within the community (e.g., in stores, restaurants, and movies and at parties and at church), and in interactions with deaf peers.

As can be developmentally expected, the adolescent stories were broader and deeper and indicated greater insight. The teens did not have the same "taken for granted" attitude they had as children, when they often took deaf and hearing differences in stride.

The phase II interviews revealed that during adolescence, the participants entered situations expecting to find barriers and were prepared to deal with them. They often emphatically articulated these painful alienating experiences, whereas in childhood, they put less emphasis on it and showed less emotion. In both phases of the study, the participants were able to identify their feelings associated with these various situations and experiences. In adolescence, however, they more readily had recommendations for dealing with them.

INACCESSIBLE FAMILY RELATIONSHIPS. While the teens in this study continue to be securely attached to their parents, some of them reported that when the family groups became larger (i.e., for holiday gatherings with extended family, or with the addition of hearing blended-family members), they saw their hearing parents as having more difficulty being available as a communication support or just as a communication oasis. Mary, whose parents and siblings are deaf, stated that deaf members of her family experienced this exclusion as well during extended family gatherings. Meanwhile, the adolescents report a variety of positive self-directed pathways when they are faced with these difficulties. A few of the stories revealed that some of the teens thought hearing people had prejudicial attitudes toward deaf family members. However, these stories were in reference to families other than their own.

> MARY: I know several deaf kids from hearing families, and some of them look down on them. They're deaf, so they send them away to school. They think they know nothing, they're obtuse—you know, dumb. They send them away, and when they come home, they don't really socialize; they're not enthusiastic about signing, most of them. But some, they are hearing families, but they love them regardless. They go to the residential school for culture, to learn about the culture, to understand them as deaf. They're eager to sign themselves. There are different kinds of people, really. Most of the time, I see different kinds.

> ALEX: My opinion is most deaf kids' brothers and sisters might not like them or they might ignore them.

SITUATIONS WITH HEARING PEERS. As in the earlier study, the adolescents described negative situations with hearing peers.

> JOE [*talking about hearing students at school*]: Like in my class, most of them, they'll gang up on me; they'll play tricks on me, and I don't like it.
> MS: What do hearing people think about deaf people?
> JOE: I would say some haven't met one or experienced one. I would say they would probably think lowly of a deaf person. Like I had a teacher who really thinks I couldn't do anything, that she had to instruct again and again and again. I'm like, I'm already doing it right. Now she understands. She didn't really think I would succeed.

> ANGIE: There's one girl who looks quiet, unhappy, frowning. The other kids are happy. I feel she's sad because she's not joining in.

> MARY: She probably wouldn't be very enthusiastic about participating in sports after school because it's hard to communicate with other hearing peers.

AUDIST ATTITUDES AND BEHAVIORS OF OTHERS. The participants frequently perceived the attitudes and behaviors of hearing people as marginalizing them. They described perceptions of hearing others as "looking down" on them, considering them "inferior" (e.g., Mary, Joe, and Danny), acting rude toward them (e.g., Alex), and being passively or actively dismissive and restrictive (e.g., Alex, Danny, Joe, Mary, Pat, and Angie). Joe and Mary suggested that in situations such as this, hearing people need to get to know them to see who they really are.

COMMUNITY SITUATIONS. We know generally that adolescence is a time of testing and exploring independence and expanding horizons out into the community without the presence of parents. This is true for the deaf adolescents in this study; however, they were learning that these expeditions could involve some uncomfortable interactions. The following quotation illustrates an example of alienation in a community situation.

> ALEX: In one restaurant, the staff people come up to me, and if I try to fingerspell, I have to stand to the side. Everybody else goes in line in front of me, and they pay and get their food. And I'm having to wait. That's rude.

IN-GROUP CONFLICT WITH DEAF PEERS. In-group conflict exists in any population, especially as identificational issues and sensitivity to differences within the peer group arise. This cohort of adolescents shared stories of rejection, rudeness, and conflict with other deaf teens (in-group rejection). They also reported incidents of deaf-on-deaf bullying. The following quotations exemplify alienating experiences that the adolescents report they experience with deaf peers:

> ALEX: Others are rejected, it's rude.

> LISA: That school is only for signs, and sometimes we fight.

> MARY: Sometimes they'll insult me, "What do you go to a hearing school for?"

> PAT: I quit! The boys were awful! It was stupid. They were bullies!

The Deaf community is an identificational community that is expected to serve as a buffer against the barriers and intolerance that deaf people face in various situations throughout life. These examples of rejection within the small confines of the Deaf community, where adolescents turn for support and nurturing, are particularly disturbing. Schools, community organizations, parent groups, and peer groups need to pay special attention to this phenomenon and develop prevention and intervention programs and policies to build responsibility and respect for the various forms of diversity within the community.

## Infinity: Future Stories

Future stories are visions that people have of their futures. In both childhood and adolescence, the participants were confident about their futures, believing they would grow up to be working, autonomous individuals who contribute to society.

*Continuing Education and Vocational Choices.* All of the participants in this study are actively thinking about their lives in the future. Most of them are considering professional careers. While the participants primarily had positive perceptions of their futures, some of the male participants were aware of the social barriers a deaf person would face in some arenas, such as politics, professional basketball, police and fire departments, and the military. These are career possibilities traditionally mentioned by many young boys. In the phase I study, police, fire, and military careers were desired by some of the boys in the study. In the adolescent study, these careers remained Pat's first choices. The other boys had moved on to other options. This may be partly due to the fact that these careers do not require a college degree and Pat, unlike the other boys in the study, does not see college as a possibility in his future.

Alex considers getting his driver's license, going to college, and possibly attending graduate school after attending Rochester Institute of Technology to study electrical technology. Danny would love to be a professional basketball player but says he will go to college to study computers. Lisa plans to attend a large hearing university and become a veterinarian. Mary is considering majoring in English or Social Work at Gallaudet University and becoming a college professor. Angie was meticulously mapping out the various tasks she would need to accomplish as she prepared for her future life as an independent adult (learning how to handle her finances, becoming aware of alerting devices, studying hard, learning to drive, going to college, learning child care techniques, understanding how to obtain medical and employment resources, using interpreters, etc.). Angie wants to travel, write a book and poetry, or possibly be a reporter. Joe wants to attend a Division I college to play football, study business, and become a business executive.

Pat seemed to struggle the most with his options. He did not envision college as a part of his future, and he wanted to join the service or a police or fire department, or even be president of the United States, but he was discouraged at the lack of opportunities in those fields for deaf adults and emphasized that he felt stuck. He was also attracted to the idea of making movies, being an artist, or working in a museum. Mostly he envisioned falling back on working as a custodian or in a fast-food restaurant.

In addition to the careers they are aspiring to themselves, the participants in the adolescent study envisioned other potential jobs for deaf adults. These jobs included physician, veterinarian, computer technologist, newspaper artist, custodian, writer, historian, architect, television and media personality, airline pilot, teacher, zoologist, inventor, scientist, psychologist, and comic book artist.

Angie was able to talk about many possible scenarios for herself and other deaf people that she anticipated would require more energy, effort, preparation, and study than what would be needed by hearing people, who have greater access to incidental communication and feedback from the environment. Although she did not refer to this process as unfair, she repeatedly described a level of concerted effort that deaf people must make to obtain the same amount of information to lead productive lives.

ANGIE: How to take care of children and school, contacting the school, bringing an interpreter to talk to the teacher, getting an interpreter for a job interview or for emergencies if you get hurt or are in the hospital and need to talk to a doctor. Deaf people need time to think about things. They can't get information from hearing, so they can't know more, like complicated things like stocks.

*Socioeconomic Potential.* Generally, the adolescents expressed the desire to earn a good income and anticipated their ability to do so. However, some considered career choices that would support this, while others perceived the earning potential of deaf adults to be limited. For some, this was compatible with what they saw as imposed limitations, such as Pat's frustration with not being able to join the army or police. He was also the only student who felt he didn't have the potential to succeed in college. Six of the seven teens saw themselves attending college, but one student reported that "most deaf teenagers don't plan to go to college because they just want to collect SSI benefits." Danny, who dreamed of becoming a professional basketball player, also saw deaf people as being more restricted in their options and income; as an alternative, he planned to work with his father so he would have communication assistance. Most of the teenagers, in addition to anticipating the possibility of college attendance, saw themselves as having their own homes and cooking their own meals. Many of their stories showed that they envision socialization with their friends (primarily deaf) into adulthood.

*Intimacy.* While the participants were not directed to discuss romantic relationships, in the phase I study, many of the children talked about marriage and offspring. In phase II, they focused more on their vision of continuing to have an active social life into adulthood and made little mention of romantic relationships or parenting. Angie, however, directly mentioned marriage as a possibility. In a discussion of her experiences in a mainstream setting, Mary mentioned the uncomfortable nature of using an interpreter when she communicates with a boy she might be interested in. Danny expressed concern about marriage based on his experiences with his parents' divorce. Angie continued to consider visual alerts and other accommodations she would need for effective parenting in her future.

*Deaf Constancy.* The concept of remaining deaf throughout one's life is called *deaf constancy*. In *Inner Lives of Deaf Children* (2001), I mentioned the observation of Schlesinger (1972) that deaf children who do not have adult deaf role models often ask if they will become hearing when they grow up. In both phase I and phase II, all of the children and adolescents saw themselves as continuing to be deaf throughout their lives.

The participants' belief in deaf constancy is particularly interesting in this age of cochlear implants. A common misconception about cochlear implants is that they make one hearing. In actuality, not all deaf people qualify as potential candidates for cochlear implants. In the phase I study, Joe talked about the possibility of having one's hearing restored, but during the phase II study, his sense of deaf constancy was consistent with that of the other participants.

It should be noted that Schlesinger's research took place in an era when deaf people had little media access and were not protected by antidiscrimination laws such as the Rehabilitation Act of 1973 and the Americans with Disabilities Act. Today's deaf youth are growing up in a more accessible society with more, although still insufficient, visible deaf adult role models. This isn't because of the lack of successfully employed and content deaf adults but rather because of the lack of opportunity to meet and interact with them. The majority of schools where deaf children and adolescents are mainstreamed do not employ deaf adults. Deaf community organizations and schools need to compensate for this by providing activities and pursuing media opportunities to increase this visibility for deaf youth.

*Independence.* All of the adolescents were pondering their futures and the options available to them. As can be seen from the examples above, they were primarily confident that they will live successful independent lives, develop careers from a wide range of options, and have a social network. Angie was particularly very inquisitive and enthusiastic, and she took an active interest in information that would help her plan and succeed in the future. She has a generally optimistic and resilient demeanor as she talks about possible future situations she will face as a deaf woman in various roles. She presents developmental responsibilities that the deaf person would confront in adulthood, such as employment, taxes, bills, home improvements, childcare, and medical care, and she discusses how she would access information and communication around these responsibilities. She anticipates the need for internal and external resources.

> ANGIE: How to know if the baby is crying or if the baby is hungry. How to take care of things if the baby needs a diaper changed. How to take care of children and school, contacting the school, bringing an interpreter to talk to the teacher. Getting an interpreter for a job interview, or for emergencies if you get hurt or are in the hospital and need to talk to a doctor.

## Covert and Overt Identity

Identity is a process that develops and changes over time, involving many aspects of one's biopsychosocial and spiritual systems. It is constructed from our understandings of the biological (i.e., disability, gender, age), psychological (drives, intellect, competencies, self-understandings), social (race, ethnicity, cultural, social roles, the resolution of conflict and crisis), and spiritual (Native American, Muslim, Jewish, Christian) aspects of our beings. It is also a compilation of our interpretations of our experiences in the past, our selves and experiences in the present, and our images of what is possible for us in the future (Tatum, 1997). It is a symbolic-interactive process of mind, self, and society (Mead, 1934). It involves our self-perceptions, which lead to self-definitions (covert identity), as well as the perceptions that others have of us and the identities they assign to us (overt identity).

*Covert Identity.* To discover someone's covert identity, or the identity one adopts but that may or may not be observed or assigned by others, we can ask, When you walk into a room, how do you see yourself first (e.g., deaf, male, or black)? What is missing from that question is information on the potential multicultural existences of the other people in the room. For example, when I interviewed Joe for the phase I interview, he considered himself hard of hearing, and he admitted that his best friend—who was also mainstreamed, had a hearing family, and used spoken English—was "deaf like me." At that point in his life, Joe, who is the only deaf member of his family, expressed his surprise at the different behavioral norms and communication patterns he observed in an all-deaf family. Since that time, Joe has grown attached to a social group of deaf adolescents who sign, and he now sometimes refers to himself as deaf rather than hard of hearing. He acknowledges that he speaks with hearing people (i.e., in his family) and signs with deaf people and appreciates social opportunities with both.

Joe encounters audism, communication barriers, and racism at his predominantly white, hearing public school. He appreciates and identifies with his deaf peer group, in which the communication barriers disappear, even though, as a black teenager, he is in the minority. When he gets together with family members for holidays, he finds himself isolated from the conversations among his hearing relatives. Thus, Joe deals with different aspects of his being in different situations. His experiences reveal that "as the deaf child develops an individual identity, his or her multiple cultures will influence the shaping of this identity" (Schirmer, 2001, pp. 120–121). For Joe, these multiple cultures include the interaction of African American, European American, hearing, and deaf cultures (Anderson & Grace, 1991). At the time of this study, Joe had not yet experienced an African American Deaf culture, though he may at some point. If he does, it will become the fifth cultural influence on his identity.

Mary has a different set of cultural influences. She is a European American female born deaf to deaf parents with multiple generations of deaf relatives. She attends a public school. She speaks of her comfort in the company of deaf peers and deaf family members and her disconnect and discomfort in the company of nonsigning hearing people. Mary's perceptions of herself in relation to hearing people have changed since our last meeting. As a child she described an easygoing relationship with her hearing classmates and relatives. During this adolescent study, her self-perceptions have shifted, and she acknowledges a much stronger identification with the communication and cultural aspects of the Deaf community and in deaf social, educational, and familial contexts.

These teenagers must confront and transition from shifting cultural orientations and realities as they move back and forth between their families, their peer groups, and the communities in which they interact. The theories discussed at the beginning of this book and in my previous book suggest that the participants have a *multicultural* existence. While many authors have discussed the deaf or hearing cultural orientation of the deaf person, it is becoming clear that in an increasingly multicultural society, deaf people are not restricted to a constant either-or dichotomy in their identities. Based on this reality, many bilingual, bicultural education programs have shifted to a multicultural approach. Developing an identity is a continuous process.

*Overt Identity.* In both the phase I and phase II studies, I showed the participants pictures of individuals and groups in photographs and asked them to create stories about the characters they observed in the photographs. Frequently, they volunteered information about the hearing status of the people in the pictures, which they determined from visible objects, actions, and clues.

In the phase I study, the children assigned a deaf or hard of hearing identity to individuals in the photographs based on visual indicators such as visual alerting and electronic devices, hearing aids, and the visible activity of signing. Mouth movement and the lack of sign language or other familiar visual cues led the informants to believe the observed was not deaf. In the phase II study, the adolescents used these same indicators and new indicators as well. They mentioned gestures; material goods and fashionable clothing and accessories indicative of a comfortable socioeconomic level; stance; emotional affect; and academic subject matter as clues to a deaf or hearing identity.

HEARING AIDS. The visible presence of hearing aids was an indicator in both studies that the characters pictured were deaf. The lack of hearing aids indicated that individuals in the photos could be hearing.

DANNY: Of course they're deaf. Several have hearing aids.

Joe: I know that most of them are deaf because some of them have hearing aids and they're chatting. Hearing. I think hearing. I don't see any hearing aids.

Use of Sign Language and Gestures. The participants interpreted the apparent use of sign language and gestures in the photographs as an indicator of the identities of the characters pictured.

Alex: I noticed if they were speaking or if they were signing. I know this person is deaf because I noticed them signing.

Danny: Hearing aid, signing, and gesturing. It looks like, maybe in Gallaudet. It looks like they're college students plus deaf.

Mary: They're deaf because they're talking to each other through sign language. You don't see deaf families act like that. You don't see deaf families do that. When deaf families get together, they tend to talk a lot and use large gestures to get people to pay attention and look at them. This looks laid back.

Joe: And some look like they're signing.

Material Goods, Fashionable Clothing, and Accessories. Danny and Mary both mentioned that characters in photographs with what they perceived as expensive fashions, accessories, and material goods were likely hearing. They indicated that it was unusual for deaf people to possess such items.

Danny: They're hearing. You don't see many deaf people with fancy watches. Not many deaf women wear these heels. Not many that I've noticed.

Danny [*describing what appears to be a group of hearing people*]: Fancy. It's nice. Looks like that's [*points to picture*] a new car. Looks like they're hearing.

Mary: I think she's probably hearing. Because most deaf people, girls I know don't dress like that. We dress kind of down to earth, not wear fancy nice clothes.

Stance. Some of the teens mentioned posture as an overt indicator of whether or not the observed person was deaf.

Mary: Looks like he's wondering about something . . . I think he's deaf . . . Maybe by the way he's sitting, sprawled back, looking to the side. Looks like the way his arms are spread out, he could sign.

DANNY [*imitating the stance of the man in the picture with his hands resting on the arms of a chair and his mouth moving*]: You wouldn't lift your hands to sign then put them back like that over and over.

PAT: He's deaf. I don't know for sure. The way he is sitting.

EXPRESSION AND EMOTIONAL AFFECT. While examining and interpreting imagined situational contexts in the photographs, the teens also implied that facial expression and apparent emotional affect were indicators of whether or not characters were deaf.

MARY: He's deaf because it looks like he's wondering about something.

LISA: I'd probably say he's deaf. His face look like, he has no idea what they're talking about.

ANGIE: I feel he's deaf, because he's mulling things over, about the future.

PAT: The one who is deaf is just sitting there bored, and the one who is hearing, maybe he was talking on the phone to his girlfriend, but the deaf one is just sitting there bored and waiting because one is hearing. So, you can see they're playing a game.

DANNY: It looks like he's talking to his grandparents far away. Maybe in another state. Something happy about his parents or his uncle or family or friends. He's happy. But the deaf kid is not happy because he has to use . . . He wishes he could hear his grandma and grandpa's voice [*shrugs*]. He looks like he's not happy . . . He's jealous. He's lucky. I have to get up and walk over and type, but hearing can talk on the phone anywhere . . . I feel that's his opinion. That he's lucky to be able to use the phone. He's frowning, maybe.

In determining whether the characters in the photographs were deaf or hearing, the participants revealed much about their perspectives of deaf people as well as their perspectives of hearing people. However, none of the adolescents differentiated among deaf, Deaf, and hard of hearing identities, nor did they indicate whether a photographed character might be an oral deaf person.

ACADEMIC SUBJECT MATTER. In discussing the photographs, the adolescents had differing opinions on how academic interests or strengths could be an indication of deaf or hearing identities. Danny, for example, said that he didn't believe science was a popular subject among deaf people, while

Alex (who likes science) and Mary commented that English was a difficult subject for deaf people.

## Images of Communication

Several findings emerged from both studies related to communication in the lives of these participants. This was a very articulate group of interviewees, and, overall, the amount and quality of information shared during both the childhood and adolescent interviews was strong. However, as can be expected developmentally, the adolescents demonstrated greatly increased depth and more direct expression of insight and feeling in their stories compared to their childhood interviews. They also provided a greater quantity of information, which was encouraged through a combination of direct and projective questioning. Creative use of photo albums and yearbooks by one participant, who attended an oral school, allowed for enhanced depth and quantity of information.

New technologies are continually emerging that are making communication more available than ever. Mary spoke of the anonymity and accessibility that instant messaging affords. The following categories of *images of communication* are discussed below: accessible versus like communication, family communication, gender issues, and community communication.

*Accessible versus Like Communication.* As discussed in the earlier section on attachment, the childhood study revealed that how a person communicates is more important than status as deaf or hearing. The adolescent study, however, revealed that there were transitions in issues of importance related to communication, comfort, attachment, and satisfaction. The adolescent study showed that *like* communication with "deaf like me" peers had become more important than the *accessible* communication the children spoke of in the phase I study. In other words, it became more important during adolescence that other teens communicate "like me," with a matching linguistic mode. This sameness in communication contributed to another important theme in adolescent communication, ease and depth. This ease and depth in communication with *self-same* individuals (domesticated others) facilitated attachment in these relationships.

ALEX: It's a lot of fun, because they can sign like me. I fit in better. It's a better match for me because I have friends. I have so many friends.

MARY: But I guess the older I get the more I want to socialize with peers who are deaf like me and can talk, and talk, and talk with me. I like that.

*Family Communication.* In both studies, the participants discussed family communication. The participants recognized the communication strengths of their parents and family members. They valued the communication they had with their parents and their generally supportive relationships. The parents of all but one of the participants in the study communicate in sign language with their teenage children. While the participants appear comfortable in this communicatively accessible relationship with their parents, some expressed a desire for their other family members to be more fluent and deaflike. All the participants expressed a general discomfort and disconnect with the lack of communication access with hearing extended family members, siblings, and blended family situations where communication was not accessible.

It was apparent that isolation and discomfort increased with larger family groups. For example, the greater the number of hearing relatives and the greater the degree of separation (i.e., separate living arrangements due to divorce and custody issues, or the addition of stepfamily members in later childhood or adolescence), the more disconnected the adolescents felt. Mary tells stories of enjoyable family activities and outings with her deaf parents and siblings but has this to say about extended family gatherings:

> Most of the time it is comfortable, but some . . . I have some cousins who are hearing. They're not enthusiastic about sign language. They get together in a group, a hearing group, and ignore the deaf people. It makes me mad because it's hard for me. We get left out.

Angie, Danny, and Pat also discussed their feelings of isolation in large family gatherings.

> ANGIE: It hurts my self-esteem a little bit if the family is talking and I don't understand what they say at all. My mom will interpret some, but I keep having to ask, "What are they saying, what are they saying?" Sometimes, like at Thanksgiving, I think my mom feels bad if she has to leave the table or if I'm in another room. It's not a lot of fun if the family is talking. I just twiddle my thumbs, I just sit and focus on my food, and I don't pay a lot of attention to the conversation . . . sometimes I feel really disheartened. My parents will interpret, or we'll write, or I'll try to watch facial expressions. Sometimes I'll ask, "What's wrong?" or "What's funny?" I scream, "What's wrong?" and my mother will explain to me and I understand, but it doesn't feel good inside. I wish they could sign.

DANNY: Most of the time the hearing people would talk and I would play my Game Boy. I would be by myself. I'm always asking them to tell me, and they get mad because they have to repeat it; they say it twice. They speak and I ask them what they said, and then they have to sign the same thing. They get sick of it. They say, "Hold." Or they look away and they just ignore me.

PAT: I wish they could sign like a deaf person or wish they were deaf. I want them to all sign . . . I want friends. I mean, I sit there and they watch a movie and I can't understand. I'm stuck . . . If I don't understand, I'm just kind of lonely and uncomfortable. I just sit there. I don't understand what they're saying. I feel kinda stuck.

Joe recognizes and speaks appreciatively of his mother's support and ability to communicate with him: "I would say that for many years my mom's been helping, and I really love her. She was there for me." He acknowledges that he is closest to his sibling who has some sign language skills, and he reports another is "stubborn" and has low expectations of him.

*Gender Issues.* In the phase I study it seemed that female family members offered the most support in communicatively inaccessible situations, but this was not the case in the phase II study. During adolescence, the participants were more independent in dealing with communication barriers. Overall, the adolescents presented their fathers as more competent, active communicators with a greater degree of linguistic matching than they did in the phase I study. They appeared to have more interaction with their fathers during their adolescent years than they had as children. This may be due partially to the fact that four of these children's parents were divorcing and the children were living with their mothers during the phase I study. The research literature suggests that hearing parents of deaf children typically grieve upon discovering that their child is deaf (Harvey, 1989, 2003; Schlesinger & Meadow, 1972) and go through a period of adjustment (Raimondo, 2001). In addition, the general literature suggests that there are gender differences in grief responses. However, there is a dearth of research examining what, if any, gender differences exist in the grief responses of parents of deaf and hard of hearing children; nor is there research on the developmental process of this grief and its effects on family interaction. Such research might offer additional insights into the adolescents' reports of more active participation and increased communication competence of their fathers at this point in their lives.

*Community Communication.* As can be expected at this point in their development, the adolescents are becoming increasingly autonomous in their interactions with their communities. As the teens venture out more on their own, or in groups of peers, they confront communication barriers. They anticipate having to deal with a lack of communication access in employment, medical care, and so forth. Alex gave examples of what he perceived as unfair treatment in restaurants when he placed an order. Pat, who desires a career in law enforcement, fire and rescue, or the armed services, projected prohibitions in these fields for deaf people. He also discussed his boredom during church services when interpreters are not available. Danny mentioned he expected to have communication difficulties in future employment. Angie experiences barriers in movie theaters and anticipates the need for interpreters in medical care, appointments pertaining to parental responsibilities, finances, and so forth. Mary shared a story about the lack of interpreting services for a theatrical event. Examples of their comments follow:

> ALEX: There was one woman who knew I was deaf. She'd seen me . . . [She] just walked away and left me. I had gone there by myself four or five times. She just ignored me, and her job is to listen to what people want, and I have my rights, but she just walked away.

> PAT: I want to be a policeman, but I can't. I'm deaf. Some jobs you can use sign, but I don't know. I can't be a fireman or work for an ambulance because I'm deaf.

> ANGIE: Some of my friends talk. I don't talk well. I have friends who can interpret for me when somebody talks. For example, if we go to a movie theater without captioning, they explain to me what's going on. Sometimes I feel bad depending on hearing or hard of hearing friends.

## PATHWAYS

In *Inner Lives of Deaf Children*, I defined pathways as the avenues that the participants took to "negotiate their relationships with disparate others, for interacting with friends and family, and for meeting their daily informational needs" (p. 219). In the phase II study, the teens still have multiple pathways for coping with situations that are inaccessible, difficult, or boring due to communication barriers. Many of the same pathways reported in the phase I study are still used by the teens. These adolescents are still quite autonomous and take the initiative in finding ways to cope with adversity. However, now they make more thoughtful decisions, rely more on technology, and report more active or anticipated assistance from their fathers, including interpreting, than they did in childhood. The increased presence of fathers is one of the most significant differences from the phase I study.

The phase II study found that the adolescents participate in more clubs and extracurricular school activities such as school sports, a deaf teen club, and the Pep Club. They are determined to force themselves to deal with difficult situations. Joe has several strategies for dealing with bullying by hearing peers—becoming a peer counselor and being a role model—and Angie makes concerted efforts to access information and learn all she can to prepare for her future. The participants also show more goal-directed coping strategies; for example, Alex plans to expand his social network when confronted with bullying at his school.

The adolescents make more intentional use of sign language interpreting than they did as children. They also have expanded their efforts to communicate with classmates and hearing friends. While in phase I they told stories about teaching others to sign, now they report teaching others about Deaf culture, the realities of being deaf, and how to succeed in their interpersonal relationships. They are more able to recognize and assert their needs and make recommendations for problem solving.

Mary, Danny, Pat, and Joe all gave examples of what they do when communication among hearing people at home, at school, or in social situations is not accessible to them.

MARY: I really don't go out often with hearing friends. Only with deaf family and friends. I socialize like that.

DANNY: Most of the time the hearing people would talk and I would play my Game Boy. I would be by myself.

MARY: If they weren't enthusiastic, I'd get a book and read.

PAT: I ask them to sign and tell them I don't understand.

JOE: I would try to work my way into the conversation . . . continue to get good grades, become active in sports . . . peer mediation . . .

Boredom was a theme for the participants in both childhood and adolescence when they were cut off from communication. Pat was particularly affected by this because of the isolation of his rural residence during the summer months and the lack of technology available to him for social contacts. His reading level and socioeconomic limitations rendered computer-based communication (e-mail, pagers, instant messaging) unavailable to him. His family does not own a TTY, so Pat is cut off from most forms of communication. Videophones were not yet widely distributed or used for home-based communication at the time of these interviews, and the cost of high-speed Internet or cable service to make this workable for Pat may have presented an additional barrier. In discussing his isolation he reports, "I go watch TV or just sign to myself in the mirror, making up stories, especially if I was bored."

Alex and Joe are assertive and defiant in their responses to situations where they feel left out. Joe actively confronts the skepticism of his teammates with his self-confidence in his athletic skills: "I'm on the team, . . . and they think, . . . 'He can't do the work.' . . . And I have to show them." Alex presented a scenario where a deaf boy was rejected by a group of deaf peers at his residential school. He demonstrated creative, autonomous problem-solving skills in his solution to this conflict. He talks about how the boy would go home and consider a strategy to begin befriending several other individuals, thus creating a new social network that eventually blends with the group that originally rejected him.

> He looks at his notes and thinks about how to make friends. He walks up to a boy sitting alone. He sits down; they talk, start to be friends. Later they meet a girl; now there are three. Every day they add more until there are eight.

Angie and Mary provided many examples of how the teens take responsibility for educating hearing others about the realities of being deaf. As noted, the adolescents revealed that they not only take it upon themselves to sometimes teach others to sign during their adolescence but also are able to share their knowledge and insights about Deaf culture, resources, and other realities.

> ANGIE: I would want to show hearing people about Deaf culture, how we are the same and different, using the TTY, visual alerts, interpreters, being successful, things like that.

> MARY: I would tell them what it's like to be me, deaf and a teenager, going to a mainstream school. I feel insulted if hearing people say, "Oh, I wish

I was deaf like you." But really, it wouldn't be that way. [*She gives many examples.*] So, they'd get an idea of what it's like to be a deaf teenager.

Angie is also assertive and resourceful in her quest for eventual independence:

> Well, if she wants to live in an apartment or a condo or a house, she would have to get an interpreter when she looked at the house, to talk to the people, to ask questions. If she decides to live in a house and be independent, she'll have to set up a TTY and a flashing light alert system, and warnings for theft and fire, or if someone comes in during the night. Or in the day, if there's a storm or tornado, you need a weather alert to go to the basement. You watch captioning on TV to know.

## GENERIC ISSUES OF ADOLESCENCE

The adolescents in this study share with hearing adolescents many concerns that include being accepted and socially regarded, wearing the clothes they want (Lisa), communicating with potential love interests (Mary), making connections with peers through the Internet (Angie, Mary, Pat), performing well in school and participating in extracurricular activities (Joe, Angie), valuing the privacy of peer group issues (Alex), and coping with changes such as divorces in their families. All of the adolescents are pondering their futures. They feel pressured to achieve and to attend college. They cherish time in social relationships with peers they feel comfortable with.

### Parent-Teen Relations and Emancipation

Interestingly, while many adolescents experience conflicts with their parents over issues related to independence, individuation, and separation, this group of deaf participants did not demonstrate such conflict. They value what they see as a supportive and loving relationship with their parents. Unique to this group of deaf adolescents, however, is the fact that they all expressed boredom and disconnect in extended family situations that are not accessible to them.

### Mood Changes and Transitional Accommodations

Another issue common to all adolescents is frequent mood changes. In addition to the hormonal changes that can contribute to fluctuating moods, environmental changes also trigger changes in emotions. Joe used the term *moody* to describe the hurt and anger he felt over mistreatment by hearing peers and in response to his own perfectionism.

As a whole, these deaf adolescents have experienced many transitions. Their families have undergone divorce, remarriage, and the addition of new family members through childbirth and blended family arrangements. Since the phase I study, several of them have transferred to different schools, which has necessitated developing new communication relationships and strategies to access information. Leaving environments (e.g., communities, schools, neighborhoods) that the adolescents and their parents have carefully constructed to accommodate the deaf teen is more stressful because it means having to start the advocacy process all over again.

### Cliques, Crowds, and Multiple Inaccessible Environments

Cliques, or peer groups, and crowds take on new meanings in adolescence. These deaf adolescents are beginning to find peer groups, particularly those who are in residential schools, where they have a larger group of students to choose from; here they also have crowds. One difference between the residential school students and the mainstreamed students that became obvious in this study is that the mainstreamed students have limited options for both cliques and crowds. They do not have a critical mass of peers from which to choose friends and acquaintances. The wider variety of education programs available to all adolescents means that deaf adolescents are spread out over a larger geographic area with little opportunity for a reference group, cliques, and crowds. These students experience aloneness in multiple environments. Danny told us this when he spoke of being with his stepsiblings when they would just talk. Mary said she was often alone at her hearing school. Pat was alone and without a peer group at home and in his community.

The adolescents experience a closer relationship with family members who sign and a disconnect with those who do not. What unhappiness or discontent they expressed about their lifeworlds centered primarily around situations where they are disconnected from communication, acceptance, and meaningful socialization with others like themselves. Danny's dismal mood seemed to be tied to this and to his notion that hearing people are "lucky." At times the teenagers were reduced to the role of passive observer rather than active participants. Like hearing adolescents, all of the participants were content in situations where they experienced a sense of belonging, attachment with their parents, and ease and depth in communication.

American teenagers are exposed to traumatic news events through television media, are aware of the dangers in a post-9/11 world, and are knowledgeable about global issues, world events, and security threats. Some of the participants talked about this, and others raised general self-protection issues in relation to bullying, dealing with strangers, and avoiding trouble when seen as "different." It is unclear if the adults in their lives are helping them process this information for accuracy or if they are receiving information for emergency preparation and coping with the threats of crises in the world around them through print media.

## Critical Thinking and Autonomy

Adolescence is a time of developing self-sufficiency, independence, and critical thinking skills, and these deaf adolescents showed signs of going through these changes. Angie is able to identify when she disagrees with the ideas of others and communicate her own opinions, but she is also able to differentiate between situations where it is or is not advantageous to express her views. She can recall previous perspectives on issues she considers and can explain how her perspectives have changed. Meanwhile, she continues to be conscious of safety issues. She loves and respects her family and knows that her parents love and respect her in turn.

All of the participants in this study indicated a very conscious and affecting awareness of the struggles they experience in communication in multiple environments that are not accessible to them. This arose in their discussions of their relationships with family and friends, at school, and in the community. This is generally not an issue for hearing adolescents, except in situations where English is a second language.

The participants in this study transferred back and forth between schools at a rate that is possibly greater than that of the general adolescent population. The reasons for these transfers often involve communication philosophies and opportunities for social development as well as perceived quality of education.

## SUMMARY

The phase II study highlights the ability of deaf and hard of hearing youth to be our teachers, our guides, and our narrators of the deaf experience. They have shown us that they can and ought to be counted upon to contribute to the knowledge base about deaf adolescents. This valuable information should guide the development of theory, policy, and practice.

The adolescent participants exhibit many strengths. While many of the perceptions and experiences emerging from the childhood study continue, we can also see the adolescents' changing images and insights in regard to their self-concepts, their relationships with and perceptions of others, their likes and dislikes, their futures, and the pathways they choose as they face their challenges. They are becoming increasingly capable of educating others about the multifaceted meanings of being deaf and demonstrating techniques for improving cross-cultural relations and communication among deaf and hearing people. They are realizing their preferred social group identities and are focusing their social energies in those directions where they experience greater depth and ease in their communication and relationships. They can identify situations that are particularly challenging, such as feeling isolated from communication in large family gatherings, and have developed strategies for dealing with uncomfortable situations. They more readily adapt, using a broader array of solutions that include turning to their deaf peer group, an otherwise accessible group, or solitary activities. The participants appear to be more prepared to deal with these challenges as their experience grows. They are also able to identify and deal with the communication and cultural issues inherent in relationships with deaf peers who possess diverse identities (e.g., hard of hearing, English signers, ASL, and culturally deaf). The participants are better able to articulate alienating experiences. The adolescent interviews were much more in depth than the childhood interviews, and the teenagers were more direct in expressing insights than they were as children. In the adolescent interviews, it was apparent that the decisions they are making in life now are more thought out. In addition, they can, and do, take advantage of rapidly changing technology in their lives.

With little exception, these adolescents continue to have confident, promising images of their futures (both for themselves and other deaf people), and they enjoy an array of vocational and professional opportunities. Most of them envision college as a possibility, yet they are more aware of the reality of barriers to certain professions. In this study, they anticipated continued socialization and intimacy with a primarily deaf social network into adulthood, and the concept of deaf constancy is inherent in their images of their futures.

# 12

# *Deaf Children and Adolescents*

## An Emerging Theory of Lifeworld Development

Learn from yesterday, live for today, hope for tomorrow.
*The important thing is not to stop questioning.*

—Albert Einstein

THROUGH THEIR narratives, Alex, Angie, Danny, Joe, Lisa, Mary, and Pat are teaching us what it means to be deaf in their social world. Their participation in this research is leading us in the direction of discovering developmental theory as it relates to their lifeworlds. From childhood to adolescence some of their ideas, beliefs, and experiences remain the same; others have changed as they mature and interact with a broadened social lifeworld. This research is ongoing, and the theory will continue to emerge from the data presented in this volume, as well as from planned interviews with the participants at future points in their lives.

In chapter 2, adolescence was discussed from various theoretical perspectives. The abundance of existing theories that attempt to explain human behavior across life do not specifically consider the unique experience of being deaf in the social world. This chapter will discuss unique developmental experiences, strengths, challenges, and considerations for deaf adolescents arising from this study and their implications for developmental theory. This discussion will not compare the development of these deaf adolescents with others but rather will help to organize their developmental lifeworlds.

The theoretical implications arising from this research involve internal and external resources, multiple systems levels (individual, group, family, organizational, community, cultural, political), and influences such as personal motivations, interpersonal and intrapsychic forces, intergroup tensions, imbalances in power, resources, and opportunities.

## LIFEWORLD DEVELOPMENT

One of the goals of this research on deaf children and adolescents was to uncover the experiences, thoughts, beliefs, and existential realities of their lifeworlds. This section describes what is emerging as a theory of the lifeworlds of these deaf and hard of hearing participants based on the themes arising from the research with this cohort to date.

Theory related to adolescence focuses primarily on the process of identity formation. In this research with deaf adolescents, it was not clear that the participants in this cohort were actively and consciously searching for an identity, but they were clearly engaged in a *psychosocial transition course*, a process of internal changes stemming from their interactions with their social worlds. This is a nonlinear process of *learning, interpreting, attaching meaning, comparing*, and *identifying preferred social contexts*.

Upon observing and interacting in various social contexts that their environments present to them, and absorbing diverse perspectives, the adolescents are learning about themselves. They are interpreting these interactions, attaching meaning to them, comparing, and identifying preferences for social conditions and groupings. They are learning where they feel comfortable and competent and have a sense of belonging and where they feel uncomfortable, stagnated, and disconnected. They are learning where and with whom they are at their best, what situations foster optimal functioning, where they are happy and at ease, and where they see themselves as different and detained. They are discovering barriers that prevent them from fully functioning and participating in a variety of situations as they encounter them. They are learning to identify situations that keep them from expressing themselves or reaching their potential and what circumstances allow them full expression. They are discovering situations that represent depth and those that represent only superficial participation or that obstruct them.

It is important to note that the teenagers in this study all have reference groups of other deaf teens, deaf adults, or deaf family members in at least some situations in their lives that enhance their opportunities for this psychosocial transition process of learning, interpreting, attaching meaning, comparing, and identifying preferred social contexts. The composition of these reference groups and the situations where they have access to them are inconsistent, changing quickly and frequently. This inconsistency allows the participants to consider and compare their various social contexts.

Mary, Pat, Alex, and Lisa exemplify a few of these inconsistencies. Mary finds herself comfortable at home with her nuclear family, where everyone is deaf and uses ASL, and in her homeroom at school with a small but diverse group of deaf and hard of hearing peers. When she moves to a classroom where she is alone with an interpreter, she becomes uncomfortable. Pat transitions from his beloved residential school for deaf students, where he enjoys full and active participation, to summers alone at home with social resources basically unavailable to him. Alex tells a story about the excitement, learning, and sudden enrichment that accompanies enrollment in a school for deaf students after being alone and without communication. He also illustrates perceived differences between his deaf peers at his residential school and his "not really deaf" peers at the hearing school where he was mainstreamed. Lisa moved from a mainstreamed elementary school that utilized total communication to an oral residential school. She works part time in a department store with hearing people and lives with a hearing family and among hearing neighbors.

These adolescents are reporting on and valuing situations characterized by depth and ease of communication, where they feel a sense of belonging and attachment, where they are stimulated by a fluid exchange of ideas, self-expression, and the sharing of information and of experiences. For the participants in this study, these affirmative exchanges happened in *like* or *self-same* relationships.

Marcia (1976) perceives adolescence as a process of exploration and commitment. For this cohort of deaf adolescents, however, the exploration is not necessarily a conscious seeking out of diverse groups with which to explore their identity. Rather, the social contexts in which these deaf adolescents find themselves are incidental. These are contexts that were given to them. Given these situations, the participants are discovering their meanings. Marcia (1976) acknowledges that adolescents have diverse means and paces of arriving at identity. Given that these deaf adolescents all have at least some other deaf people in their lives to serve as reference groups, it would be interesting to explore the difference between the deaf adolescents in this study and those who become deaf or meet other deaf people later in their lives in terms of the pace and the process and their experiences of self-discovery and self-understanding.

The participants in this study report close, supportive relationships with their parents. Schlesinger (1972) suggests that as deaf adolescents adopt a deaf identity, they may experience a greater source of conflict with their parents over such things as individuation, values, and behaviors than hearing adolescents do. This conflict is not apparent in this cohort. The parents appear to be aware and supportive of the adolescents' need for a social reference group and avenues for communication. In this study, the concept of *parents as allies* has emerged as an important, positive factor in the adolescents' lives.

Based on the informants' narratives, it seems that their parents have been experiencing a *corresponding adaptation* process that resulted from their acknowledgment of their adolescents' developmental needs and enabled them to help their adolescents realize individuation. It is unclear to what this dual developmental process can be attributed. Do the adolescents in this study just happen to have an exceptionally committed group of parents? Are the schools doing a good job of educating their parents? Could it be a combination of both? One element that could be explored in further research is whether the parents' longstanding role as advocates for their deaf children in an adverse world has made them heroes in the eyes of their children and given their children the expectation that they will "always be there for me" because they always have been, as Joe implied.

The greater source of tension and conflict for these informants is not separation and individuation in their relationships with their parents, as Schlesinger (1972) suggests, but rather increased interactions, or the prospect of such, in their communities and schools. These tensions arise in numerous situations, and are often the result of

- dismissive attitudes of employees during attempts to place orders at restaurants,
- the prospect of communicating with health care professionals,
- communicating with a hearing person with whom they hold a romantic interest,
- general attempts to participate and to be understood at school,
- imagining future employment situations, and
- lack of access to movies in theaters.

These tensions fall in the category of *layers of alienation* in the theme of alienation and disparate others arising out of this study. These participants are attached to and confident in their relationships with their parents; they value their support and affection. In this study, the hearing parents often serve as allies, and this seems to be a source of security for the participants. In a follow-up study, it will be interesting to explore the role of their parents, if any, in the participants' lives as they continue to progress toward their independence. Will this sense of security and alliance remain or change? Will conflicts arise in young adulthood as the teens ease into their forthcoming years?

The participants are anticipating new roles and relationships (employee, college student, spouse, parent, homeowner, etc.) and considering their choices in increasingly responsible positions in life, as Havinghurst (1972) suggests. The participants express a sense of *deaf constancy* in their visions of their futures and their future roles and responsibilities. They speak of future employment possibilities, college or vocational preparation, and adult responsibilities such as personal finances, as well as concerns such as personal safety, homeland security, and equal access to information and communication. With a sense of dignity they display a work ethic and aim to be responsible, contributing citizens, valuing their continued growth and relationships. They are also considering socialization, problem-solving strategies in various potential scenarios (i.e., child rearing, communication access, health education information, denial of civil rights), and personal interests and characteristics.

Vygotsky (1978) theorizes that development flows from the transmission of knowledge from the more experienced to the less experienced. Relationships that avail the communication and language matching necessary for this transmission are in short supply for many of these teenagers. Nonetheless, the participants in this study each have and value at least one relationship where such exchanges occur. Although it is often unclear how communication in these relationships is transmitted (e.g., by signing or lipreading) or how good or deep the communication is, these transmissions are meaningful for the participants in this study.

While examples of positive transmissions are evident, there are also examples of distress and anxiety related to the absence of such opportunities. Joe recognizes that he has had to work extra hard for his achievements. He told us of a teacher who suggested that he could become a peer mediator and prevent problems by becoming "part of the solution" at his hearing school. He mentions role models and speaks of how he has also positioned himself as a role model for younger students. He has a close relationship with an older sister who signs and whose advice he respects. He can talk to his sister about his challenges. He also describes his admiration for his mother, who signs, and her ongoing support.

Realizing the restrictions that her environment presents for her, and clearly frustrated by them, Angie conveys a profound passion and curiosity for information, instruction, modeling, media, experiences, and relationships that would contribute to her personal growth and success. She acknowledges that her parents and teachers have taught and guided her, and she continually seeks out and values their help. Lisa reports close respectful relationships with her teachers. She also reports that her sisters assist and guide her in her summer conditioning program for swimming. Mary, whose family is deaf and uses ASL, shares amusing stories about family vacations and relates dialogues that reveal how she affectionately learns from her older siblings' blunders.

Alex has created a story about a class of deaf students where the teacher, who signs, instructs them on pregnancy, prenatal care, and childbirth. Some of the participants have had the opportunity to join a weekend deaf teen club that sponsors deaf adult presenters on a variety of topics including careers, leadership, and life skills. In the absence of deaf adult role models, Pat and Danny each express great disappointment in the perceived impossibility of attaining their dream jobs and desired socioeconomic status. In light of this, Danny seems resolved to settle for less while Pat is particularly stuck for vocational ideas. Pat also reports that his favorite "class" at school is his visits with his counselor, where he receives help with his "mistakes" and learns to relax.

The absence of easy communication with more experienced people from which Angie can learn is a source of anxiety for her in her quest for self-improvement and her preparations for her future. For the participants who have good English language and reading skills, the Internet is surfacing as a compensatory resource for information (e.g., for Mary and Angie). While it is evident that these opportunities are valued and are making contributions to the development of these teens, their reports of and emotional reactions to ongoing barriers to information and participation in multiple areas of life and society demonstrate the need for increased opportunities for these positive transmissions.

The participants' narratives support the notion that deaf and hard of hearing children and adolescents do not experience average supportive developmental milieus. Broad institutional change in society is needed to maximize developmental opportunities for deaf and hard of hearing adolescents—change that facilitates a more nurturing and less traumatic transition from childhood to adulthood—so that they can achieve their potential and aspirations and be who they want to be, as opposed to who they believe society intentionally or unintentionally restricts them to being. These participants see who they think they are, what they dream of doing with their lives, who they want to be, and what their passions are, yet they are experiencing social environments that are not supporting them in their efforts to meet their goals and the social demands of adolescence. Schools, families, advocates, legislators, and community organizations are vital to this process.

Technology is beginning to help us create an increasing number of visually stimulating environments that facilitate incidental and formal lifelong learning opportunities. While technology has advanced our information access and communication channels, the English language barriers that Pat, Mary, and Angie note are real, as are socioeconomic factors. These deaf and hard of hearing participants gravitate toward opportunities for intellectual and social stimulation and personal development in visually rich environments. It will be interesting to see the long-term developmental outcomes of the positive advancements of technology.

*Resilience* is an important factor in the lives of these participants. One of their greatest strengths is that they have achieved tremendous developmental accomplishments and demonstrate a passionate drive for continued growth. But their often harsh, restrictive, and biased environments are not stimulating their *full potential*, and the emotional burden of this truth is evident in their interviews.

With reference to moral development, this study suggests that the participants have experienced many uncomfortable situations that range from exclusion from communication in extended family situations to bullying at school and in-group rejection. Even with the evident disconnect in their extended families and diverse social situations and their general lack of access to information, as a whole, the participants' behaviors and their narratives demonstrate their positive moral character and conscience.

The research reveals both internal and external components that contribute to the participants' moral lifeworlds. The internal strengths or components include *purpose, constructive coping skills, problem-solving skills, resilience, self-direction, motivation, self-interest,* and *personal responsibility.* The external factors contributing to their moral lifeworlds include *supportive relationships* with their parents, teachers, and peers and *access to information and resources* when it is available.

The participants demonstrate purpose and direction in their lives and constructive ways of dealing with alienating situations. They show respect for their parents, teachers, and others in authority; they demonstrate a work ethic and personal responsibility for their personal success. Angie considers moral dilemmas such as balancing her personal safety while understanding the perspective of someone who could be potentially dangerous to her and desiring to help the person change their destructive behaviors. She also is aware of the personal and social responsibility she has to make informed and ethical decisions concerning personal finances. Pat and Joe both have experienced bullying at the hands of their peers but maintain a standard of high moral character for themselves and seek constructive avenues for dealing with such injustice. Alex speaks of how he has been dismissed by peers and restaurant workers, yet he also demonstrates constructive moral responses to this mistreatment. Angie and Joe report receiving support from their parents and teachers in resolving moral dilemmas. All of the participants also demonstrate independent, self-directed, problem-solving skills in the face of difficulty. Some of them discuss participation in a deaf teen club that also supports their problem solving in situations involving peer interactions and provides education about adult life. Pat has been especially mistreated by peers and has been particularly isolated from potential interactions and resources that could enhance his moral development and moral intelligence. Yet he continues to uphold genuine moral character. Increased access to stimulating information, resources, and supports in their environments will allow these participants to enhance their moral development further as they face new and challenging situations coinciding with their continued development toward adult independence and success in their lives.

Research has indicated that deaf and hard of hearing students who use interpreters in mainstreamed settings are not learning the same amount of information as their hearing classmates, due, in part, to the fact that an interpreted education does not provide equal opportunities for intellectual stimulation (Schick, Williams, & Kupermintz, 2006). The adolescents' narratives illustrate how even with an interpreter in the classroom, misunderstandings, aloneness, discomfort, and harassment occur in interactions and the learning process.

The narratives demonstrate the importance of stimulating social environments where deaf and hard of hearing children and adolescents can uncover and absorb the depths of knowledge to be availed. These participants are finding this satisfaction in relationships and visually rich environments that allow for ease of communication with peers and adults who share their language. As a whole, these participants generally do not demonstrate low self-esteem, as some studies suggest we might expect, although some express ambivalence related to career outlook (Danny, Pat), and some have negative internalizations about general competence (Danny). For the most part, the informants feel good about themselves, their capabilities, and their internal resources; they believe they are worthy of the love they receive from their parents, family members, and others, and with little exception they know they will succeed in their futures and have much to offer the world. However, they are dissatisfied with and frustrated by their frequent encounters with hurtful environmental challenges and restrictions. Regardless, they have an abundance of individual and collective strengths that contribute to an overall sense of well-being.

## Multisystemic Literacy in the Developmental Environment

Through these narratives, we have witnessed the developmental transactions of deaf children and adolescents with a variety of environmental systems. We have seen them describe their personal satisfaction in their relationships to this point in their lives with systems that are accessible and match their language needs; that permit them to experience a gratifying depth of connection, exchange of information, personal stimulation, and growth; and that allow them to feel wholly human. We have also witnessed their disheartening stories of discomfort, disappointment, and disconnection in mismatched disparate relationships and communication with others. In these disparate relationships and inaccessable situations, they report feeling alone, bored, thwarted, and devalued.

The importance of the social environment to the well-being of the participants is evident. Yet research investigating the impact of factors external to the personal characteristics of deaf and hard of hearing people, their home life, and school environment is almost nonexistent. The critical components of a deaf child's successful social-emotional development include early identification through infant hearing screening (e.g.,

Yoshinaga-Itano, 2003), parental involvement in deaf children's educational programs (e.g., Calderon and Greenberg, 2000), parental communication patterns and language use (e.g., Desselle, 1994; Vernon & Andrews, 1990), type of educational placement (e.g., Kluwin, 1993; Polat, 2003; Ramsey, 1997; Oliva, 2004), and whether or not parents are deaf or hearing (e.g., Polat, 2003). Most research investigations, however, have focused on the developmental effects of the child's individual characteristics such as hearing level, age at which the child became deaf, the presence of disabilities (Meadow-Orlans & Sass-Lehrer, 1995), and the child's communication skills (Hintermair, 2006). Very little attention has been given to other potential influencing systems such as extended family, neighborhood and community, and informal networks; the availability of social opportunities for deaf children outside of school in their natural environments; the social, cultural, and political structures that devalue their very existence; and the accumulating effects of these systems individually or collectively.

The dearth of research stems from several factors. First, most researchers have assumed that these supports are nonexistent (which is largely true), and they have not considered them to be individually or collectively important to the child's well-being. They have assumed that children and adolescents are not directly affected by these systems' influences. Second, much of the research inherently values changing the child, as opposed to changing the environments in which the child interacts. Research has typically not taken a holistic ecosystems approach. Third, most of the research about the growth and development of the deaf person has primarily examined developmental influences on school-aged deaf children and adolescents and has not given as much attention to social-emotional well-being beyond the school years into adulthood and later life.

This study has demonstrated the striking inconsistencies across multiple environments and multiple systemic levels that the participants encounter. These inconsistencies require the adolescents to adapt, yet most environmental systems do not reciprocate in that adaptation. This is in essence what Humphries (1996) calls *audism*, a culture that is hearing centered and that values sound, spoken language, and expectations of behavior similar to that of hearing people. It is a social structure that discriminates against individuals who cannot hear, and it is deeply engrained in our culture, beliefs, and behaviors (Bauman, 2004; Lane, 1992). From an audist perspective, deaf people are seen as the problem (Brueggemann, 1999), and deaf children and adolescents bear the burden of adaptation.

The effects of systemic audism are deeply engrained in our culture and can be seen in Danny's notion that deaf people are intellectually inferior to hearing people; Angie's desperate drive to be nourished with information that is not readily available to her and her perception that deaf people have to work much harder to simply be informed, let alone to be well-versed and prepared for life's various roles and tasks; Joe's persistence in transcending the harsh behaviors of his hearing peers at school; Pat's disappointment in his career options; Mary's dissatisfaction with the superficial nature of her relationships with hearing people who don't speak her language; and Alex's disenchantment with the behaviors of restaurant workers when he wants to place an order.

This brings us to the concept of *multisystemic literacy*. Literacy involves much more than reading and writing language; it is the power to find and exchange meaning in order to participate in, make contributions to, and achieve goals in the social world (Freire, 1985; Moll, 1994). Each of the participants confronts varying levels of literacy among the multiple systems with which they interact on a regular basis. An optimal environment for the social-emotional development of a deaf person will involve multiple systems that are literate in the language, culture, adaptations, behaviors, needs, strengths, and resources that deaf and hard of hearing people bring to their interactions. If a restaurant is unable to achieve the goal of serving its customers equally, and if classmates, teachers, peers, extended family members, churches, employers, public servants, health care institutions, the media, and so forth, are unable to provide deaf and hard of hearing people with the same quality and quantity of information, then these systems are not *deaf literate*. The absence of *deaf literacy* is part of the reason audism exists; at the same time, this absence is the reason that multisystemic literacy is part of the solution.

*Compatible, Partially Compatible, and Noncompatible Systemic Literacies.* Looking closely at the developmental environments of the deaf children and adolescents in this study, we can see that they routinely move back and forth across multiple systems comprised of their home, school, community, peer, neighborhood, and organizational environments. As the adolescents transition across these systems, they encounter inconsistencies in awareness, language and communcation competencies, and attitudes. In other words, they face inconsistent systemic literacy in their developmental environments. Systemic literacy can be broken down into three types: *compatible literacies*, *partially compatible literacies*, and *noncompatible literacies*.

*Compatible literacy* systems provide a good match, or a *goodness of fit*, that results in successful transactions, mutual adaptation, and mutual development. *Partially compatible literacy systems* provide for limited interactions and limited adaptation and development. *Noncompatible* systems fail to match the literacies of the deaf or hard of hearing person and may contribute to failed interactions and divergent development where the two systems, such as child and parent, do not mutually adapt to each other.

Mary's description of her peer and nuclear family interactions, which contribute to her social-emotional well-being, is an example of compatible systemic literacy. Mary's account of her limited and unsatisfactory interaction with hearing peers through an interpreter is an example of a partially compatible literacy environment. Angie's frustration with and anxiety over the lack of forthcoming information and access in multiple systems in her environment provides us with examples of noncompatible systemic literacy.

*Corresponding and Noncorresponding Developmental Processes.* When a deaf child is born to hearing parents who have no preparation, information, or background experience to help them respond immediately to the unique needs of their deaf child, they begin their family journey without the literacy they need for optimal growth and development of both the child and family systems. However, the reports of the children and adolescents in this research to date have shown us that their hearing parents embarked on a developmental journey and learned and grew from the experience, demonstrating their love and support for their children.

In most of these families, there was a *corresponding developmental process* in which both the child and family were developing needed literacies for successful family interaction and growth. This is not to say, however, that the child and the family always developed at the same pace or with the same breadth and depth. With this in mind, then, it is possible that deaf children and their hearing families may experience divergent or *noncorresponding developmental processes*, such as when one or more members of the family depart or discontinue their growth in communication, language, and understanding of the deaf family member and the many and varied aspects of their being in the world. In addition, subsystems of families, such as siblings, grandparents, stepparents, and extended family members, may not be on corresponding pathways to deaf literacy and literacy development. This is where the participants in this study expressed discontent in the family system.

Preexisting compatible literacies conducive to development may exist in systems, as well; for example, in Mary's intergenerational family system, her parents, siblings, and grandparents are deaf. We would expect, then, that Mary's family paradigm already includes the experience of being deaf. Therefore, the birth of a deaf child in her family is likely be what Reiss (1981) calls a *first-order issue*, a predictable event or transition that the family is prepared for and that does not require significant adaptation of the family paradigm. When hearing parents discover by hearing parents that their child is deaf, we would expect that to be a *second-order issue*, an unpredictable traumatic event that forces the family to reexamine and adapt the beliefs, assumptions, and orientations that construct its family paradigm (Reiss, 1981). Interestingly, the informants in this research who have hearing parents give little indication that the discovery that they were deaf had this profound, traumatic second-order impact on their family systems. Phase I and phase II interviews both revealed that the participants sometimes saw their parents as initially worried and embarking on a learning course to adapt, but the children did not see their parents as grief stricken, shocked, angry, or traumatized. They reported they were loved and wanted above all else.

Contrary to what many people assume, then, literacy is not and should not be a linear process where the deaf person bears the bulk of the responsibility for adaptation. This should be an ongoing, reciprocal, intergenerational, and multisystemic developmental process that realizes diverse means toward compatible systemic literacies. This is an enormous task indeed, but so is the socially unjust and unrealistic alternative of expecting deaf children and adolescents to bear the responsibility for adaptation. Suggestions for developing multisystemic literacies can be found in the final chapter of this book.

Angie's frustration over the lack of captioning in movie theaters is an example of a system that is not deaf literate and that impacts upon her and her own English literacy skills. Pat's difficulties with the printed word in media technologies demonstrates the need for more widespread literacy in technologies compatible with the deaf person's literacy needs. The Deaf and Hard of Hearing Consumer Advocacy Network (DHHCAN), a national coalition of organizations representing deaf and hard of hearing people and their supporters, continues to use their advanced deaf literacies to lobby, advocate, and provide mass education to legislative policy makers, Internet and telecommunications providers, and software and electronics design companies to increase the number of compatible systemic deaf literacies in the technology field. The coalition is working to achieve a corresponding developmental process and compatible literacies for the benefit of deaf and hard of hearing people in society. This is but one example of how the literacies of deaf and hard of hearing people are more advanced than those of the systems with which they interact. It is representative of the strengths and resources that lie within the Deaf community for conquering passive and active audism. It is an example of how these literacies can be used to achieve compatible systemic literacies and corresponding developmental processes. From an existential perspective, the participants in this research continue to transcend multiple social barriers through their strengths and pathways.

## Into the Future

The development of a theory is an emerging process. The nature of this research is also emerging as our participants grow and change throughout their lives. While I could end this book with a prediction of what is to come for Alex, Angie, Danny, Joe, Lisa, Mary, and Pat, the life course is unpredictable, and qualitative research is time and context bound. I wish to remain faithful to one of the most important aspects of this research, the voices of the participants, who are our teachers, for they are the choreographers in the dance of their lives and in the emergence of grounded theory.

The ideas presented herein are unfolding as this research and the lives of our teachers unfold. As these ideas have emerged, so have new questions. It is my hope to meet our teachers again during their young adult lives. At that time, it will be interesting to see if their expectations for and views of themselves and others remain the same or change. Will they enter the careers they anticipate? Will their hopes and dreams come true? What will their adult relationships encompass? What will their multiple environments present to them, and how will they respond? How will they continue to change and grow? How will their individual and collective strengths and resources support them? Will they develop and utilize new strengths and resources? Will they continue to be the teachers of their lifeworlds, creating a more deaf-literate environment? Will they all arrive at the same or different ends with the same or different means? And so much more . . .

# 13

# *And Finally . . . Tomorrow's Leaders Paving the Way*

For tomorrow belongs to the people who prepare for it today.
—African proverb

The future is not some place we are going to, but one we are creating. The paths are not to be found, but made, and the activity of making them, changes both the maker and the destination.
—John Schaar

IN THIS study, I sought the narratives of deaf adolescents so that I could learn about their experiences and perceptions and the existential realities of their lifeworlds. The research uncovered belief systems that these deaf adolescents have about belonging and culture, their views of themselves and others, and how they perceive their relationships with their parents and significant others. It explored the realities of their experiences in their environments and relationships. It provided us with a deeper understanding of the developmental issues and tasks they face. The study revealed the pathways the teenagers use to transcend the challenges that they face at this point in their lives and taught us about their multiple strengths. Furthermore, as a follow-up study to the earlier phase I study on deaf children, this phase II study reveals how the adolescents' perceptions of their lifeworlds have changed over these developmental periods. Through their own narratives, they shared with us their thoughts about being a deaf adolescent and their views of their futures.

Part of the task before us is to create multiple environments that are visually stimulating and responsive to deaf and hard of hearing people throughout their lives, to challenge the absence of multisystemic deaf literacies. The value of and basic human need for relationships and interaction with self-same peer groups was clearly evident in the phase II interviews, and it is becoming increasingly important in today's social context. The recommendations that follow take into consideration these and other findings emerging from the research. These recommendations are in no way comprehensive, and it is expected that the reader, and even deaf adolescents themselves, will have much to add.

## Reinforce Strengths

A large amount of data pertaining to the strengths of these children and adolescents emerged in the studies. It is imperative that educational and community programs, families, and professional training programs incorporate, focus on, and reinforce the strengths that deaf youth and their families possess. We need to continue to move away from disempowering, low expectations and proceed into the future, recognizing, promoting, and utilizing the strengths that the participants in this study have demonstrated. While we are promoting a healthy sense of individual and collective strengths, we can provide realistic opportunities for transcending limitations and environmental restrictions. It is important to understand what restrictions exist, what forces are imposing them, and how we can develop programs and policies to defeat them. By emphasizing our individual and community strengths, we can overcome the unrealistic and negative expectations and labels that society has imposed on deaf people in research, policy, and practice, as well as elsewhere. A participatory approach draws from individual and collective strengths of the community and can aid in the development of model programs and the encouragement of a healthy sense of competence in our youth that will prepare them well for their futures. The following recommendations reinforce and incorporate the strengths identified in this book.

### National and International Conferences on Multisystemic Deaf Literacies

There is a need for national and international conferences focused on building agendas and making plans to increase the responsiveness of multiple systems to deaf and hard of hearing people. These conferences could be forums for networking, information sharing, and brainstorming about effective programs and models. They should include professionals from the media to encourage collaboration and dissemination of ideas.

## Creative Arts and Media

Today, many deaf and hard of hearing youth are finding themselves alone in public schools without the benefit of a nurturing peer group or deaf adults to mentor them. Identifying these youth to provide them with information and resources is becoming increasingly challenging. Creative arts and media programs have great potential for outreach and should be aggressively pursued. There are a number of opportunities that can utilize and refine the strengths of deaf and hard of hearing children and adolescents and take them to greater depths, as well as build their communities and link them to other deaf and hard of hearing children scattered throughout the world.

Some schools already have drama and media programs that they can build upon. Other schools can obtain grants to begin these programs. Schools should consider sponsoring artists in residence and summer and weekend enrichment programs. Community organizations such as community centers, state associations, and clubs for the deaf can also play important roles by obtaining arts and media grants. Collaborative efforts pulling from the strengths of these community and educational resources can develop theatrical productions about career opportunities; the vocations, achievements, and career paths of famous deaf adults; Deaf culture and history; and ordinary deaf adults and their day-to-day lives (work, parenting, continuing education, socialization, health care, diversity, legal rights, recreation, finances, etc.). These productions can serve as creative avenues for deaf and hard of hearing youth to express their ideas, feelings, hopes, and desires about their own day-to-day experiences of being in the world (at home, at school, and in the community). This would give them the opportunity to make recommendations that can lead to positive change in their environments. Psychosocial educational productions aimed at bullying and assault prevention, dating, peer pressure, and other issues of importance to the teens could be developed.

The productions can incorporate and feature deaf folklore, monologues, poetry, drawings, posters, and other expressive arts that the students themselves create as school, extracurricular, or personal hobby projects. Deaf children and teens in schools can collaborate with deaf adults, deaf actors, their teachers, and parent volunteers on topics, script development and ideas, prioritization of audiences, and so forth. Touring productions can travel to public schools where deaf children are mainstreamed, to residential schools, to summer camps and leadership programs for deaf youth, and to conferences and programs in the Deaf community. They can be presented at parent conferences and PTA meetings, at school board meetings, at corporate and employee training programs, at public facilities where communication occurs, at vocational training programs, at colleges and universities, at libraries, and at medical and nursing schools.

To reach even broader audiences, including deaf students who may be isolated in the mainstream (whom Oliva, 2004, calls *solitaires*), network and cable televisions programs and Web-based media such as video clips, signed vlogs (video blogs), and written blogs, can be created by deaf and hard of hearing children and adolescents. Importantly, deaf students should play lead roles in the creation, planning, delivery, dissemination, and evaluation of these productions. Such activities utilize, reinforce, and deepen the strengths and resources of the students and their schools, families, and communities and serve to empower them while educating deaf and hearing others about the many and varied aspects of their individual and collective lives.

These experiences allow students to construct or expand meaning and purpose in their lives and the lives of others. They contribute to social change by filling existential voids in the lives of other deaf students who have not yet met their self-same peers and of parents of deaf children without networks. They can educate potential employers, educators, restaurant workers, theater managers, hearing classmates, and others about the strengths, feelings, and needs of our deaf youth. Of course, all of the responsibility for this type of social change should not rest on the shoulders of deaf children and adolescents alone; it should never become a burden. Some deaf children and teens may choose not to participate, but the opportunities should be available for those who can benefit because the possibilities are endless. Such activities can be incorporated into classroom learning and will help deaf students develop a sense of pride in themselves and their communities. These productions need not be restricted to deaf life issues. The very presence of deaf and hard of hearing students in these endeavors creates the potential for change and growth on multiple systems levels.

## Collaboration with Our Students

Rarely have we as a society demonstrated to our deaf students that we value their input and ideas. The research in this book reveals that deaf adolescents are able to participate in a research process that values their input and allows them to teach us about their lifeworlds and their needs. This empowering process demonstrates to the students that they can make a difference in their communities and situations in life. We should aim to show our students that their ideas, input, strengths, and participation are valued in the development of our knowledge, programs, and policies. It is important that we not wait until adulthood to seek the retrospective narratives of what was and what could have been. The painful narratives of deaf adults about their formative years may not be repeated if we monitor and seek to understand how current practices affect the lives of children and adolescents while they are at critical points in their development. This will allow us to intervene and prevent ineffective or potentially damaging practices and identify and continue our successes.

## Education about Legal Rights, Assertiveness, and Conflict Resolution

While all of the adolescents in the phase II study told stories of alienating experiences and exclusion in society, only one indicated an awareness of the rights and laws that prohibit discrimination. Information on the rights to communication and participation and the prohibition of discrimination should be incorporated into educational curriculums and community programs. Assertiveness training, as well as training and information on conflict resolution, can also be of benefit to them. Deaf adults in the community can serve as role models and mentors in this process.

## Community-Based Clubs and Activities for Deaf Youth

All of the participants in this study responded positively to structured weekend activities sponsored by local community organizations. These events provide an oasis for the mainstreamed students who have few opportunities for such socialization with peers at school or in their neighborhoods. Clubs for deaf children and teens fill a social and recreational void for these participants by giving them space and opportunities for support around issues of concern (i.e., group sessions dealing with dating, drug and alcohol prevention, peer pressure, career and postsecondary choices, self-defense and protection, etc.), as well as organized recreational activities. Alex and Danny also enjoy going to summer camps with deaf peers.

All the participants value opportunities and spaces for socialization with self-same peers.

These programs are few and far between, but they hold immense promise for positive support in the growth and development of deaf children and adolescents. Collaborative efforts between Deaf communities, community organizations, and schools, in partnership with state and local departments of education, could increase the number of offerings. Funding may be available from local arts councils, parks and recreation services, departments of education, private foundations, and local and state governments. Supporting organizations that adopt participatory approaches will facilitate self-determination, empowerment, social development, and leadership skills. Aggressive outreach and public relations strategies should market the programs to an increasingly isolated and diverse population of deaf and hard of hearing students.

## Reinforcement of Parents' Belief that Children Know They Are Loved

Contrary to anecdotal and published assumptions about deaf children's negative perceptions of their parents regard for them, the informants in this study overwhelmingly report strong positive perceptions of their parents' love and regard. This should be reinforced in programs for parents of deaf children. Parents should be helped to see what they are doing right, what their children appreciate, and how their children perceive them. Parental strengths should be recognized and reinforced by early intervention and other programs to ensure that they are contributing to this positive phenomenon and to support families where this attachment might not be occurring.

Other ideas for parent support include forming local chapters of the American Society for Deaf Children; developing Web-based forums, vlogs and blogs, Listservs, and video clips on informational topics; and providing increased opportunities for family learning vacations, mentoring with deaf adults for families, and assistance with transportation and technology grants for access to information, community events, and programs. Cable network programs focusing on a variety of deaf life issues are also important. Creative outreach to minority and immigrant families, language translations for programs and materials, and multilingual and culturally competent professionals are urgently needed.

## Mentoring

Mentoring activities can benefit deaf youth and their families in a number of ways. Using Take Your Child to Work Day as a model, deaf children and teens should have the opportunity to shadow deaf adults on their jobs in various careers, particularly careers that are of interest to them. Danny is interested in a career in computers but has concerns about how he would communicate with his coworkers. It would be beneficial for him to see how deaf adults communicate at work. Angie is bubbling over with curiosity and excitement about learning about the future. She had many questions for me after our interviews about my life and work. Being mentored by deaf adults in various daily situations would be a welcome opportunity for her. Matching families with deaf adult mentors does not have to be limited to career opportunities. The implementation of programs such as the Laurent Clerc National Deaf Education Center's Shared Reading Project, which pairs deaf adults with families of deaf children, offers one such model. More such enrichment programs around a variety of life themes would be important to pursue.

## Extended Family Sign Classes and Activities

All the participants in this study reported becoming bored in inaccessible situations with their extended families. While many educational and community programs already offer sign language classes for parents and immediate family members, they must find ways to encourage extended families to participate in classes and activities. This will result in a fuller, more compatible, growth-enhancing language environment in the family. Many schools and community programs that provide family learning vacations and activities also sponsor additional opportunities for improved family communication. Creativity in dealing with financial assistance and transportation for families in need, offerings at satellite locations, and creative outreach to minority and immigrant families will help to reach families not currently able to participate. Programs should pull from the strengths of their deaf and hard of hearing children and youth in the planning process and even at the instruction and activity leadership levels. Mentoring with deaf adults should also include extended family members. Another mechanism for making sign language instruction more assessable to parents and families is to allocate public and private funds for Internet and telecommunications video instruction technology. Families should also consider hiring interpreters for family gatherings such as holiday parties, weddings, funerals, reunions, retirement events, and birthday celebrations.

## Community Support Workers

Community organizations and schools can provide social workers to assist with case management, daily living skills, and parent education programs, all of which can help the deaf child's family develop knowledge about language and communication skills and general child development. These social workers can also build the deaf literacy skills of multiple community environments with which deaf children and adolescents interact.

## Bully Prevention Programs in Schools and Community Organizations

The participants in this study identified several situations involving bullying, teasing, and harassment by both deaf and hearing peers and rejection and discrimination by others in their environments. There is a dearth of research and literature on this very serious phenomenon as it relates to deaf children and teens and a serious need to examine and address this issue through research, prevention, and intervention programs (Miller & Weiner, 2006). Bullying prevention and programs that promote respect for diversity among deaf and hard of hearing people need to be established in our schools and community agencies.

Rejection, bullying, and assault within one's own community of peers is doubly traumatic. Organizations and environments such as educational programs for deaf children and teens and the Deaf community should support and nurture intellectual and psychosocial development and provide safe havens. As discussed in *Inner Lives of Deaf Children*, a panethnic or multicultural approach to unity should be established to promote respect and harmony in our increasingly diverse Deaf community. This needs to be deeply ingrained as a value base in the attitudes and systemic processes at the institutional level. Educational programs and community organizations need to examine their mission and implementation processes to ensure their commitment to diversity.

## Sign Language and Deaf Awareness Programs in Schools Where Deaf Children Are Mainstreamed

The adolescents participating in the phase II study who were mainstreamed into public schools indicated discomfort in their relations with hearing peers in mainstream settings. A systematic response to this could include the establishment of ASL and Deaf culture programs in the schools to make them more deaf centered. An empowering approach would allow the deaf adolescent the opportunity to participate in the planning and delivery of this activity, perhaps for academic credit. More schools and school districts should be offering ASL as a foreign language for high school credit.

*Outreach: Connecting through Technology and Transportation-Based Solutions*

Creative use of technology and transportation offers many possibilities for outreach to individuals and families who are underserved, isolated, or unable to afford equipment. One solution to the isolation caused by weekends and summers away from the accessible environment of the residential school and by mainstreaming lies in technology. Direct grants for the provision of digital pagers, computers, and videophone technology should be made available to fill this social and communication void. There is a need for more school and community partnerships that effectively reach out to rural, socioeconomically disadvantaged, and minority and immigrant families. These outreach partnerships would help isolated deaf students such as Pat and other underserved groups who experience financial, geographic, and intrapersonal barriers to information, resources, and connections to a supportive and growth-enhancing community.

Universities, community agencies and organizations, telecommunications companies, schools, and education agencies should collaborate to provide direct grants for technology and equipment that will enable deaf and hard of hearing children to stay in touch with peer, school, and other support systems by way of things like video-enhanced webcasting and instant message services; mentoring programs that could include the matching of college students, faculty, and staff, as well as deaf professionals, to deaf elementary and high school students; online psychoeducational programming and sign language instruction for parents and families; technology training programs that can be taken to local communities and into the homes of deaf youth and their families to get them connected with a nurturing community; transportation grants obtained by community agencies and local education programs; and Gallaudet University Regional Centers to enable children to participate in the deaf children's clubs, summer camps, and workshops recommended in previous sections, as well as programs for immediate and extended family members. Strengthening linkages between effective state and national advocacy organizations and deaf and hard of hearing students through schools and community programs will help to prepare deaf and hard of hearing adolescents for leadership and mutual aid.

## Scholarship/Sponsorship Opportunities

It is imperative that private and public funding be made available for scholarships and sponsorships that will allow deaf children and teens to attend programs that will enhance their development and opportunities. The teens in this study have continued to place high value on the learning and relationships they have developed in formal and informal peer-group settings with other deaf and hard of hearing children and adolescents. Such programs can include weekend and summer clubs, workshops and camps for deaf and hard of hearing youth, and family learning vacations. Scholarships and sponsorship should also be made available for family enrichment programs that include extended family members and give them access to language and communication development and resources.

## Emergency Preparedness

Crisis and trauma response programs in local communities need to learn to work with local Deaf communities and make their information, training, and services available to deaf and hard of hearing people. Mainstream education programs need to be sure that they include a response plan that is accessible and inclusive of deaf students and their deaf or hearing parents.

## Research

Although many research questions arise regarding different aspects of the lifeworlds of deaf and hard of hearing children and adolescents, my recommendations focus on suggestions for further research growing out of this study. The participatory research methods used in this study, which incorporate the voices of participants, should be adopted for the purpose of developing effective systemic responses that facilitate the development of meaningful and healthy deaf lives. Participatory research should translate into participatory programs.

This study focused on a cohort of deaf and hard of hearing youth who are now entering their young adult years. Similar studies should continue to take place to inform us of the lifeworlds and the needs of new cohorts of deaf and hard of hearing children and adolescents, including minority and immigrant populations and deaf youth with cochlear implants. Similar studies can also focus on families and on parents of deaf and hard of hearing children to tell us more about their lifeworlds and needs.

To understand more about the relationship between healthy self-esteem in deaf children and communication and language at home, we may explore the variety of parent-child dyads (i.e., one or two hearing parents and a deaf child; one or two deaf parents and a deaf child; one hearing parent, one deaf parent, and a deaf child; and more than one deaf child in the family).

We need to understand what programs are effective in meeting the various needs of diverse groups of deaf and hard of hearing youth and their families and provide opportunities for dissemination of exemplary programs for replication. We are also in need of research that will lead to the development and support of programs that will increase the resilience and graduation rates of deaf high school and postsecondary students.

Research is also needed to understand the incidence of, and solutions to, alienating situations that deaf children and adolescents and their families report. Some of the most pressing issues are assault and bullying and evaluation of pilot programs to prevent such incidents, multicultural attitudes of deaf and hard of hearing people, and evaluation of multicultural responsiveness and cultural competence programs in schools and community agencies. To supplement the availability of traditional interpreting services, we need to identify effective means of increasing communication ease in public and private settings such as movie theaters, restaurants, shopping malls, medical offices, and places of employment.

It will be informative to visit these teenagers again when they are young adults to explore the developmental processes they have experienced and to discover how they define and perceive themselves and their lifeworlds at that point in their development. In that way, we can identify the similarities and differences in themes across time. This will also allow us to further analyze the issues they face in terms of identity and existential being in the world and the diverse choices they have made in their lives.

## Concluding Thoughts

Clearly, these youth are affected by the many biopsychosocial, cultural, political, and economic forces in their environments. They reveal transactions with an array of supportive as well as prohibitive social systems. Yet these participants obviously possess strengths. The pathways they take as they navigate the various channels throughout their formative years are evidence of their abilities to transcend unfavorable environments through existential creativity, defiance, freedom, and responsibility and to create meaning and purpose in their lives (Frankl, 1969).

We must consider and accept the realities that deaf and hard of hearing people present. One such reality is the desire for self-same relationships. As we move forward, it is important to note that our active responses to what these adolescents have shared with us should be respectful of their expressed realities and should occur on a variety of system levels: individual, family, community, organizational, policy, governmental, and cultural. For example, to facilitate the development of self-same relationships and to reach out to isolated deaf and hard of hearing students, we may have to become their partners in advocacy on the policy, governmental, community, and organizational level.

It takes a child to teach a village. Chapter 2 in this book presented many of the contextual realities in the lives of deaf adolescents today. These changing social contexts are contributing to new challenges of self-definition for the Deaf community. Yet the adolescents in this study were able to share with us that in the face of these social changes, they are resilient and they are able to tell us what they want and need to achieve actualization in their lives. They were able to teach us the multiple meanings of being deaf in multiple systems in their lifeworlds. We will need to embrace these multiple realities and participate in a collective response to creating a more welcoming and nurturing social environment. From this research we are moving toward a developmental theory of the lifeworlds of these deaf and hard of hearing participants. One of the most important lessons we have learned from this research process is that through their narratives, deaf and hard of hearing children and teenagers can make valuable contributions to our knowledge base, our professional practices, and to their own lifeworlds. They have taught us well; they have lifted our souls and touched our lives, and for that we are more whole.

# References

Adams, G. R., Montemayor, R., & Gullotta, T. P. (Eds.). (1996). *Psychosocial development during adolescence: Progress in developmental contextualism.* Thousand Oaks, CA: Sage.

Adams, J. E., Coelho, G. V., & Hamburg, D. A. (1974). *Coping and adaptation.* New York: Basic Books.

Akamatsu, C. T., Musselman, C., & Zwiebel, A. (2000). Nature versus nurture in the development of cognition in deaf people. In P. E. Spencer, C. J. Erting, & M. Marschark (Eds.), *The deaf child in the family and at school* (pp. 255–274), Mahwah, NJ: Erlbaum.

Allen, T. E., Rawlings, B. W., & Schildroth, A. N. (1989). *Deaf students and the school-to-work transition.* Baltimore: Brookes.

Americans with Disabilities Act of 1990, 42 U.S.C.A. #12101 et seq. (West 1993).

Anderson, G. B., & Grace, C. A. (1991). Black deaf adolescents: A diverse and underserved population. *The Volta Review, 93,* 73–86.

Andrews, J. F., Leigh, I. W., & Weiner, T. (2004). *Deaf people: Evolving perspectives from psychology, education, and sociology.* Boston: Allyn & Bacon.

Bakan, D. (1971). Adolescence in America: From idea to social fact. *Daedalus, 100,* 979–995.

Bat-Chava, Y. (1993). Antecedents of self-esteem in deaf people: A meta-analytic review. *Rehabilitation Psychology, 38*(4), 221–234.

Bauman, H-D. L. (2004). Audism: Exploring the metaphysics of oppression. *Journal of Deaf Studies and Deaf Education, 9*(2), 239.

Beck, B. (1988). Self-assessment of selected interpersonal abilities in hard of hearing and deaf adolescents. *International Journal of Rehabilitation Research, 11*(4), 343–349.

Berger, P. (1963). *Invitation to sociology.* Garden City, NY: Doubleday.

Berger, P., & Luckmann, T. (1967). *The social construction of reality.* Garden City, NY: Doubleday.

Bloom, M. (1992). *Changing lives: Studies in human development and professional helping.* Columbia: University of South Carolina Press.

Bloom, M., & Germain, C. B. (1999). *Human behavior in the social environment: An ecological view* (2nd ed.). New York: Columbia University Press.

Bodner-Johnson, B., & Sass-Lehrer, M. (2003). *The young deaf or hard of hearing child: A family-centered approach to early education.* Baltimore: Brookes.

Bogdan, R. C., & Biklen, S. K. (1992). *Qualitative research in education: An introduction to theory and methods* (2nd ed.). Boston: Allyn & Bacon.

Braden, J. (1994). *Deafness, deprivation and IQ.* New York: Plenum.

Brice, P. (1985). A comparison of levels of tolerance for ambiguity in deaf and hearing school children. *American Annals of the Deaf, 130*(3), 226–230.

Brooks, H. C., & Ellis, G. J. (1982). Self-esteem of hearing-impaired adolescents: Effects of labelling. *Youth & Society, 14*(1), 59–80.

Brueggemann, B. (1999). *Lend me your ear: Rhetorical constructions of deafness.* Washington, DC: Gallaudet University Press.

Bruner, J., Goodnow, J., & Austin, A. (1956). *A study of thinking.* New York: Wiley.

Burkitt, I. (1991). *Social selves: Theories of the social formation of personality.* London: Sage.

Calderon, R., & Greenberg, M. T. (2000). Challenges to parents and professionals in promoting socioemotional development in deaf children. In P. E. Spencer, C. J. Erting, & M. Marschark (Eds.), *The deaf child in the family and at school* (pp. 167–185). Mahwah, NJ: Erlbaum.

Calderon, R., & Greenberg, M. T. (2003). Social and emotional development of deaf children: family, school and program effects. In M. Marschark & P. Spencer (Eds.), *Oxford handbook of deaf studies, language, and education* (pp. 177–189). New York: Oxford University Press.

Cates, J. A. (1991). Self-concept in hearing and prelingual/profoundly deaf students: A comparison of teachers' perceptions. *American Annals of the Deaf, 136* (4), 354–359.

Cobb, N. J. (1995). Adolescence: *Continuity, change, and diversity* (2nd ed.). Mountain View, CA: Mayfield.

Cole, S. H., & Edelman, R. J. (1991). Identity patterns and self and teacher perceptions of problems for deaf adolescents: A research note. *Journal of Child Psychology and Psychiatry, 32*(7), 1159–1165.

Coles, R. (1990). *The spiritual life of children.* Boston: Houghton Mifflin.

Collins, W. A., & Shulman, S. (Eds.). (1997). *Romantic relationships in adolescence: Developmental perspectives.* San Francisco: Jossey-Bass.

Cooley, C. H. (1902). *Human nature and the social order.* New York: Schocken.

Corker, M. (1996). *Deaf transitions: Images and origins of deaf families, deaf communities, and deaf identities.* Philadelphia: Jessica Kingsley.

Desselle, D. D. (1994). Self-esteem, family climate, and communication patterns in relation to deafness. *American Annals of the Deaf, 139*(3), 322–328.

Dweck, C. S. (1999). *Self theories: Their role in motivation, personality, and development.* Philadelphia: Psychology.

Elkind, D. (1984). *All grown up and no place to go.* New York: Addison-Wesley.

Erikson, E. H. (1959). *Identity and the life cycle.* New York: Norton.

Erting, C. J., Johnson, R. C., Smith, D., & Snider, B. (Eds.). (1994). *The Deaf way: Perspectives from the international conference on Deaf culture.* Washington, DC: Gallaudet University Press.

Erting, C., Prezioso, C., & Hynes, M. (1990). The interactional context of deaf mother-infant interaction. In V. Volterra & C. Erting (Eds.), *From gesture to language in hearing and deaf children* (pp. 97–106). Heidelberg, Germany: Springer.

Foster, S. (1989). Social alienation and peer identification: A study of the social construction of deafness. *Human Organization, 48*(3), 226–235.

Foster, S. (1994). Outsider in the deaf world: Reflections on an ethnographic researcher. *Journal of the American Deafness and Rehabilitation Association, 27*(3), 1–11.

Frankl, V. E. (1969). *The will to meaning: Foundations and applications of logotherapy.* New York: New American Library.

Freire, P. (1985). *The politics of education: Culture, power, and liberation.* South Hadley, MA: Bergin and Garvey.

Furth, H. (1964). Research with the deaf: Implications for language and cognition. *Psychological Bulletin, 62*, 145–162.

Geertz, C. (1973). *Thick description: Toward an interpretive theory of cultures.* New York: Basic Books.

Germain, C. (1973). The ecological perspective in casework practice. *Social Casework, 54*, 223–230.

Germain, C. (1980). *The life model of social work practice.* New York: Columbia University Press.

Germain, C. (1987). Human development in contemporary environments. *Social Service Review*, 565–580.

Glickman, N. (1996). The development of culturally deaf identities. In N. Glickman & M. Harvey (Eds.), *Culturally affirmative psychotherapy with deaf persons.* Mahwah, NJ: Erlbaum.

Goffman, E. (1974). *Stigma.* New York: Jason Aronson.

Gould, K. (1987). Life model versus conflict model: A feminist perspective. *Social Work, 32*, 346–351.

Greene, M. (1978). *Landscapes of learning.* New York: Teachers College Press.

Harkins, J. E., & Bakke, M. (2003). Technologies for communication: Status and trends. In M. Marschark & P. E. Spencer (Eds.), *Oxford handbook of deaf studies, language, and education* (pp. 406–419). New York: Oxford University Press.

Harter, S., & Pike, P. (1984). The pictorial scale of perceived competence and social acceptance for young children. *Child Development, 55*, 1969–1982.

Hartman, H. (1939). *Ego psychology and the problem of adaptation.* New York: International Universities Press.

Harvey, M. (1989). *Psychotherapy with deaf and hard of hearing persons: A systemic model.* Mahwah, NJ: Erlbaum.

Harvey, M. A. (2003). *Psychotherapy with deaf and hard of hearing persons: A systemic model* (2nd ed.). Mahwah, NJ: Erlbaum.

Havinghurst, R. J. (1972). *Developmental tasks and education.* New York: David McKay.

Hewitt, J. P. (1998). *The myth of self-esteem: Finding happiness and solving problems in America.* New York: St. Martin's.

Heyman, S. J. (2000). *The widening gap: Why America's working families are in jeopardy and what can be done about it.* New York: Basic Books.

Hill, J. P. (1973). Some perspectives on adolescence in American society. Unpublished position paper for the Office of Child Development. United States Department of Health, Education, and Welfare.

Hintermair, M. (2006). Parental resources, parental stress, and socioemotional development of deaf and hard of hearing children. *Journal of Deaf Studies and Deaf Education, 11*(4), 493–513.

Humphries, T. (1996). Of deaf mutes, the strange, and the modern Deaf self. In N. S. Glickman & M. A. Harvey (Eds.), *Culturally affirmative psychotherapy with deaf persons* (pp. 99–114). Mahwah, NJ: Erlbaum.

Karchmer, M. A., & Mitchell, R. E. (2003). Demographic and achievement characteristics of deaf and hard of hearing students. In M. Marschark & P. E. Spencer (Eds.), *Oxford handbook of deaf studies, language, and education* (pp. 21–37). New York: Oxford University Press.

Katz, C. (1996). *A history of the deaf community in Beaumont, Texas.* Unpublished manuscript, Lamar University, Beaumont, TX.

Kluwin, T. (1993). Cumulative effects of mainstreaming on the achievement of deaf adolescents. *Exceptional Children, 60,* 70–81.

Kohlberg, L. (1963). The development of children's orientation toward a moral order: Social experience, social conduct and the development of moral thought II. *Vita Humana, 6*(1–2), 18–19.

Kusche, C. A., Garfield, T. S., & Greenberg, M. T. (1983). The understanding of emotional and social attributions in deaf adolescents. *Journal of Clinical Child Psychology, 12,* 153–160.

Ladd, P. (2003). *Understanding Deaf culture: In search of Deafhood.* Clevedon, UK: Multilingual Matters.

LaGreca, A. M. (1990). *Through the eyes of the child: Obtaining self-reports from children and adolescents.* Boston: Allyn & Bacon.

Lane, H. (1992). *The mask of benevolence: Disabling the Deaf community.* New York: Knopf.

Lincoln, Y. S., & Guba, E. G. (1985). *Naturalistic inquiry.* Newbury Park, CA: Sage.

Marcia, J. (1966). Development and validation of ego identity status. *Journal of Personality and Social Psychology, 3,* 551–558.

Marcia, J. (1976). *Studies in ego identity.* Burnaby, British Columbia, Canada: Simon Fraser University.

Marschark, M. (1993). *Psychological development of deaf children.* New York: Oxford University Press.

Marschark, M. (2003). Cognitive functioning in deaf adults and children. In M. Marschark & P. E. Spencer (Eds.), *Oxford handbook of deaf studies, language, and education* (pp. 464–477). New York: Oxford University Press.

Martinez, M., & Silvestre, N. (1995). Self-concept in profoundly deaf adolescent pupils. *International Journal of Psychology, 30*(3), 305–316.

Mead, G. H. (1934). *Mind, self and society.* Chicago: University of Chicago Press.

Meadow, K. P., & Dyssegaard, B. (1983). Social-emotional adjustment of deaf students. *International Journal of Rehabilitation Research, 6,* 345–348.

Meadow-Orlans, K. P. (1990). Research on the developmental aspects of deafness. In D. Moores and K. P. Meadow-Orlans (Eds.), *Educational and developmental aspects of deafness* (pp. 282–298). Washington, DC: Gallaudet University Press.

Meadow-Orlans, K. P., Mertens, D. M., & Sass-Lehrer, M. A. (2003). *Parents and their deaf children: The early years.* Washington, DC: Gallaudet University Press.

Meadow-Orlans, K. P., & Sass-Lehrer, M. (1995). Support services for families of children who are deaf. Challenges for professionals. *Topics in Early Childhood Special Education, 15*(3), 314–334.

Miller, M., & Weiner, M. T. (2006). Deaf children and bullying: Directions for future research. *American Annals of the Deaf, 151*(1), 61–70.

Mindel, E. D., & Vernon, M. (1971). *They grow in silence: The deaf child and his family.* Silver Spring, MD: National Association of the Deaf.

Mindel, E. D., & Vernon, M. (1987). *They grow in silence. The deaf child and his family* (2nd ed.). Boston: Little, Brown.

Mitchell, R. E., and Karchmer, M. A. (2004). Chasing the mythical ten percent: Parental hearing status of deaf and hard of hearing students in the United States. *Sign Language Studies, 4*(2), 138–163.

Moll, L. C. (1994). Literacy research in community and classrooms: Sociocultural approach. In R. B. Ruddell, M. R. Ruddell, & H. Singer (Eds.), *Theoretical models and processes of reading* (4th ed.) (pp. 179–207). Newark, DE: International Reading Association.

Moores, D. F. (2001). *Educating the deaf: Psychology, principles, and practices* (5th ed.). Boston: Houghton Mifflin.

Moores, D. F. (2004, June). *No Deaf/hard of hearing child left behind.* Keynote presentation, Intermountain Special Study Institute on Deafness, Idaho State University.

Moores, D. F., Jatho, J., & Dunn, C. (2001). Families with deaf members: American Annals of the Deaf, 1996–2000. *American Annals of the Deaf, 146,* 245–250.

Nash, J. E. (2000). Shifting stigma from body to self: Paradoxical consequences of mainstreaming. In P. E. Spencer, C. J. Erting, & M. Marschark (Eds.), *The deaf child in the family and at school: Essays in honor of Kathryn P. Meadow-Orlans* (pp. 211–227). Mahwah, NJ: Erlbaum.

National Center for Education Statistics. (1999). Home page. Retrieved July 24, 2006, from http://nces.ed.gov/.

Oliva, G. A. (2004). *Alone in the mainstream: A deaf woman remembers public school.* Washington, DC: Gallaudet University Press.

Padden, C. (1980). The deaf community and the culture of deaf people. In C. Baker & R. Battison (Eds.), *Sign language and the deaf community* (pp. 89–103). Washington, DC: National Association of the Deaf.

Padden, C., & Humphries T. (2005). *Inside deaf culture.* Cambridge, MA: Harvard University Press.

Paige, R. (2004). *Leading American education in the 21st century: Reflections on four years of fundamental reform.* Farewell address to the Heritage Foundation. Retrieved July 24, 2006, from http://www.ed.gov/news/speeches/2004/12/12142004.html.

Paige, R. (2005). U.S. Department of Education Releases National Education Technology Plan, January 7, 2005. Retrieved July 24, 2006, from http://www.ed.gov/about/offices/list/os/technology/plan/2004/site/edlite-default.html.

Parasnis, I. (Ed.). (1996). *Cultural and language diversity and the deaf experience.* New York: Cambridge University Press.

Piaget, J. (1952). *The origins of intelligence in children.* New York: International University Press.

Pintner R., & Patterson, D. (1917). A comparison of deaf and hearing children in visual memory span for digits. *Journal of Experimental Psychology, 2,* 76–88.

Polat, F. (2003). Factors affecting psychosocial adjustment of deaf students. *Journal of Deaf Studies and Deaf Education, 8,* 325–329.

Powers, S. (1990). Self-perceived competencies of a group of hearing-impaired pupils in a unit setting. *Journal of the British Association of Teachers of the Deaf, 14*(3), 61–68.

Raimondo, J. D. (2001). Early intervention for infants with hearing loss: Parents' perspectives. *International Pediatrics 16*(1) 1–3.

Ramsey, C. L. (1997). *Deaf children in public schools: Placement, context, and consequences.* Washington, DC: Gallaudet University Press.

Reiss, D. (1981). *The family's construction of reality.* Cambridge, MA: Harvard University Press.

Revenson, T. A., & Singer, D. G. (1978). *A Piaget primer: How a child thinks.* New York: Penguin.

Rönnberg, J. (2003). Working memory, neuroscience, and language: Evidence from deaf and hard of hearing individuals. In M. Marschark & P. E. Spencer (Eds.), *Oxford handbook of deaf studies, language, and education* (pp. 478–489). New York: Oxford University Press.

Rosenberg, M. (1989). *Society and the adolescent self-image.* Middletown, CT: Wesleyan University Press.

Sadowski, M. (Ed.). (2003). *Adolescents at school: Perspectives on youth, identity, and education.* Cambridge, MA: Harvard Education Press.

Saleebey, D. (2005). *The strengths perspective in social work practice* (4th ed.). Boston: Allyn & Bacon.

Scheetz, N. (2001). *Orientation to deafness* (2nd ed.). Boston: Allyn & Bacon.

Schick, B., Williams, K., & Kupermintz, H. (2006). Look who's being left behind: Educational interpreters and access to education for deaf and hard of hearing students. *Journal of Deaf Studies and Deaf Education, 11,* 3–20.

Schirmer, B. R. (2001). *Psychological, social and educational dimensions of deafness.* Needham Heights, MA: Allyn & Bacon.

Schlesinger, H. S. (1972). A developmental model applied to problems of deafness. In H. S. Schlesinger & K. P. Meadow, *Sound and sign: Childhood deafness and mental health* (pp. 7–29). Berkeley: University of California Press.

Schlesinger, H. S., & Meadow, K. P. (1972). *Sound and sign: Childhood deafness and mental health.* Berkeley: University of California Press.

Searls, M. (1993). Self-concept among deaf and hearing children of deaf parents. *Journal of the American Deafness and Rehabilitation Association, 27*(1), 25–37.

Shantz, C. U. (1983). Social cognition. In P. H. Mussen (Ed.), *Handbook of child psychology* (Vol. 3, pp. 495–555). New York: Wiley.

Sheridan, M. (1995). Existential transcendence among deaf and hard of hearing people. In M. D. Garretson (Ed.), *Deafness, life and culture II* (pp. 103–106). Silver Spring, MD: National Association of the Deaf.

Sheridan, M. (1996). Emerging themes in the study of deaf children. Ann Arbor, MI: UMI Dissertation Services. Retrieved July 24, 2006, from ProQuest Digital Dissertations database; Publication No. AAT 9639344.

Sheridan, M. (2001). *Inner lives of deaf children: Interviews and analysis.* Washington DC: Gallaudet University Press.

Smith L. L., & Elliott, C. H. (2001). *Hollow kids: Recapturing the soul of a generation lost to the self-esteem myth.* Roseville, CA: Prima.

Stein, S. J., & Book, H. E. (2000). *The EQ edge: Emotional intelligence and your success.* Toronto, Ontario, Canada: Multi-health Systems.

Stinson, M. S., & Walter, G. G. (1992). Persistence in college. In S. B. Foster & G. G. Walter (Eds.), *Deaf students in postsecondary education* (pp. 43–64). London: Routledge.

Stone, W. L., & Lemanek, K. L. (1990). Developmental issues in children's self reports. In A. M. La Greca (Ed.), *Through the eyes of the child: Obtaining self-reports from children and adolescents* (pp. 18–82). Boston: Allyn & Bacon.

Tatum, B. (1997). *"Why are all the Black kids sitting together in the cafeteria?" And other conversations about race.* New York: Basic Books.

U.S. Department of Education, Office of Educational Technology. (2004). *Toward a new golden age in American education: How the Internet, the law and today's students are revolutionizing expectations.* Washington, DC: U.S. Department of Education.

Vernon, M., & Andrews, J. F. (1990). *The psychology of deafness: Understanding deaf and hard of hearing people.* White Plains, NY: Longman.

Vygotsky, L. S. (1978). *Mind in society.* Cambridge, MA: Harvard University Press.

Vygotsky, L. S. (1993). *The collected works of L. S. Vygotsky: Vol. 2. The fundamentals of defectology (abnormal psychology and learning disabilities)* (J. E. Knox & C. B. Stevens, Trans.; R. W. Reiber & A. S. Carton, Eds.). New York: Plenum.

Wallis, D., Musselman, C., & MacKay, S. (2004). Hearing mothers and their deaf children: The relationship between early, ongoing mode match and subsequent mental health functioning in adolescents. *Journal of Deaf Studies and Deaf Education, 9,* 2–14.

Walsh, J. (2006). *Theories for direct social work practice.* Belmont, CA: Thompson.

Yachnik, M. (1986). Self-esteem in adolescents. *American Annals of the Deaf, 131,* 305–310.

Yoshinaga-Itano, C. (2003). Universal newborn hearing screening programs and developmental outcomes. *Audiological Medicine, 1,* 199–206.

# INDEX